IRISH MIGRANTS IN MODERN BRITAIN, 1750–1922

Donald M. MacRaild

First published 1999 by
MACMILLAN PRESS LTD
Houndmills, Basingstoke, Hampshire RG21 6XS
and London
Companies and representatives throughout the world

ISBN 0–333–67761–7 hardcover
ISBN 0–333–67762–5 paperback

A catalogue record for this book is available from the British Library.

This book is printed on paper suitable for recycling and made from
fully managed and sustained forest sources.

10	9	8	7	6	5	4	3	2	1
08	07	06	05	04	03	02	01	00	99

Printed in Hong Kong

 Published in the United States of America 1999 by
ST. MARTIN'S PRESS, INC.,
Scholarly and Reference Division
175 Fifth Avenue, New York, N.Y. 10010

ISBN 0–312–22032–4

For my parents, Wendy and Neil

CONTENTS

TABLES

Acknowledgements

A work of synthesis such as this inevitably rests heavily on the work of other scholars. I hope such debts are adequately acknowledged in the notes and in the bibliographical essay. However, I wish to make additional remarks on the contribution of a number of close academic friends and colleagues. I am deeply grateful to Colin Holmes and David Martin, who read and commented on the entire typescript. Enda Delaney, Sheridan Gilley, Tony Hepburn, Frank Neal, Alan O'Day and Roger Swift each helped to improve individual chapters. Thanks also to my colleagues Sylvia Ellis, Matt Perry and Peter Waldron for their encouragement during the writing of this book. I owe a significant debt to my special subject students of 1994–5 and 1997–8, who sharpened my thinking on the Irish in Britain. As this book was written without any period of study leave, and with the usual burden of teaching and administration, it is more important than usual to acknowledge the love and support of my wife and son, Lisa and Michael. All those evenings and weekends should have been theirs; but any errors are mine.

INTRODUCTION

Until the advent of 'New Commonwealth' migration after World War II, the Irish were by far the largest ethnic group in Britain. However, this prominence was not unique to the modern period. Irish sojourners were finding their way to Britain as early as the Middle Ages and had begun to form permanent settlements in London by the Elizabethan period. The eighteenth century saw further developments of this type, with Irish migration mirroring the wider growth of urban and industrial centres. The emergence of the northern towns, and the establishment of the great commercial and industrial cities, prompted the appearance of much larger and more closely observed Irish settlements. The flow of migrants from Ireland reached new heights after the French Wars (1793–1815), with thousands entering British ports each year. By the 1830s, parliamentary commissioners and local observers were expressing concern about this rising rate of Irish settlement. In the 1840s, the impact of the Famine and a pattern of long-lived cultural antagonisms conspired to make the Irish in Britain the 'largest unassimilable section of society'; 'a people set apart and everywhere rejected and despised'.[1] Perhaps unsurprisingly, most historians have focused on this key phase; but the influx did not end there. As late as World War I, a continuing migration meant that even less fashionable Irish centres, such as Whitehaven in Cumberland and Hebburn on Tyneside, bore the cultural and political hallmarks of their long-established Irish communities, whether in the form of thriving Catholic churches or Orange lodges.[2]

The growth and development of Irish communities provide key themes for analysis here. The first part of this study looks at departure from Ireland and the nature of settlement in Britain. Chapter 1 asks why so many Irish left their homeland and examines the changing nature of emigration. Chapter 2 then considers the migrants' arrival in Britain over the long term, including temporary and permanent influxes, pre-industrial as well as industrial migration. A second theme is the development and adaptation of Irish communities (Chapters 3–5). By focusing on the two most important aspects of Irish migrant culture, religion and politics, these chapters attempt to show not just the stresses and strains of Irish life but also the impressive feats of cultural survival and growth which knitted migrant communities together. A third theme, which is discussed in chapter 6, addresses the complex and important question of anti-Irish animosity. Why did the Irish in Britain meet with such acute antipathy from the host populations of England, Wales and Scotland? This chapter takes us through the main forms of aggression against the Irish, covering middle-class opposition as well as working-class violence. By analysing these important elements, *Irish Migrants in Modern Britain* attempts to illustrate that a sense of Irishness – a resilient idea of nationality and ethnicity – was maintained by the Irish in Britain long after the mass migration of the Famine era. This book further suggests that historians are wrong to argue that anti-Irish animosity and violence died out quickly after the mid-Victorian years.[3] There can be no denying that times were particularly turbulent when Queen Victoria was new to the throne, but many of the key instruments of violence – not least a pervasive culture of anti-Catholicism – were still functioning when the old queen died.

Although there has been an explosion of historical interest in recent years, the Irish in Britain are still a relatively little-known group in British society, a fact which is thrown into sharp relief by the huge volume of writings on their American counterparts. The transatlantic interest in migration and ethnicity is, of course, partly explained by the fundamentally greater significance of incoming groups in the history of the United States. Most historians would subscribe to Handlin's dictum: 'Once I thought to write a history of the immigrants in America. Then I discovered that the immigrants *were* American history.'[4] As a result, research on America's migrants began much earlier than in Britain, with notable exponents such as Adams, Blegen and Hansen all publishing key works before World War II.[5] The relative neglect of Britain's Irish community is also explained by the sheer size of the Irish flow to America. By the 1840s the United States had become by far the major recipient of all Irish migrants. In 1850 America's Irish-born population was 30 per cent larger than the British; ten years later the American Irish were twice as numerous; and by 1891 this differential was threefold.

Although incoming groups have never been as important in British history, they are more significant than the weight of historical scholarship would suggest.[6] In the case of the Irish, while the United States' stream eclipsed the combined totals of all other receivers of Irish migrants, Britain remained an important destination. Even in 1901, there were more than 600 000 Irish in Britain. Moreover, if we attempt to count first- and second-generation offspring, the wider Irish community was probably in excess of two million. Britain attracted a steady flow of Irish settlers long after cheap crossings opened up the United States; and until the 1830s more Irish crossed the Irish Sea than the Atlantic. The importance of the British share is further emphasised by Cormac Ó Gráda's revelation that the three main sources of emigration statistics seriously underestimate the movement of people from Ireland to Britain. Whereas a standard reading puts at one-eighth of all Irish emigrants the number who went to Britain, Ó Gráda argues that figure is nearer to one-fifth or even one-quarter.[7] Furthermore, in the twentieth century things turned full circle. The British stream, which was reinvigorated by the demands of post-war reconstruction in the 1940s and 1950s, eventually outstripped the traffic to America.[8]

The British dimension of Irish emigration also has been less well studied because of the commonly held, though rather controversial, view that the Irish in Britain were merely temporary sojourners whose ultimate destination was America. No doubt some of the Irish in Britain saw residence in a northern pit village or a Scottish shipbuilding town as part of some grander plan to emigrate to the New World, but what proportion held or realised this dream? Still others may have intended to return to Ireland after their working life was over, as was often the case in the twentieth century. This notion of transience has long influenced historians of the Irish Diaspora, though few writers have gone as far as Ruth-Ann Harris, who suggests that a *majority* of the Irish in early industrial Britain eventually made it to America.[9] There are examples which support Harris's perspective, most notably the resolve of the Famine Irish emigrants to reach American destinations. Despite the disease and abject poverty of their circumstances, many of these migrants were still able to move on: some 500 000 Irish entered Liverpool during the desperate year of 1847, but around 300 000 of these subsequently headed for the United States. Harris's view is tempered, however, by the fact that most of the remainder were paupers, with little chance of moving very far at all, which in turn tells us something else about the Irish in Britain and the way they have been perceived. Britain may have been a temporary haven for better-off migrants, but it was also a rather more permanent and bleak berth for the abjectly poor who lacked the wherewithal to leave.

Such was clearly the case with the Doorley family from King's County, whose life history has been so carefully recovered by David Fitzpatrick. How many of the Irish in Britain were like Maria Doorley's mother and sisters, women who never realised their dream of an Australian ending? While Maria and her father, brother and one sister emigrated to Queensland in the 1860s, the rest of the family made it only to Lancashire and the 'squalor of Bolton', where they lived out the remainder of their lives in poverty. The letters exchanged by the two branches of the family 'provide a searing impression of the penury and misery experienced by many Irish expatriates in industrial Britain.'[10] Examples such as these confirm the view that the Irish in Britain were the poorest element of the migrant stream; after all, surely more pressing economic factors restricted the Bolton Doorleys to Lancashire than had propelled their relatives on to Australia? Many, like the Doorleys, dreamed of America or Australia, but others, perhaps even a majority, found that Britain was a permanent home once they had landed there. At the same time, we must not forget that the migration from Ireland to Britain was not without a significant element of planning. Just because migrants were going to Britain did not mean they did not think about the families and friends they might look for. Even in the worst of times, such as during the Great Famine, many had destinations other than America or Australia fixed in their minds. The case of Jeremiah Sullivan, who fled Ireland during the Famine, illustrates this point well. When four of his children died of starvation in a village near Cheltenham in April 1847, the coroner's inquest learned that the family had been on their way from Skibbereen to London, via South Wales, to find Sullivan's aunt, who owned a shop.[11] Despite eviction and starvation, indeed because of it, families such as the Sullivans knew where they wanted to be.

The study of Irish migration to Britain has also foundered on problems of measurement. Unlike other outflows, the British stream was a movement *within* the United Kingdom and so evaded the meticulous counting that from the 1850s marked passages to America. Migration to Britain was – geographically and thus psychologically –

less permanent than going to America or Australia. If a member of the Irish community in Britain had regular work then returning to Ireland for a funeral or a wedding would not have been impossible. Indeed, from the 1820s, with the advent of cheap steam crossings, coming and going between Ireland and Britain became increasingly common, as is shown by the thriving spalpeen trade (see Chapter 1), which adds further to this idea of impermanence and fluidity. These factors obscure the apparent solidity which marked most Irish communities in Britain by the 1850s and is shown by their strong social and cultural presence.

The Irish in Britain have traditionally been associated with poverty and hardship, with their perceived Catholicism and rural origins proving particularly of interest to historians. Yet the image of the Irish in Britain as the flotsam and jetsam of the migrant flow is dispelled by deeper reading into the subject. Although migrants in Britain may not have achieved the kind of economic or political power enjoyed by their brethren in the big cities of east-coast America (which is to be explained partly by the fluidity of American municipal culture and the contrasting conservatism of British institutional life), we must nevertheless acknowledge the vibrancy of both Catholic and Protestant networks in Liverpool, Glasgow and other large centres, before a full picture of Irish life in Britain can be drawn. Despite its limitations, the widespread Home Rule movement of the generations after 1870 further indicates the expression of a coherent migrant identity, while the Irish role in the labour movement from the later 1880s points to deeper roots in British life. While it is right to say the Irish in Britain were a 'peculiar tramping people', occupying a 'curious middle place' in nineteenth-century Britain, there was more to their communal life than poverty, Catholicism and drink.[12]

The Victorians themselves are responsible for the persistence of this Irish migrant stereotype, for most contemporary writings exaggerated Irish poverty, immorality, drunkenness and Catholicism. Even the briefest reading of Carlyle's or Kay's outpourings reveals how the image of the Irish has crowded out any notion of their lived reality. The Irish were portrayed as the greatest nuisance of the new industrial and urban world; they were the scapegoats for a host of problems that their arrival did not manufacture and scarcely worsened. The Irish scapegoat was meant to explain the negative features of the Victorian city and perhaps to assuage those who feared them. Yet the image of the Irish as a negative and alien presence had more to do

with the urban world in which they lived than with the character of
the Irish themselves. For Victorians, the words 'Irish' and 'slum' were
virtually interchangeable, each epitomising middle-class attitudes
towards working-class lifestyles. In this respect, Mayne's depiction of
the classic slum is instructive:

> Slums are myths. They are constructions of the imagination ... I do
> not mean that slums were not real. They were after all, a universal
> feature of big cities. Their reality, however, lay in the construction
> of common-sense conviction, and in the certainties of public
> knowledge which common-sense understandings sustained, rather
> than in the material conditions of everyday living.[13]

For 'slums' read 'Irish'; the fact that so many Irish lived in the
poorest districts adds to the irony of this analogy. The idea of the
classic slum, like the Victorian image of the Irish, presents us with a
series of 'words', 'discourse' and 'signs'; and with a language of
prejudice which informed images of British life.[14] In this formulation,
Irishness became encoded with the same bourgeois values as informed
images of other slum dwellers, such as prostitutes and criminals. In
sum, Irishness became a synonym for decaying moral values. What is
more, every potential good point could be read negatively: for
example, overcrowded living conditions, which might be seen by
economic historians as a measure of mutual support, were a sign of
degeneracy to the Victorian onlooker. The Irish imagined by 'Condition of England' writers were, thus, far worse than the 'real' Irish.
While Irish communities clustered into distinct ethnic neighbourhoods, the classic 'Irish ghetto' was either non-existent or greatly
exaggerated. Few ghettos actually existed and none seems to have
been entirely closed off from the outside world. However, their
currency remained strong with the Victorians, and it is not surprising
that the Irish developed a state of mental or psychological ghetto-
isation as a defence mechanism against the opprobrium they faced.[15]

If the Industrial Revolution and urban growth provide key contexts
for our examination of the Irish in Britain, we must also recognise
the political background provided by the Act of Union. The Act had
been intended by Pitt to improve Anglo-Irish relations. Yet this study
of the Irish in Britain shows how far, in this one respect, Pitt's mission
failed. The Act of Union, taken as a neutral constitutional fact, should
have obviated the language of 'aliens' and 'outsiders' when discussing

Irish migration because these settlers were migrants *within*, not emigrants *into*, the United Kingdom. No Act of Parliament, however, could change attitudes overnight. The Irish, particularly Catholics, opposed the Union, and as time went by a movement sprung up to seek its repeal. Union was supposed to mean a linking of equals; but instead Ireland became England's 'social laboratory', a testing ground for harsher forms of legislation than even England's own poor had to bear, as was the case with the Irish Poor Law (1838). In fact, there was no strengthening of bonds in this era (except between Unionists and Westminster); and, if anything, historic tensions between Britain and Ireland were much increased. The idea that constitutional arrangements would filter down into the lives of ordinary Irish people was utterly destroyed by wild reactions to social or political forces such as migration and nationalism. More broadly, too, the Act of Union illustrated how clearly emergent ideas of Britishness (perhaps more properly the expansion of 'Englishness') excluded the Irish. For centuries English colonial designs on Ireland had failed to forge a wider and inclusive identity. Key elements of English or British identity, such as the Protestant Ascendancy and the importance of anti-Catholicism, immediately excluded Ireland's major ethnic group. Irish Catholics were not seen as fellow nation builders; they were more like the French, a people whose exclusion and enmity underpinned national identity.

This study also stresses how the Irish were divided *within* themselves. While the Irish *generally* were outcast in British minds, Irish Catholics *specifically* were further threatened by their difference from Irish Protestants. The Irish were not an homogenous group. As Akenson points out, a never-ending procession of colonisers – from Norman lords and Scots planters to Victorian civil servants – helped to create a cascade of competing identities within Ireland, from old Irish or old English to Scotch Irish and Irish Catholic.[16] Not all of these shared the same idea of what Irishness meant, and the competition to define the nation resulted in significant turbulence. What is more, as the Ulster loyalist idea of Irishness melted into Britishness during the Home Rule crisis, Catholics gradually became the only meaningful and distinct Irish race. This was partly because Catholics themselves increasingly linked 'Catholic' and 'Irish' with 'nationalist'; but it was also because, for the British, *meaningful* and *distinct* Irish simply meant *bad Irish*. The national and religious differences between the Protestants and Catholics of Ireland inevitably did much to shape social relations among migrants in the new communities of Britain, and so these occupy a major strand of the following discussion.

Irish Migrants in Modern Britain examines many important issues. It describes various aspects of Irish life in Britain, both good and bad, from the communally minded to the sectarian and violent. Much of what follows points to the long-run and developmental nature of Irish settlement, and considers the impressive feats of communal cohesion and mutual support which all migrant groups can demonstrate. The church and other social agencies provided Irish settlers with a sense of shared identity, and these are examined in detail. At the same time, however, we are constantly reminded that antipathy and alienation were major motivations for internal solidarity.

1

Economy, Poverty and Emigration

Introduction

Since the early eighteenth century around eight million people have emigrated from Ireland.[1] Of this number, perhaps five million left in the first seven decades of the nineteenth century. In the mid-nineteenth century, young Irish men and women had a one in three chance of emigrating. In fact, the scale of departure was so large that by 1890 some 40 per cent of all Irish-born people were living outside their country of birth.[2] Hobsbawm's vivid description of the forces at work in Europe at this time have a particular resonance for Ireland:

> The nineteenth century was a gigantic machine for uprooting countrymen. Most of them went to cities, or at any rate out of traditional rural pursuits, to find their way as best they could in strange, frightening, but at best boundlessly hopeful new worlds, where city pavements were said to be paved with gold, though immigrants rarely picked up more than some copper.[3]

While in most countries, the passage of people was dwarfed by enormous natural increases in population, in the case of Ireland massive rates of departure were exacerbated by the effects of increased celibacy, a higher mean age at marriage and other lifestyle factors, which combined to ensure that her population fell into steep decline. Between 1841 and 1901, the Irish population halved from more than eight million to approximately four million. Finally, mass emigration became a feature of Irish life long before other European countries. Ireland emitted a higher proportion of her people than any other country, and a greater absolute number of emigrants than even much larger countries like England and Germany. As a consequence, whatever the impact of emigration upon European society in general, the overall effects were many times greater in Ireland's case.

The earliest significant migration from Ireland occurred in the early eighteenth century from the Dissenting communities, particularly those of Ulster. Despite interruptions from wars and legislation prohibiting the loss of valuable labour (especially artisans), the century before 1815 saw upwards of 300 000 Irish departing for the Americas. Around 100 000 of these departed during the French Wars, while a larger number crossed the Irish Sea to Britain. After 1815, moreover, there was a great increase in the numbers of those who left. By 1845, the eve of the Great Famine, around one million had already departed for America and perhaps 500 000 had made their way to Britain. And yet, greater departures were still to come. The period of the Great Famine (1845–50) and its aftermath saw the greatest emigration in Irish history, with over two million departures in little more than a decade. Even in the 1860s and 1870s, when agriculture was more buoyant than it had been since 1815, people continued to leave. By the latter decade, emigration was so fundamental to Irish life that probably no Irish family was untouched by it.

Although the migrant stream carried resisting groups, such as Dissenters in search of religious freedoms and political rebels fleeing the gallows, the majority of those who headed for new lives outside the country of their birth simply left in search of economic opportunities. They also left for a variety of destinations. North America was an important journey's end in the eighteenth century, although from 1815 to around 1840 Britain was by the far most important attraction for Irish migrants. Canada was also a more important centre of Irish settlement in this period than the United States. This is because legislation was introduced in Britain after the American Revolution to prevent the loss of human capital to the new republic. Successive British governments then continued to encourage Irish and other migrants to travel to British North America, thus simultaneously bolstering the last North American colony and depriving American industry of much needed labour. Although many settlers disembarked in Canada for these reasons, a large proportion of them are thought to have walked south along the coast of New Brunswick, crossing the border into Maine before reaching the growing American cities.[4] When restrictions were relaxed and crossings became cheaper, especially in the late 1830s and 1840s, the United States quickly eclipsed Canada as a direct route for Irish settlers. In the second half of the century, Australia, New Zealand, South Africa and Argentina also attracted significant flows of Irish migrants, while a still under-studied form of emigration is that which took Irish soldiers, sailors and civil servants to promote and protect the British empire, not least India.[5] The vast majority of these population movements, however, can be viewed in the context of an expanding Atlantic economy in which Britain and the United States vied for supremacy and Ireland provided vast quantities of labour. Indeed, in the post-Famine period, the United States accounted for around one-half of the entire stream and Britain for about one-fifth.

These migrants responded to a combination of 'push' and 'pull' factors. They were driven from Ireland by the chronic effects of meagre and unevenly distributed resources, perpetual hardship and by moments of acute crisis. But they were drawn to Britain or America by perceived opportunity and the prospect of sharing in the relative prosperity of those countries. Yet emigration does not easily fit into models or patterns. It neither selected one social group nor concentrated on only one region. The poorest elements of society did not emigrate first, and the prosperous did not necessarily remain behind. The earliest large-scale departures came from the wealthier north and east during the eighteenth century, while the poorest province, Connacht, maintained disproportionately low emigration rates until after the Famine. The decision to leave was not taken lightly or for the same reasons by different individuals and families. Even in the worst times, such as at the height of the Famine, the leaving was not simply desperate *and* unthinking. Emigration, in fact, must be seen as an element of the life-cycle: a survival strategy as well as a means of adapting and improving the lives people knew. Moreover, emigration was an economically sensitive indicator of the state of the nation, rising and falling as crops failed or as harvests were good, as trade boomed or slumped, and according to economic conditions in the receiving country. The decision to leave was intensely personal, often prompted by a letter from a friend or relative containing stories of milk and honey and a pre-paid ticket.

Irish emigration was like that of no other country, except perhaps Sweden, in terms of its gender balance. Whereas men dominated most outflows from Europe, Ireland sent an equal number of women. Even before the Famine, women constituted two-fifths of the Irish outflow. Moreover, this symmetry was achieved without strong traditions of family migration, other than in eastern Ulster.[6] While married couples, Fitzpatrick has shown, accounted for around one-third of all English migration in the later nineteenth and early twentieth centuries, in Ireland single men and women aged 20–24 accounted for two-fifths of all emigrants in this period. The traditional image is of women being pushed out of the labour market by men, although it has been suggested that technological innovation, by reducing the importance of muscle power, actually increased the woman's position in rural work. A more likely explanation of the uniquely high rate of female migration, therefore, is the improved prospects for women in the receiving countries. These factors of gender, age and marital status were due not just to problems in Ireland but also to the migrant's pursuit of a number of personal goals, especially a good job and improved status.[7]

The scale of emigration from Ireland caused a good deal of contemporary concern. The one-time Young Irelander (see Chapter 5) John Mitchel, for example, argued that those who left were exiles rather than emigrants.[8] Even at the time, however, it was not just activists such as Mitchel who viewed emigration as a cause for concern. For example, more conservative Irishmen would have endorsed David Ricardo's view, expressed in 1816, that emigration was a cause for concern because 'the young, the strong, the enterprising and industrious families leave us, whilst the idle and the indolent portion stay with us'.[9] This contemporary concern with depletion has led to debate in recent years among historians trying to assess the loss of 'human capital' which the emigrant trade involved.[10]

Whether we view emigration as the result of political injustice or of economic necessity, the fact remains that it derived from a deeply complex mixture of social, economic and cultural phenomena. Before we can begin to appreciate the nature of Irish communities in Britain, therefore, it is necessary to discuss the Irish preconditions of mass departure. No attempt is made to be totally inclusive.[11] Instead, the focus rests firmly on the key 'push' factors which sustained Europe's greatest migration, and an attempt is made to evaluate some of the elements of Irish life which explain both the nature and patterns of Irish emigration.

Ireland before the Famine

'By 1800', Hoppen has argued, 'a recognisably nineteenth-century Irish rural society was already in place, though the wealth, size, and experiences of its component parts were to change significantly during the succeeding hundred years'.[12] At the top were the 10 000 or so landlords who owned the land; next came the farmers, who rented lands of varying values; the third category, those who worked the land, accounted for the overwhelming majority of the Irish population. In practice, these distinctions were blurred, with each group containing numerous gradations. Many landowners and large farmers were deeply in debt, while even the poorest members of rural society aimed to rent a scrap of land under the 'Conacre system'. Land nevertheless conferred status in proportion to the size of the holding; ownership might provide a sense of security, although a saleable tenancy could just as easily finance migration. In a pastoral society, such as Ireland, the individual's relationship with the land was paramount because ownership 'marked out a crucial line of division between those enjoying some prospect of planning for the future and those who could merely live from one moment to the next'.[13] Whether land was subdivided (as was increasingly the case among potato-dependent smallholders) or passed on to the eldest son (as was the case with the wealthier farmers and landowners), the prospect of inheritance determined an individual's outlook on life. When population pressure pushed subdivision to crisis levels, or when younger sons or daughters had no prospect of inheriting their father's farm, emigration became a likely option. These problems certainly came to bear in the 30 years after 1815.

The Great Famine has long been viewed as the turning point of Irish history: a series of events which, by promoting emigration, economic change and population decline, destroyed traditional society and ushered in a new Ireland, in some senses, the modernisation of Irish society. W. F. Adams and later R. Crotty were first to suggest that the Famine, rather than setting new trends, actually enhanced demographic and economic patterns that were already noticeable in the generation after 1815 when the return to a peacetime economy ended a generation of rural prosperity.[14] Evidence for this view is provided by reference to the contrasting economic fortunes of the Irish during and after the French Wars. Whereas the period from 1780 to 1815 had been characterised by increases in tillage, potato cultivation and population, conditions thereafter became favourable for a return to less labour-intensive dairy and pasture farming. From 1815 to the 1840s Ireland's agricultural economy was marred by falling prices, banking collapses and failed speculations. The period also witnessed increasing pressure on the scant resources, especially of small farmers and farm labourers, with poverty becoming more marked.

It is this combination of factors which led Crotty, and others, to declare that 1815 and not 1845 was the great 'watershed' of Irish history.[15] While Crotty's argument is controversial because it plays down the Great Famine, which was by any measure an horrific social catastrophe, as well as an important symbol for nationalist thought in Ireland and America, we do have to recognise that many indicators of demographic and economic change were apparent in the generation between 1815 and 1845. Indeed, it is common now to argue that the Famine was a tragic accident rather than an inevitable result of the post-1815 economic crisis and population growth.

The geographical distribution of the emigration which occurred after 1815, for example, reflected the pressure upon the commercialised, or commercialising, sector, with movement from the south midlands becoming especially marked. In the 1820s and 1830s, moreover, the counties with the highest incidence of emigration were those in the midlands and south Ulster, which were most affected by the decline of domestic industry.[16] Low levels of urbanisation were also instrumental in encouraging a regionally distinct depletion of counties near to Dublin and Ulster and the counties of Leinster and Connacht nearest to the main east-coast ports. In addition, a majority of those who went to Australia in this period came from a corridor of counties stretching from Clare and Limerick in the west to Tipperary, King's and Kilkenny further east.[17] These regional factors are also generally apparent in terms of chosen destinations. Thus, while most movement to Canada and Scotland came from Ulster, the American Irish were most likely to come from Connacht and the English-bound from southern and eastern counties. Although Australia mainly attracted those from the south-west and north midlands, New Zealand was popular with Ulster people.[18]

The volume of emigration increased markedly and became more general in the 1820s, with North America taking an ever greater share. In 1825, some 13 719 crossed the Atlantic, 60 per cent of whom went to Canada.[19] In 1826 the figure was approximately 18 500. More than 50 000 went to Canada alone in both 1832 and 1833, when the United States' figure had crept up from under 5000 in 1825 and 1826 to around 13 000. As the 1830s progressed, Canadian emigration began to die away and the United States became the favoured transatlantic destination. Although many of these migrants obtained assisted passages, the majority went completely by dint of their own resources, or with the help of friends and especially family members. Although departures were provoked by the desire for economic improvement, and though hardships were forcing many people to leave Ireland, especially for Britain, those departing at this stage were neither entirely poverty stricken nor uniformly desperate.

Reliable figures for pre-Famine emigration to the Americas are difficult to come by, and those measuring the flow to Britain are non-existent, although it is possible to derive some sense of the scale of arrival from censuses. These returns show that the two decades after 1815 were formative in the establishment of permanent Irish communities in urban Britain, where the flow of migrants increased annually. Indeed, until the Famine, Britain was by far the most popular destination for Irish migrants. It was not until 1851 that the Irish-born population of the United States (962 000) had exceeded that of Britain (727 000). By the 1830s, the Irish presence in industrial Britain was sufficiently important to merit separate investigation as part of Sir George Nicholls's huge study of Irish poverty. The subsequent report, written by Sir George Cornewall Lewis, and published in 1836, revealed substantial migrant populations throughout western and central Scotland, north-west England, and into Yorkshire and the Midlands. Lewis's report ignored the development of a very significant Irish community in the north-east of England. While industrialisation and urban growth were clearly leading to the spread of permanent settlements, there was also a more transient flow to Britain at this time.

Population and Potatoes

The emigrant tide was propelled by many factors, with population growth undeniably important among them. Between the mid-seventeenth century and the 1830s population grew rapidly. A total numbering somewhere near three million in 1785 had more than doubled to 8 175 124 in 1841. The Famine, however, led to a

Table 1.1: Population of Ireland, 1821–1901

	Total	Percentage change
1821	6 801 827	
1831	7 767 401	+14.19
1841	8 175 124	+5.25
1851	6 552 385	-19.85
1861	5 798 967	-11.50
1871	5 412 377	-6.67
1881	5 174 836	-4.39
1891	4 458 775	-9.08
1901	4 390 219	-5.23

Source: Census of Ireland, 1831–1911.

spectacular reversal of these patterns. In 1851, the population was recorded at a little over 6.5 million; it had fallen to nearly 5.8 million in 1861. Although Ireland's rate of decline fell into single figures during the 1860s, it was not until 1936–7 that Irish censuses recorded a rise, and then at a rate of only 0.46 per cent (Table 1.1).

Unsurprisingly, social observers of pre-Famine Ireland had long noticed the unparalleled development of the Irish population. Arthur Young, writing in the 1770s, offered this explanation of the phenomenon:

> There are several circumstances in Ireland extremely favourable to population, to which must be attributed that country being so much more populous than the state of manufacturing industry would seem to imply. There are five causes which may be particularised among others of less consequence. First, there being no Poor Laws. Second, the habitations. Third, the generalities of marriage. Fourth, children not being burdensome. Fifth, potatoes the food.[20]

Subsequent historical studies have emphasised Young's third point, showing how Irish couples tended to marry earlier than their European counterparts, a point which has been confirmed by detailed statistical comparisons with the English, Danish and French examples.[21]

Fifty years after Young wrote this assessment, observers had become far more critical of the Irish freedoms which he had viewed so favourably. In fact, a sea change in attitudes had occurred. The end of wartime prosperity had made people frightened of the twin effects of population rise and growing poverty, so that a general clamour for an Irish Poor Law had come to replace Young's criticism of the English version. The link was being made between early marriage, large families and Irish poverty, and Malthusian forebodings became common currency.

However, more recent analyses have questioned the idea that Ireland was caught in a Malthusian trap. It has since been shown that by the 1820s the rate of population growth in Ireland had fallen into line with general European trends, with even the poorer counties in the west of Ireland experiencing a downturn. An annual growth rate of around 1.5 per cent between 1790 and 1821 fell below 1 per cent in the 1820s and to 0.5 per cent between 1830 to 1845. The pattern of decline was due partly to emigration, but other restrictions such as delayed marriage and celibacy were coming into play.[22] Reproduction rates were already falling before the Famine and the median marriage age in Ireland in the 1830s was similar to England's at between 22.7 and 24.2 for women and 26.7 to 28.2 for men, though class, occupational and regional differences prevailed. Yet contemporary foreboding is borne out by regional disparities in pre-Famine population growth, with poorer counties growing most rapidly. The velocity of population growth may have slowed down by the 1830s but this development did not entirely offset the huge increases of previous decades, especially in the west and south. Thus in the 1820s, while Connacht's five counties and Munster's six increased by up to 25 per cent, no county in Ulster grew at much more than 16 per cent and none in Leinster at more than 12 (see Table 1.2).

The perceived juxtaposition of widespread population growth and economic backwardness in pre-Famine Ireland led many contemporaries to consider that the country was on the brink of a subsistence crisis. The horrors of the Famine, with more than one million dead, and perhaps double that figure emigrating, enforced such a view. To the Victorians, however, questioning land distribution in Ireland was less important than moralising about the alleged fecundity and laziness of her peasantry. Malthus's classic thesis, which contemporaries applied indiscriminately to the poorer classes, appeared to offer a further endorsement of this position, striking a particular chord in the Irish case. Malthus declared that 'population has this constant tendency to increase beyond the means of subsistence',[23] and

Table 1.2: Population change in Ireland, by county, 1831–91 (continuing opposite)

	1831	% change	1841	% change	1851	% change
Leinster						
Carlow	81 988	3.85	86 988	5.17	68 078	-21.05
Dublin	176 012	11.90	140 047	-20.43	146 778	4.81
Kildare	108 424	9.45	114 488	5.59	95 723	-16.39
Kilkenny	193 868	6.45	202 420	4.51	158 748	-21.57
King's	144 225	10.02	146 225	1.82	112 076	-23.68
Longford	112 558	4.64	115 491	2.60	82 348	-28.70
Louth	124 846	4.79	128 240	2.72	107 662	-16.05
Meath	176 826	11.08	183 828	3.96	140 748	-23.43
Queen's	145 851	8.62	15 393	5.54	111 664	-27.46
Westmeath	136 872	6.25	1 413	3.23	111 407	-21.15
Wexford	182 713	6.97	202 033	10.57	180 158	-10.83
Wicklow	121 557	9.74	126 143	3.77	98 979	-21.53
Munster						
Clare	258 322	24.00	286 394	11.00	212 440	-25.82
Cork	810 732	10.99	854 118	5.35	649 308	-23.98
Kerry	263 126	21.71	293 880	11.68	238 254	-18.92
Limerick	315 355	13.65	330 029	4.65	262 132	-20.57
Tipperary	402 563	16.05	435 553	8.10	331 567	-23.88
Waterford	177 054	13.12	196 187	10.80	164 035	-16.39
Ulster						
Antrim	272 328	16.58	285 567	4.86	259 903	-8.98
Armagh	220 134	11.50	232 393	5.57	196 084	-15.62
Cavan	227 933	16.84	243 158	6.68	174 064	-28.41
Donegal	289 149	16.47	296 448	2.52	255 158	-13.93
Down	352 012	8.17	361 446	2.86	320 817	-11.24
Fermanagh	149 763	14.33	156 481	4.49	116 047	-25.84
Londonderry	222 012	14.51	222 174	0.07	192 022	-13.57
Monaghan	195 536	11.93	200 442	2.51	141 823	-29.24
Tyrone	304 468	16.27	312 956	2.79	255 661	-18.31
Conacht						
Galway	414 684	22.92	440 198	6.15	321 684	-26.92
Leitrim	141 524	13.41	155 297	9.73	111 897	-27.94
Mayo	366 328	24.98	388 887	6.16	274 499	-29.41
Roscommon	249 613	19.59	253 591	1.59	173 436	-31.61
Sligo	171 765	17.46	180 886	5.31	128 515	-28.95

Source: W. E. Vaughan and A. J. Fitzpatrick, *Irish Historical Statistics: Population, 1821–1971* (Dublin, 1978), pp. 4–15.

1861	% change	1871	% change	1881	% change	1891	% change
57 137	-16.07	51 650	-9.60	46 568	-9.84	40 936	-12.09
155 444	5.90	158 936	2.24	169 308	6.53	174 215	2.90
90 946	-4.90	83 614	-8.06	75 804	-9.34	70 206	-7.38
124 515	-21.56	109 379	-12.15	99 531	-9.00	87 261	-12.33
90 043	-19.66	75 900	-15.70	72 852	-4.02	65 187	-8.20
71 694	-12.94	64 501	-10.03	61 009	-5.41	52 647	-13.70
90 713	-15.74	84 021	-7.37	77 038	-7.54	65 820	-7.35
110 373	-21.58	95 558	-13.42	87 469	-8.47	76 987	-11.98
90 650	-18.81	79 771	-12.00	73 124	-8.33	64 883	-11.27
90 879	-18.42	78 432	-13.69	71 798	-8.46	65 109	-9.32
143 954	-20.09	132 854	-7.84	123 854	-6.64	111 778	-9.75
86 479	-12.63	78 697	-9.00	70 386	-10.56	62 136	-11.72
166 305	-21.72	147 864	-11.00	141 457	-4.33	124 483	-12.00
544 818	-16.09	517 076	-5.09	495 607	-4.15	438 432	-11.54
201 800	-15.30	196 586	-2.58	201 039	2.27	179 136	-10.89
217 277	-17.11	191 936	-11.66	180 632	-5.89	158 912	-12.02
249 106	-24.87	216 713	-13.00	196 612	-7.90	173 188	-13.24
134 252	-18.16	123 310	-8.15	98 251	-8.55	87 187	-12.87
256 986	-1.12	245 758	-4.37	237 738	-3.26	215 229	9.47
190 086	-3.06	179 260	-5.70	163 177	-8.97	143 289	-12.19
153 906	-11.58	140 735	-8.56	129 476	-8.00	111 917	-13.56
237 395	-6.96	218 334	-8.03	206 035	-5.63	185 635	-9.90
299 302	-6.71	277 294	-7.35	248 190	-10.50	224 008	-9.74
105 768	-8.86	92 794	-12.27	84 879	-8.53	74 170	-12.62
184 209	-4.07	173 906	-5.59	164 991	-5.13	152 009	-7.87
126 482	-10.82	114 969	-9.10	102 748	-10.63	86 206	-16.1
238 500	-6.71	215 766	-9.53	197 719	-8.37	171 401	-13.31
271 478	-15.61	248 458	-8.48	242 005	-2.60	214 712	-11.28
104 744	-6.39	95 562	-8.77	90 372	-5.43	786 618	-13.00
254 796	-7.18	246 030	-8.44	245 212	-0.33	219 034	-10.68
157 272	-9.32	140 670	-10.55	132 490	-5.82	114 397	-13.66
124 845	-2.86	115 578	-3.39	111 578	-3.39	98 013	-12.16

Ireland appeared to be, in the eyes of many contemporaries, a case in point. But what factors encouraged Irish population to increase so rapidly? Subdividing or subletting land certainly played a part, until land became so divided that it could not adequately support eking out a miserable existence. However, the suggestion that this system encouraged early marriages, and thus large families, is not sustainable, given that such trends had long been a feature of Irish life. The 80 years between 1741 and 1822 were relatively free of food shortages, and major famines were certainly absent. These factors, along with wartime demand, predisposed many people to early marriage. The most powerful inducement to marry young, however, was the availability of a cheap, efficient and reliable staple foodstuff: the humble potato. This foodstuff was not adopted overnight, but became increasingly important as the eighteenth century wore on.[24]

As the nineteenth century approached, contemporary observers made much comment on the role of potato, many viewing it as Ireland's saviour, and more besides. Although Malthus warned of the hazards of over-reliance, the potato was generally considered to be a buffer against, not the creator of, hunger and privation, for it was both efficient to grow and cheap to consume. As early as the 1770s, Adam Smith pointed to the potato diet as an explanation of why 'the strongest men and most beautiful women perhaps in the British dominions, are said to be … from the lowest ranks of the people in Ireland'.[25] The potato became increasingly important as the poor adopted it as their main food, supplemented only by a little salt, buttermilk and the odd herring or pieces of bacon. Observers in both Ireland and Britain noted how Irish workers chose the potato above any other food; some thought this was a terrible state of affairs which encouraged the wastage of surplus cash on drink and tobacco. Most, however, simply marvelled at the strength and stamina which Irish men and women displayed on an essentially potato-based diet. Arthur Young went as far as to repeat Smith's observation that the potato explained both the athleticism of the men and beauty of the women. More than that, Young felt critics of the potato-based diet were misinformed:

> The food of the common Irish, potatoes and milk, have been produced more than once as an instance of the extreme poverty of the country, but this I believe is an opinion embraced with alacrity more than reflection. I have heard it stigmatised as unhealthy, and

not sufficiently nourishing for the support of hard labour, but this opinion is very amazing in a country, many of whose poor people are as athletic in their form, as robust, and as capable of enduring labour as any upon earth. This idleness seen among many when working for those who oppress them is a very contrast to the vigour and activity with which the same people work when themselves alone reap the benefits of their labour.... When I see the people of a country in spite of political oppression with well formed vigorous bodies, and their cottages swarming with children, ... I know not how to believe them subsisting on an unwholesome food.[26]

Historians also have viewed the potato as a kind of 'nutritional miracle', with the potato spawning a whole historiography of its own.[27] Yet as Mokyr, and some contemporaries, observed, the potato was not uniformly advantageous. It contributed little to commercial farming, because it was not a cash crop, and only two per cent of production was exported. The fact that potatoes, unlike grain, could not be stored meant that bumper harvests were often wasted and the impact of poorer ones could not be cushioned. The potato may have stabilised human life under most ordinary circumstances, but it had a negative impact upon those features of farming – especially live-stock – which may have offered some commercial possibilities for poorer elements in society. Pigs, horses and hens were the chief beneficiaries of overproduction, and ate well at those times, but they were the first to suffer in years of low yields.

However, Malthus was most concerned to point out the human consequences of the potato:

A very striking instance of the disadvantageous effect of a low relative price of food on the consumption of the poor may be observed in Ireland. In Ireland the funds for the maintenance of labour have been increased so rapidly during the last century, and so large a portion of that sort of food which forms the principal support of the lower classes has been awarded to them, that the increase in population has been more rapid than in almost any known country, except America. The Irish labourer paid in potatoes has earned perhaps the means of subsistence for double the number of persons that could be supported by the earnings of an English labourer paid in wheat; and the increase of population has been nearly in proportion to the relative quantities of the customary food awarded to the labourers in each.[28]

Malthus, of course, could make no reference to the poor-quality
Lumper potato, which began to spread in earnest in Ireland only
during the 1820s.[29] However, his words do capture a growing concern
that was being expressed about the balance in Irish life between
humans and nature. The potato *was* – despite its calorific content and
dietary advantages – an indication of the sort of poverty and hardship
which prompted, among other things, emigration. Donnelly captures
this well: 'Ultimately, the successive failures of the potato claimed as
many victims as they did in Ireland because so high a proportion of
the population had come to live in a degree of poverty that exposed
them fully to a horrendous accident of nature which it was difficult to
escape'.[30]

Temporary migration was an important element in Irish migration
to Britain. It was also a key factor in keeping poor cottiers in the west
of Ireland in possession of their small landholdings and became an
increasingly important way of deriving cash earnings until well after
the Famine.[31] Increasing commercialisation of British farming in the
early decades of the nineteenth century led to a greater demand for
day labour on British farms which could not always be serviced by
local workers. Technological innovation also led to sharp contrasts
between winter and summer work, and this change, too, expanded
the Irish labourer's opportunity for seasonal work. In addition, Irish
labour proved to be inherently superior to that of the local paupers
who were normally employed at harvest time, while much indigenous
rural labour was at that time being lost to towns and cities, where
wages were higher.[32]

The logic of these workers spending half the year roaming for work
is not difficult to deduce. Women and children were quite capable of
tending the home farm, while a wandering reaper (spalpeen) could
bring back between £10 and £12 from a summer season in Britain,
which was enough to pay the rent and to purchase the few
commodities that the family could not make. For many poorer
households this was the only source of cash income. While the
spalpeen's living could be precarious (a poor season might last just a
few weeks and yield little more than 5s), Irish circumstances dictated
that it be tried by more and more people each year. While temporary
labour was the first step to permanent settlement in an unknown
number of cases, the majority of spalpeen came from the traditional
counties of western Ulster and Connacht, of which Donegal and
Mayo had perhaps the longest tradition, where this annual trek was

meant to cement, not weaken, the cottier's grip on the land of Ireland.[33]

Seasonal work often began with a drift to the large farms of eastern Ireland, although the animosity of indigenous labour and contracting opportunities quickly pushed these workers to Britain, where competition was less intense. From 1815, during the months of May and June, London's Irish community could be swollen by up to 5000 spalpeen, who idled their time waiting for the harvesting work to begin in the Home Counties. The 1820s and 1830s witnessed large increases in the flow, due to upturns in demand, as well as the advent of steam packets. By this time, the annual migration of agricultural labourers was significantly higher than the once generally accepted figure of 10 000. Ó Gráda's analysis of parliamentary reports suggests that in the mid-1830s between 35 000 and 40 000 were crossing the Irish Sea for this type of work. The 1841 census puts the figure at 60 000, though, as Ó Gráda points out, this does not include travellers from minor ports. Various committees of inquiry in the 1860s touched on the subject of temporary migration, and from these Ó Gráda has shown that the Famine did not drastically reduce the flow of seasonal workers. The Irish Midlands railway ran a special 'fourth-class' fare, known as a 'harvest ticket', to transport men from the outlying counties to Dublin and then on to Liverpool or other west coast ports. This railway company alone sold 78 000 such tickets annually in the four years before 1865, leading Ó Gráda to suggest that around 100 000 annually made this journey.[34] In counties such as Mayo, where the spalpeen culture was strongest, reliance upon this supplementary economy was enormous.

Land and Inequality

Irish poverty, which provided the main impetus for emigration, was not a unified or monocausal occurrence. Instead, it arose, as Mokyr has argued, from a 'series of related but separate phenomena which did not necessarily share the same causal mechanism'. These were: Irish agricultural backwardness; the absence of an Irish Industrial Revolution (or perhaps the absence of the transference of industrial development to Ireland, apart from eastern Ulster); and the failure in the 1840s of the potato crop, which impoverished so many who relied upon it.[35] Market conditions in Ireland made or exacerbated these problems, taking away potential outlets for surplus population. Thus, while displaced cottars from the Highlands of Scotland were able to find work in Glasgow or Edinburgh, and English agricultural labourers were absorbed to some extent into growing towns and cities, such opportunities were not apparent in Ireland. Belfast accounted large quantities of migrant labour during the nineteenth century, but neither this city nor Dublin could provide for the sheer volume of Irish migrants that rural poverty was creating.[36]

We have already noticed how attitudes towards the Irish population changed greatly in the 50 years after Arthur Young's tours in the 1770s. He had believed that Irish mobility, which was encouraged by 'Ireland being free from the curse of the English Poor Laws',[37] was a positive factor in Irish rural life. Young argued that the English Poor Law and Acts of Settlement had simply crystallised English pauperism, preventing a natural flow from poorer areas to prosperous ones; for him, migration to areas with labour shortages might have eliminated the problem of poverty altogether. By the 1830s, rapid Irish migration to Britain and the huge simultaneous increases in rural poverty encouraged a new generation of social writers to view the absence of an Irish Poor Law as an invidious influence. By the 1830s, rural poverty was so extensive that many demanded the English system of 1834 be superimposed on Ireland. Both Sir George Nicholls and Sir George Cornewall Lewis, who conducted studies of poverty and the Poor Law, concluded that the English system would not work in Ireland. In 1838, however, the Whig ministry drove through a harsh Poor Law for Ireland which banned outdoor relief and provided workhouse places for a little over 60 000 individuals. The system, which accounted for a fraction of Ireland's needs, was an accident waiting to happen. The Poor Law (Ireland) Act of 1838 was meant to instil discipline, cure Irish poverty and stem the tide of migrants; the legislation achieved none of these things.

The contrast between rich and poor in Ireland was widely remarked upon. As early as 1812, E. G. Wakefield noted the 'lowest state of misery' that marked aspects of Irish rural life – and the situation worsened considerably in the generation after 1815. Writing in 1834, H. D. Inglis considered that poverty to be 'shocking for humanity to contemplate'. Inglis was, moreover, horrified by the lack of sensitivity in Dublin society. 'With few exceptions', he remarked, 'a Dublin tradesman who has realized 10 000*l*. or perhaps a greatly less sum, ... sets up his jaunting-car, becomes the possessor of a villa, and entertains company'. He contrasted this with the paucity of bacon and cheese shops to be found in Dublin: 'but what would be the use of opening a bacon shop, where the lower orders, who are elsewhere the chief purchasers of bacon, cannot afford to eat bacon, and live on potatos [sic]?'[38] Comments of this sort were becoming increasingly voluminous when, in late 1843, Peel's government attempted to address the complex issues of Irish poverty and landholding by appointing the Devon Commission, which reported in 1845 with a series of radical proposals. As well as noting the 'exemplary patience' with which the Irish poor bore their sufferings, the Devon Commission also identified nearly four million improvable acres of land. Although this land had not been improved by the time of the Famine, critics argued that any land improved in line with the commissioners' recommendations would not have been turned over to tillage and, thus, would not have helped the poorest elements of society. Indeed, the nationalist John Mitchel argued that the Devon Commission was a great conspiracy between English rulers and Anglo-Irish landlords. He saw the commissioners' insistence that Irish landholding should be revamped – that the tiny properties of Ireland's million or so landholders needed to be accumulated into larger units – as a plan to extirpate the peasantry of Ireland.

There is no doubt that land lay at the heart of Ireland's problems. It was unfairly distributed and its place in the social fabric was artificial. Ireland's landholding system encouraged social division, created poverty and promoted large-scale emigration. Many contemporaries were highly critical of landlords. For outsiders, such as J. G. Kohl, a German observer who visited Ireland ten years before the Famine, the Irish landlord class was the worst in Europe: 'even worse than the great Polish and Russian proprietors, who at least build houses for their peasants, and furnish them with food in times of Famine. This the Irish landlord does not do, because his tenant is a *free* man, though with only the inconveniences of freedom – such as hunger, want, and care – without any of its advantages'.[39] This conception of the evils inherent in Irish land ownership questions has fired nationalist historians, such as Dennis Clark, who considered that the 'ownership of the land was vested in a landlord class composed largely of parasitic absentees' who maintained a system that was 'deeply exploitative and inefficient'.[40] Much of this rhetoric is of course driven by what happened during the Famine, as well as by a need to attach blame. The fact that cottier landholders declined from

310 375 to 88 083 in the 20 years after 1841 has served to emphasise the argument.

Yet, Irish nationalists were not alone in attacking the Irish landholding system. John Stuart Mill, writing during the early years of the Famine, was one of the sternest critics, making similar observations on the great evils of Irish society.[41] While Mill believed the cottier system must be swept away, he expressed deeper contempt for the attitude of Irish landlords, especially their failure to pay adequate taxes to care for their own poor. Mill contrasted the understandable exhortations for charity from the poor with the importunate demands of the landlords:

> The cry of some persons is, let England give; and give to the peasantry, to those who are really in want. There is charity in this proposal, if not wisdom, when it comes from this side of the Irish Channel; when from the other side, it is something else; it is the conduct of him who begs for charity, which, if rarely meritorious or dignified, is excusable when there is nothing to be done. But the Irish landlords next present themselves, and exclaim, give to *us*. Lend to us below the market rate of interest, that we may pay off our mortgages; we shall then have a large income for our own use, with part of which we will employ the poor.[42]

Some historians have defended landlords against the charges of writers like Mill. Crotty, for example, suggested that Irish landlords were no meaner or sadistic than their counterparts elsewhere, arguing that evictions and high rents – two especially common complaints – were the products of changing agricultural demand in the post-1815 market and the historic precariousness of landholding in Ireland, where until the 1870s only Ulster had a comprehensive system of 'tenant right', guaranteeing fixity of tenure and the right to benefit from improvements made to the land.[43] There is no doubting the lack of protection for tenants in Ireland, but it was the vagaries of economic circumstances which exposed the Irish cottier, and his flimsy legal rights, to the impulse of the improving landlord. With labour-intensive tillage farming giving way to more labour-efficient pastoral farming, the pressure upon land became more acute, so that rentals, evictions and emigration increased.

One consequence of the instability of landed relations was a very low quality of accommodation for the rural poor, who either could not, or would not, invest time and money on dwellings that they might so easily lose. Even as far back as the 1770s, Arthur Young registered shock at these conditions:

> A wandering family will fix themselves under a dry bank, and with a few sticks, furze, fern, etc. make up a hovel much worse than an English pigstye, support themselves how they can, by work, begging and stealing; if the neighbourhood wants hands, or takes no notice of them, the hovel grows into a cabin.[44]

Nor was he impressed with the conditions with which the rural poor were accustomed:

> The cottages of the Irish, which are called cabins, are the most miserable looking hovels than can well be conceived; they generally consist of only one room. Mud – kneaded with straw – is the common material of the walls; these have only a door, which lets in light instead of a window, and should let the smoke out instead of a chimney, but they had rather keep it in.... The roofs of the cabins are ... raised from the tops of the mud walls, and the covering varies; some are thatched with straw, potato stalks, or with heath, others only covered with sods of turf. The bad repair these roofs are kept in, a hole in the thatch being often mended with turf, and weeds sprouting from every part, gives them the appearance of a weedy dunghill, especially when the cabin is not built with regular walls, but supported on one, or perhaps on both sides by the banks of a broad dry ditch; the roof then seems a hillock, upon which perhaps the pig grazes.[45]

Such single-roomed mud-walled huts were still widespread in pre-Famine Ireland. The census of 1841 recorded 491 278 of them, and, though mortality and emigration during the Famine years reduced the number of inhabitants who lived in such places, these dwellings still numbered 135 589 ten years later.

Poverty and what some have seen as the inadequacies of Irish landlordism were not the only explanations for the state of such dwellings. Although the age-old custom of *buailteachas*, or trans-humance (travelling between different places and occupations with the seasons: fishing, herding, farming), had probably died out by the early nineteenth century, there were many factors to spur a culture of migration. A propensity among the poor to wander was undoubtedly encouraged by the threat of expulsion from unleased marginal land. This system also prevented Irish families from becoming attached to homes and domestic possessions. Such sentiments were, as many social commentators noted, slow to die from Irish culture, even when it was transplanted to Britain or America.

While the potato and buttermilk diet kept Irish rural workers healthy in times of plenty, poverty determined the poor quality of peasant clothing, and visitors were shocked by it. A German observer in 1844 commented with thinly veiled disgust at the dress of the Irish: 'In no country is it held disgraceful to wear a coat of a coarse texture, but to go about in rags is nowhere allowed but in Ireland.... In Ireland no one appears to feel offended or surprised at the sight of a naked elbow or a bare leg'.[46] However, epithets about domestic backwardness or semi-naked barbarians came from observers who knew little of the Ireland that had nurtured these alleged offenders.

The Limits of Industrial and Urban Growth

A major reason why people left Ireland was the great decline in rural and semi-rural cottage industries. This decline was especially true of cotton and linen, though other activities, such as nail-making, were similarly affected. Increased economic activity in these trades in the 50 years before 1815 had reduced the domestic worker's reliance on agriculture, as was common elsewhere in Europe where cottage industries were thriving. The lessening importance of agriculture, and the development of a monied economy in areas where domestic textiles prospered, encouraged population growth as well as reliance upon the potato as a food of nutritional and agricultural efficiency. In the 1820s, however, competition from the rapidly industrialising British textile industry placed enormous stresses on the traditional domestic sector in Ireland.

In the eighteenth and early nineteenth centuries, domestic spinning and weaving provided vital supplementary income for thousands of small farmers and agricultural workers throughout Ireland. Often farming land provided little else but subsistence levels of production, and these workers needed extra income to buy goods at market. When factory production became more common, pressure was placed upon these handicraft workers; and only Ulster developed a mechanised system to compete with that in Britain. Production of Irish cotton and linen came to be concentrated around Belfast and other north-eastern towns, and rural outworkers, squeezed by rapidly diminishing demand, were faced with just two options: potato-reliant agricultural work in Ireland or emigration.[47]

The crisis in domestic textiles was characterised by regional disparities. The coarse yarns produced in Connacht were the first to be hit by factory competition, whereas Ulster's fine cambric and damask linens were not affected till later. As mechanisation spread, rates of pay in the domestic sphere were forced down and hours lengthened accordingly. The Irish workers who were pinched in this way were not dissimilar to the hand-loom weavers or wool-combers of northern England. In fact, it is important to regard Ireland's marginalised domestic textile workers as victims of a wider structural-economic shift which saw concentrated units of production in Lancashire, west Yorkshire and Belfast eclipsing traditional pro-duction in a range of regions, for example Norfolk and the West Country as well as in rural Ireland. In each area migration offered a possible solution. What is more, the demise of domestic production pushed men as well as women towards leaving.

The failure of Ireland to develop towns on a scale to compare with the rest of northern Europe was partly the result of this failure in the industrial sphere. This situation clearly affected the rate of emigration. Although it is possible for a place to be urban without being industrial, the most marked European urban development in this period occurred in the industrialising areas where coal, iron and steel, shipbuilding, engineering, textiles and other labour-intensive, mech-anised and often factory-based systems of production were emerging. Aside from Belfast, which fitted these criteria, Ireland lacked such manifestations. The countries with the lowest levels of urbanisation tended to be those also registering fewest signs of industrial advance-ment, with Ireland foremost among them. Comparison of European rates of urbanisation shows just how stark the Irish picture was. Only Austria, Poland, Scandinavia and Switzerland had smaller relative urban populations and witnessed urban population growth at a rate slower than in Ireland. When compared with the industrialising nations of England and Wales, Scotland, Germany and the Low Countries, Irish levels of urban development were very low.

There were sharp national and regional differences in the Atlantic archipelago, with Ireland lagging far behind her close neighbours.

Scotland, where the population remained smaller than Ireland's throughout the nineteenth century, and which had similarly under-developed pastoral regions, offers the most telling of contrasts. In 1800, there were eight centres of over 10 000 population both in Ireland and in Scotland, though the Scottish examples were larger, accounting for 17.3 per cent of the population against Ireland's seven per cent. While Ireland and Scotland shared many similar features, from climate and geography to the existence of traditional communities in crisis, Scotland's disadvantages were less stark and her advantages more numerous. In Scotland, mineral wealth was immense and helped to promote the industrialisation of the central belt. By the 1850s, this thin strip of Scotland was perhaps the most densely urban and actively industrial region in the world. By 1890 Scotland's 37 urban centres of over 10 000 population housed 50.3 per cent of Scots, whereas Ireland's corresponding figures were just 18 and 17.6 per cent.[48]

In the nineteenth century, Ireland had only three cities that were significant on a British scale: Dublin, Belfast and Cork. Yet Dublin's population increased by no more than 50 per cent in this period, while Cork's declined by one-quarter. Only Belfast could be compared to the great industrial cities of Europe. Most other urban centres were tiny in 1901 and had grown little in the preceding century. Few Irish towns had populations of more than 10 000 in total. Urban growth, therefore, failed to match population increases. In Cork between 1821 and 1841, for example, the urban population increased by about five per cent, whereas in the county itself the increase was 22.8 per cent. In Limerick, the figures were respectively 14.2 per cent and 23.5; for Galway 16.8 and 42.4.[49]

Ireland, therefore, lacked the cushion against rural discontent and massive emigration which towns and industries provided in Britain. An Irish agricultural labourer might find work in tanning, brewing or house-building in Cork, Dublin or elsewhere; and males and females alike were drawn with increasing regularity from rural Ulster's domestic spinning wheels and looms to Belfast's textile factories; but none of this activity was enough to service the demand for work. Comparisons with industrial Britain are stark. In 1901, Dublin and Belfast had a combined population of 640 000, which was much smaller than either Liverpool or Manchester alone. The Irish may have become a 'model urban proletariat'[50] in New York or Glasgow, but there was no hope of their becoming such in the Ireland that lay beyond Belfast.

The Great Famine, 1845–50

Despite the claim of scholars such as Crotty and Foster that 1815 marked *the* watershed in Irish economic and social history, the Great Famine nevertheless remains crucial in any explanation of Irish emigration. The potato blight which struck Ireland in the autumn of 1845 had a devastating impact. Viewed by some in Britain as a providential punishment for purblind landlordism and peasant fecundity, the Famine swept rapid changes through Irish society. Terrible mortality, floods of emigration and sickening incidents of destitution gripped the country. Poverty and hunger were not new to Irish society; nor did the Famine create cottier emigration.

What made the Famine unique was its scale and intensity: the levels of death, disease, privation and emigration that were thrown up in its wake. It also presents one of the most spectacular failings of government social provision in the nineteenth century: food supplies, work schemes, assisted emigration, poor houses and private charity all proved to be inadequate in the face of this social disaster. Irish commentators felt that Peel's and especially Russell's governments did too little, and it has been argued recently that successive British administrations viewed the Famine crisis an ideal opportunity to 'engineer' Irish social structure, by removing the poorest elements who farmed tiny scraps of land, in a way that had been suggested by the Devon Commission in 1845. Certainly, there can be no other explanation of punitive legislation such as the 'Gregory clause' of the Poor Law Amendment Act 1847, which forbade the administration of poor relief to those who held more than one-quarter of an acre of land. Seen on this level, it is no surprise perhaps that the Famine entered the consciousness of Irish nationalists at the time and has been a powerful instrument, as well as a deep social tragedy, ever since.[51]

The potato blight proved to be both acute and chronic: it struck in 1845 and returned each year until 1849, rendering partial and complete failure upon the potato crop. Its effects were undeniably dreadful; the disaster proved to be an insurmountable challenge to a poor rural population which struggled at the best of times to survive on a foodstuff now being destroyed by fungal infection. In Trevelyan's words, the Famine amounted to a 'great calamity'. For nearly a decade people died or fled from its effects. Exact mortality and emigration figures are unavailable, though numerous historians have attempted to calculate Ireland's losses.

In 1845, the Irish population was probably more than 8.5 million; six years later it had fallen by around two million or more to 6 552 385. Cousens suggests that between 1846 and 1850 excess mortality (deaths over and above those who would have died anyway) accounted for 800 645 persons (nearer 860 000 if the figures for the first three months of 1851 are included). More recently, Mokyr and Donnelly have revised these figures upwards to take account of entire families which were wiped out (and thus not reported to census enumerators) and averted births (incidents of children not being born due to the Famine) to arrive at a figure of between 1 082 000 and 1 498 000.[52] Yet these general statistics reveal only so much about emigration, for the Famine struck selectively, by social class and region. It tended to impact most heavily upon the potato-dependent cottiers of the west, and left alone rich farmers in Carlow, which is why Cullen has argued that the Great Famine was 'less a national disaster than a social and regional one'.[53] The average across the country was in the low 20s per 1000, while the number of counties experiencing a rate of more than 25 was in double figures.[54] Figures for the four provinces reveal interesting features of excess mortality: worst hit was Connacht (40.4 per 1000), then came Munster (30.3), Ulster (20.7) and Leinster (8.6).

Although there was massive variation in the excess mortality rates by province and county, only County Dublin was unaffected. Elsewhere, the figure for excess mortality between 1846 and 1851 ranged from the very low in Wexford, to the harrowingly high rates in Roscommon, Sligo and Mayo. Variations can also be traced within provinces, with Leitrim (also in Connacht) much less affected than either of these three worst-hit counties. In Ulster, southern counties such as Cavan, Fermanagh and Monaghan suffered much worse than central or eastern parts, where Londonderry experienced the lowest excess mortality and Armagh the highest. The counties which suffered most suggest an inter-regional distribution, taking in a combination of densely populated and economically backward counties where small-holding and subsistence were most common. This state of affairs is starkly illustrated by the rate of population decline (Table 1.2). Thus, to these Ulster and north Connacht counties should be added Galway, Cork and Clare. Even in counties which appear to have escaped relatively lightly, such as Kerry, there were coastal pockets of marginal cultivation where communities experienced devastation in the shadow of the Famine. Only a multitude of local, perhaps parish-level studies might reveal the precise consequences of this social disaster.

Emigration during the Famine was different from that which went before, not only in scale but also in terms of the attitude underpinning it. The first signs of blight in 1845 had summoned up little of the panic that accompanied the near universal crop failure in the summer of 1846. This latter event 'had an instantaneous and unmistakable effect', wrote Oliver MacDonagh. 'For the first time in Irish history, there was a heavy autumn exodus', in which 'thousands risked their lives upon a winter crossing'.[55] In so doing, many perished, travelling in infamous 'coffin ships' across cold and stormy seas without adequate provision. Sea-born mortality rates reached almost one-fifth in 1847, and Canadian officials were said to be shocked by the state of the people disembarking at their ports. Conditions were greatly improved after 1847. However, from this point Famine emigration became a mass exodus of the half-starved, the diseased and the desperate; people who were poorly clothed, ill-provisioned and with bleak prospects. Even so, sea-born mortality on the trip to Canada was 'seldom greater than two per cent'.[56] Some of the worst problems for migrants occurred after they had arrived (as we shall see in Chapter 2). At least 20 000 (30 per cent) of migrants to Canada had died by the end of 1847. In that year nearly 220 000 people emigrated from Ireland, and though the figure fluctuated thereafter, with a high of more than 350 000 in 1851, only one year (1855) saw emigration drop below 100 000. Throughout the period from 1847 to 1855 the average rate of exodus stood at 200 000 per annum.

In these years, it has been calculated, somewhere around 2.1 million people fled Ireland: 1.2 million before 1851 and up to 900 000 after that date. The United States was the main recipient, accounting for nearly three-quarters (1.5 million), with Canada taking around 340 000, Britain up to 300 000, and a small fraction going elsewhere, mainly to Australia. Indications are that this pattern was already in place before the Famine. In the eight years before the Famine perhaps 350 000 had made their way to America. This was an annual rate of 50 000 – or 10 000 more than crossed each year in the later 1820s and early 1830s. Without the Famine, however, the scale of loss would have been much smaller, or much less compressed. As Miller has shown, the Famine doubled the emigration rate so that 'more people left in just eleven years than during the preceding two and one-half centuries'.[57]

The nature of population loss was also different during the Famine. For the first time, a substantial proportion of emigrants came from the poorer classes, with up to 90 per cent between 1851 and 1855 recorded as labourers. Even in the United States, where emigrants were traditionally of higher status, approximately three-quarters were drawn from the labourer class. The majority of these people were poor, from Irish-speaking regions and were Catholic: factors which did not smooth their passage into the new communities. Cheap transport helped to prime the emigrant pump, and another significant spur lay in the development of chain migration through the system of remittances, whereby family members sent back cash or pre-paid tickets to assist relatives. In the period between 1848 and 1851 alone some £2 947 000 came back to Ireland this way. Landlord-assisted schemes had existed for some time in Ireland, though the Poor Law of 1849, which brought into being for the first time a system of government-assisted emigration, accounted for less than 20 000.[58]

In general, during the Famine, an inverse relationship existed between the poverty and population pressure in a particular county and its rate of emigration. The exceptions to this rule were north Connacht and south Ulster, where both mortality and emigration were high. Elsewhere, the heavily populated and poverty stricken areas (Mayo, for example) provided proportionately few emigrants in the Famine years. Generally, the places with the highest destitution rates witnessed high mortality rather than high emigration. The logic of these patterns was twofold: first, that people *either* died *or* departed; and, secondly, that destitution denied potential migrants the means and the spirit to leave. Thus, Galway, Clare and west Cork experienced high mortality rates but low emigration. In Limerick, Donegal and a number of Leinster counties (Kildare, Kilkenny and Louth) the opposite was true, with low mortality and high emigration. Overall, the greatest numbers of departures came from northern Connacht, the Leinster midlands and south Ulster.[59]

These regional factors are explained by contrasting pictures of poverty and population density, but also by deteriorating relations on the land, with evictions and clearances a common feature of life in some parts. Evictions of smallholders led to sizeable migrations in counties such as Leitrim, Roscommon, Longford and Queen's, while areas with heavy poor rates also experienced significant emigration among classes of ratepayers who were not far from the bottom rung of society themselves, usually with property valued at around £4.

During the Famine, landlords were roundly condemned for failing to take care of their poor. Although there were many examples of landlords doing their bit for tenants, this is still perceived to be much less common than in Scotland, where men such as Norman MacLeod of MacLeod of Skye bankrupted themselves trying to keep their cottars from starving.[60] In fact, Ireland had good landlords too: men such as Lord George Hill of Dunfanaghy, County Donegal, who was able to boast that none of the tenants on his land died of starvation.[61] Moreover, what landlord could be more cruel than the Scotsman Gordon of Cluny? Between 1848 and 1851, more than 2700 tenant debtors on his lands on Barra, South Uist and Benbecula were sent to Canada, many of whom were hunted with dogs, bound and despatched against their will.[62] Some Irish landowners abnegated their responsibilities, and in many areas eviction rates were very high. No doubt many of these expulsions were the result of opportunism, but some were the result of Poor Law legislation that made the lessor responsible for rates collected on properties valued at less than £4. While in normal times this benefited smallholders, in times of hardship it increased the likelihood of eviction. The perilous position of many poorer ratepayers in the areas hardest hit explains why small farmers in Queen's county and north-central Ireland were a significant part of the emigrant stream.[63]

Thus emigration, whether through private initiative or on the public purse, was but one answer to the tribulations of Irish life in the 1840s and 1850s, but it was not a new response, and it did not end with the Famine.

Beyond the Famine

Despite the commonly held view that the Famine destroyed traditional Irish society, poverty and subsistence persisted as features of Irish life, especially in the west, which for many years 'remained to a considerable extent a potato economy, dependence on the root being almost as great as in the pre-Famine years'.[64] In the 1870s, the counties of Munster and Connacht lost their populations at a generally lower rate than was experienced in the north and east. By 1871 many of the areas which had been most terribly ravaged by the Famine had recovered to achieve 1841 population levels and it was in this same seaboard region of the west that the harvest failures of 1879 and

1880, which were almost bad as those experienced during the Great Famine, and the demise of seasonal harvest migration created further social problems. As a consequence, population loss from the western counties in the 1880s became as acute as it had been in Ulster and Leinster during previous decades (see Table 1.2).[65]

This decline was not restricted to the poorer west: with the exception of Dublin, all counties experienced it. The most striking contrasts in falling population, however, occurred in the 1860s and 1870s, between the traditional west and south, and other parts of Ireland. In Munster and Connacht, percentage population loss in this period, with one or two exceptions (Limerick in 1871, Roscommon in 1881) mostly ran in single figures, whereas much greater flows were recorded in Ulster and Leinster before 1871. The 1880s was clearly an important decade for emigration, with 18 out of 32 counties witnessing doubled-figured losses, including all five of Connacht's and all six of Munster's.

By 1880, Fitzpatrick has remarked, 'the national "haemorrhage" has long since become a structural element of the post-Famine social order'.[66] And in the 50 years before the creation of the Irish Free State (1922), some 2.5 million Irish emigrants left their homeland. Despite the allure of the United States for the people of Europe's other nations, Ireland's emigrant flow was by far the most voluminous. Ireland's nearest competitors were Norway, Sweden and Scotland, but none of these mustered more than half Ireland's emigration rate; and 'even at the height of the "new immigration" of the 1890s, net movement from Italy was less than half as brisk as that from Ireland'.[67]

The rapid decline of the Irish population in the century after the Famine cannot be explained by emigration alone. K. H. Connell once argued that the Famine delivered the Malthusian check that contemporaries had long feared. For him, the Famine instilled a fear factor into the lives of the poor, eliminating the 'haphazard, happy-go-lucky marriages of the eighteenth and early nineteenth centuries'. However, more recent research has shown that a decline in the rate of population growth had actually begun before the Famine. The calamity of the 1840s amplified, rather than created, changing patterns of nuptiality and fertility. While there is no doubt that the Famine further reduced reproduction rates (which in the post-Famine decades became among the lowest in Europe), recent writers have rightly questioned Connell's view that late marriage (and, therefore, fewer children), improved living standards and a new-found materialism followed. Guinnane points out that, while celibacy increased (which it did very markedly), many of those who remained single into old age, thus accruing material benefits to themselves, were actually better-off farmers, mainly household heads.[68] For the poorer elements of Irish society, however, emigration remained the most viable option for economic improvement, and the post-Famine years witnessed a marked upturn in emigration from the poor counties of the west.

One of the most compelling reasons to emigrate from Connacht and western Munster was the demise of the large-scale harvest migration, which had provided a vital supplement to household incomes. The demise of the wandering reaper in the 1880s tells us as much about traditional Irish life as does the Famine. Society in the west had resisted the sort of mass migration that had been the response in most regions to the potato failure of the 1840s. Here supplementary incomes remained vital if potato-dependent cottiers and landless poor were to maintain their precarious existence on the margins of what was a changing Irish society. Indeed, it was not until the onset of widespread mechanisation and the agricultural depression of the 1870s that temporary migration began to fall (reaching 42 000 in 1880) and a permanent exodus became more noticeable. Reaping and threshing were increasingly performed by machines, which reduced labour demand and left Irish spalpeens to harvest potatoes, turnips and other roots crops which were more difficult to mechanise. In response, there was sustained population drift from the poorer west, where, in Ó Gráda's trenchant observation, 'partial proletarianisation in Britain was exchanged for the prospect of fuller proletarianisation in America and elsewhere'.[69]

These encroachments on the spalpeen way of life constituted part of a wider process of change in Irish rural society. Irish historians have long noted the 'social revolution' between the Famine and World War I which led to the emergence of a widespread system of landed proprietorship by small-scale occupiers. Accompanying this transformation, and an important companion to the demise of seasonal migrant labour, was the relative disappearance of the Irish agricultural labourer.[70] Contemporaries themselves noted that peasant proprietorship and the more equitable distribution of land, which had been facilitated by successive legislation between the 1870s and the early 1900s, in addition to a widespread change from tillage to pasture, dealt successive blows to the poorest elements of Irish society, for

Table 1.3: Emigration from Connacht and Munster in the later nineteenth century

Decade to:	1871	% increase	1881	% increase	1891	% increase	1901	% increase
Connacht								
Galway	38 758	-23.8	23 665	-38.9	51 121	116.0	36 820	-28.0
Leitrim	13 980	-16.9	12 683	-9.3	21 008	65.6	9 830	-53.2
Mayo	27 496	-6.2	24 705	-10.2	42 368	71.5	40 703	-39.3
Roscommon	21 393	-22.9	13 790	-35.4	23 128	67.7	16 332	-29.4
Sligo	12 049	-9.6	11 708	-2.8	23 594	101.5	14 065	-40.4
Munster								
Clare	31 667	-36.7	18 796	-40.6	32 421	72.5	18 031	-44.4
Cork	118 669	-19.8	74 209	-37.5	83 533	12.6	77 072	-7.7
Kerry	40 480	-29.6	27 036	-33.2	50 855	88.1	38 599	-24.1
Limerick	46 339	-25.5	22 132	-52.2	33 081	49.5	14 426	-56.4
Tipperary	47 269	-41.7	26 645	-43.6	32 762	23.0	19 050	-41.9
Waterford	19 681	-48.7	12 732	-35.3	19 428	52.6	10 058	-48.2

Source: Census of Ireland, 1881–1911; Emigration returns, 1911–20.

Table 1.4: Total post-Famine emigration by province

Decade to:					Four-decade
	1871	1881	1891	1901	total
*Province**					
Ulster	201 240	240 110	216 524	86 455	744 329
Munster	304 105	181 370	252 080	177 236	914 791
Leinster	149 838	110 619	138 282	49 552	448 291
Connacht	113 676	86 551	161 219	117 750	479 196

*Provinces are ranked in accordance with their population size in 1871.
Source: Census of Ireland, 1881–1911; Emigration returns, 1911–20.

whom the sale of labour and the precarious, untenanted working of tiny plots of marginal land had been so vital. At the same time, the upturn in emigration, encouraged by the disappearance of paid agricultural labour, does not seem to have increased the value of the labour which remained behind. The regions in flux saw no increase in non-agricultural employment, and emigration was further encouraged, a process shown in rates of emigration from the west (Table 1.3).

The most significant emigrations of the period came from the western seaboard counties, a cross-regional mix taking in Kerry, Clare, Galway and Mayo, with Roscommon the only inland county to rank among the highest senders of emigrants. Galway and Mayo experienced the most considerable population loss, particularly in the 1880s, although a question of proportion must be borne in mind: Leitrim and Sligo, for example, had little more than half the population of these two larger counties, and so their rates of loss, notably in the 1870s and 1880s, are of particular significance. As Table 1.4 illustrates, the counties of Munster, most notably Cork and Kerry, witnessed some of the largest gross levels of emigration in this later period, although only Cork decanted a greater number of emigrants than Galway and Mayo. Here too we must remember proportions: Cork's population was the largest in Ireland by a considerable degree, twice the size of its nearest rivals. Counties Tipperary and Limerick lost more people by emigration at various times in this period, and at a slightly higher proportional rate than the counties of Connacht. What is noticeable from Table 1.4 is the great leap in emigration from Connacht during the 1880s.

Table 1.5: Major emigrations from Ireland, 1876–1900

	United States	Canada	Australia and New Zealand	Britain
1876–80	139 622	6 501	27 836	84 753
1881–85	313 682	27 484	26 102	46 199
1886–90	293 691	12 302	17 427	24 587
1891–95	222 460	4 211	5 181	10 766
1896–1900	165 029	2 376	4 191	17 195

Source: Emigration returns of the Registrar General, 1876–1900.

Much is made of Britain's eclipse in many different spheres in the later nineteenth century, and the attraction of Irish emigrants was but one of them. Britain's position as the main recipient of the Irish stream was undermined in the 1840s with the Famine and cheap steam packets to America. Although Britain's share of the emigration trade fell off markedly in the post-Famine period, until 1880, the journey across the Irish Sea was still attracting more than half the number of emigrants who went to the United States; thereafter the transatlantic share grew rapidly as Britain's dwindled (see Table 1.5).

Conclusions

While emigration was a key element of Irish demographic history, nationalist writers have viewed its contexts and consequences as far broader than mere numbers can capture. The nature of departure, especially during the Famine, enforces the view that emigration was more than simply a response to social pressures and economic change: it was a result of the unequal, colonial relations between Britain and Ireland. Emigration threw up questions about a 'brain drain', a depletion of human resources, which we do not have the evidence to answer. Yet this is an interesting point upon which to conclude, given that many contemporaries in Britain were critical of the value of Irish labour, while some extolled its virtues. Poor Law guardians, magistrates, the police and many clerics tended to view the Irish as a pernicious influence on the morals of their countrymen; but employers usually shared the view of Alexander Carlile, cotton master of Paisley, who said that it would be 'most detrimental to the town and neighbourhood, were the Irish immigrations stopped or even seriously interfered with'.[71] Since then, many economic historians have emphasised the importance to British industrial development of Irish 'mobile shock troops'. Whether or not migrants were representative of the Ireland they left behind will never be known, although it is clear that those who left were tremendously adaptable. They became prominent in a whole host of trades that were uncommon in Ireland, such mining, iron- and steel-making and shipbuilding. At the same time, we cannot know the sum of all individual motivations for migration. While key explanations lie at the macro-economic level, migrants were not selected randomly nor drawn in equal proportions from all classes of society. Yet we do know that by the 1830s emigration was more than an economic necessity; it had become a part of the Irish people's culture. In the same period, moreover, it had also become part of Britain's culture because the massive 'pull' factor of the Industrial Revolution made this phenomenal movement of people more likely.

2

CONCENTRATION AND DISPERSAL: IRISH LABOUR MIGRATION TO BRITAIN

Introduction

Irish emigration might have been, as Foster claimed, 'the great fact of Irish social history from the early nineteenth century', but it also had an enormous influence upon receiver nations.[1] Ireland's close proximity to Britain meant that the two had always been linked by interactions such as migration. In the late eighteenth and early nineteenth centuries, however, what had previously been a noticeably two-way flow of people developed into a much more one-sided affair. Ireland's relative economic prosperity during the French Wars slowed, but did not stem, the flow altogether. By the 1820s there were noticeable Irish settlements in many towns outside the major ports of entry and the capital. These communities grew considerably in the 1830s and early 1840s and were swollen greatly by the emigration of the Great Famine period (1845–50) (see Table 2.1). What is more, they continued to be augmented for a long time after this mass exodus had subsided. Distinct Irish communities were still visible in the inter-war period in the large cities of Liverpool, Manchester, Glasgow, Birmingham and more recently in Luton and Coventry.

Historians have rightly viewed Irish settlement during the Industrial Revolution as heroic, hectic and tragic. Irish settlers were well represented in the social reportage of the day as figures of pity and loathing in equal measure. Many were also acknowledged to be at the

Table 2.1: The Irish-born population of England and Wales and Scotland, 1841–1911

	England and Wales	%	Scotland	%
1841	289 404	1.8	126 321	4.8
1851	519 959	2.9	207 367	7.2
1861	601 634	3.0	204 083	6.7
1871	566 540	2.5	207 770	6.2
1881	562 374	2.2	218 745	5.9
1891	458 315	1.6	194 807	4.8
1901	426 565	1.3	205 064	4.6
1911	375 325	1.0	174 715	3.7

Source: Census of England and Wales, 1841–1911; Census of Scotland, 1841–1911.

frontier of industrial expansion: hewing canals, laying railways and blasting docks. They also dominated the building trades which constructed the redbrick towns and cities of Victorian Britain, of which Manchester is the classic example. Many migrants fell into the worst jobs in textiles, tanning and chemicals, while the Irishman's often-cited feats of strength and endurance were perceived to be vital in some of the heaviest work, for example dock labour, quarrying and mining. The Irish also seemed to dominate the marginal street economies of the big towns and cities: 'The Irish deal in old things of all descriptions, [such as] bones, old tools, old clothes', said the Procurator Fiscal of Greenock, George Williamson, who added, in true Engels style, that 'they also rear pigs in considerable numbers, and sometimes keep them in their houses'. Williamson, like Mayhew, observed a great company of Irish hawkers, who sold everything from 'fish, oysters, salted meat, eggs' to 'hare-skins, and shells from the West Indies and Honduras', noting that 'they turn their hand to every description of low trade which is the fruit of industry, and requires almost no capital'.[2]

Despite the great number of Irish arrivals in the 1830s and 1840s, and the huge body of negative opinion which welled up against them at this time, Irish settlement was not simply an early industrial phenomenon. Long after the cataclysmic events of the Great Famine,

Irish workers continued to seek out new lives in the manufacturing heartlands of Britain. Table 2.1 shows that, although the most significant increase in the Irish-born population of Britain occurred between 1841 and 1861, the Irish-born presence was still important on the eve of World War I, and in Scotland it remained even more apparent. It is also important to recognise that national averages hide very significant regional clustering. There were virtually no Irish people in the market towns of Buckinghamshire or Dorset, whereas in the main centres of the industrial north the Irish might easily represent up to one-third of the male labour force. Moreover, in the long-run phenomenon of Irish settlement the experience of settlers was often richly variegated. Irish migrants were flexible and available; and, while they remained most noticeable in places such as Liverpool and Glasgow and the other major industrial centres throughout the whole of the nineteenth century, dozens of smaller places – such as Stafford and Ormskirk, Maryport and Consett – also developed Irish communities.

Itinerant Migration

Irish migrants had entered Britain in notable numbers since the medieval period, a process which, at various times, evoked considerable consternation. As early as 1413 a statute ordered that all 'Irishmen and Irish clerks, beggars called chamberdekyns, be voided out of the realm', whereas a more permanent nuisance was perceived by an Elizabethan commentator who described the Irish in England as 'like crickets to the crevice of a brew-house'.[3] During the hungry years of 1629 and 1633 working people across the south, from Pembroke to Essex, London to Somerset, complained about the influx of Irish vagrants, and, as migration became more commonplace, a system of removal was established so that Poor Law legislation could be deployed to send the Irish home.[4] Peddlers, drovers and travelling tradesmen were often Irish, though they captured the imagination rather less than the regular traffic in 'Wild Geese', the 'idle swordsmen' who sought livings as mercenaries in European armies. It was common for Irish to fight Irish while in the pay of France, Spain, Austria or of other Catholic monarchies. The numbers of 'Wild Geese' increased greatly in those times (for example, 1603 and in the 1650s) when Irish armies were vanquished by the English.

Today, there are still Irish settlements in France and Spain as testimony to the ancient tradition of Irish mercenaries.[5]

However, the most important transient pre-industrial migration, as we saw in Chapter 1, was that of seasonal harvesters or spalpeens. Although such movement was probably going on earlier, seasonal passage had become a key part of both Irish and British life in the mid to late eighteenth century. Although itinerant migration has been viewed by some historians as a kind of precursor to permanent settlement, it was, in fact, a parallel movement which did not peak until long after the Famine. Some seasonal migrants stayed on in Britain, though this summer work was more important, we have noted, as a contribution towards the peasants' struggle to hold on to their Irish lands, rather than a step towards a new life across the water. Cheap fares made temporary migration more popular in the 1820s, and by this time few regions – from the Highlands of Scotland to Norfolk and Kent – were without regular supplies of Irish agricultural labour. These workers travelled from most Irish ports, including smaller ones such as Dundalk, Drogheda and Londonderry, and by 1841 one in 37 of Mayo's residents sought work on farms throughout England and Scotland.[6]

Irish harvesters met with a mixed response in the communities where they searched for work. William Cobbett was typical of his day when he described the spalpeens passing through London as 'squalid creatures ... with rags hardly sufficient to hide the nakedness of their bodies'.[7] These workers, however, were popular with farmers, who came to rely on their labour, even if constables and magistrates looked at them, and their occasional drunken rowdyism, with an unfriendly eye. The real tension, though, derived not from their appearance or drinking, but from their place on the economic ladder. Spalpeens found themselves encroaching on those indigenous workers – for example Scots cottars – who were themselves feeling the pressures of commercial agriculture. The two groups were thus thrown into competition with one another. By the 1790s, for example, Irish competition had ensured that the number of Highland reapers working in the Scottish Borders had declined, and this competitive struggle caused native resentment.[8] What is more, similar pressures were also pushing poor agricultural labourers from southern England to compete with Irish labourers for work of this type.

The Irish reaper was probably just as noteworthy for acts of piety – for example, walking six miles to the nearest Catholic chapel – as for drinking and fighting, or for poor living and working conditions, which in any case varied considerably. Some farmers treated Irish reapers well, others poorly. Pay rates fluctuated and varied across regions, depending on the amount of work there was to be done. Tatie hokers, for example, were paid much more for harvesting than they were for the hoeing and milking which occupied the time between early and late crops. Spalpeens sometimes received food, such as potatoes, soup, buttermilk, bread and beer, whereas others received only skimmed milk and had to find their own comestibles. Larger farms might have what amounted to rough dormitories for their workers; in the Scottish Borders, at the turn of twentieth century, conditions were often favourable, with cottages provided for the itinerant Irish workers. Border farmers also tended to hire labour for a longer period – usually between June and December – with the men hoeing turnips, making hay, bringing in corn and digging potatoes. Yet at about the same time, one farm near Warrington provided only 'Paddy houses', cleared outhouses, for their roving labourers, and it was common for such workers simply to be directed towards draughty chicken shacks or pigsties. Across the country, though, food rations were more generous during harvests, with bread, cheese and beer provided as standard.[9]

These seasonal farm workers were not the only ones who sought a living by moving about the country following work. Another group that did so was the navvies. Navvies were renowned for hard work and hard living; brute force, drinking and violence were part of their folklore. Navvies were said to live by their own code, moving their hastily constructed shanty towns with them as they went. Yet these men possessed an array of talents as well as great physical endurance. Contemporaries reckoned it took a year to turn a countryside labourer into a navvy, and even then many did not make it. The navvies were set apart from their fellow workers – physically, culturally and mentally. They were generally better paid and lived on a diet that was said to be rich in beef and beer, although their working lives were usually short. The term 'navvy' became a common insult in Victorian society, a term of derision, an epithet that mothers uttered to frighten their children.[10]

The proportion of navvies who were Irish varied considerably. Brooke's examination of railway builders in Yorkshire, Derbyshire, Durham and Cumberland between 1841 and 1871 suggests that the Irish comprised only about four per cent, whereas Handley considered

Irish labour in Scotland to be more important than native labour. Further evidence from Patmore's micro-study of navvies working on the Nidd Viaduct in Knaresborough in 1851 puts the Irish at one-quarter.[11] Overall, it does not seem unreasonable to suggest the Irish accounted for more than ten per cent of the navvying workforce. Irish labour played a vital part in the great railway construction projects of the nineteenth century, and was still a substantial component of this labour force in the 1860s and 1870s, when great dock basins were being excavated in, for example, the Lancashire boom town of Barrow-in-Furness.

Irish paupers were another important itinerant group in this period. Wandering beggars had long been the butt of critical comments, but the post-war slump after 1815 precipitated both permanent settlement and pauper migration, with the latter appearing altogether more desperate and disorganised. The north-west of England seems to have been worst hit, and when pauper numbers increased so too did complaints about them. It has often been written that the Poor Law reforms of the 1820s and 1830s, which climaxed with the Poor Law Amendment Act of 1834, were the products of an ideological sea change, and, while this is partly true, the factor of cost – and most evidently the cost of Irish paupers – played a major part by generating a desire for reform among local ratepayers. As early as 1817, the Cumbrian ruling elite was expressing concern about the proportion of the county's poor rate that was being spent on the Irish. John Curwen, a prominent landlord and mine-owner, told the Sturges-Bourne Select Committee on the Poor Law that in his parish of Rockliffe, near Carlisle, the figure was nearly 50 per cent. He added:

> I believe it will be found in all the principal towns of the county, there is almost the same proportion of Irish and Scotch pressing on the poor rates; so that we may assume one-third of the whole charge on the county of Cumberland is paid to Irish, who have no settlement, and who have surreptitiously intruded themselves upon us.[12]

Such complaints had not dissipated by the 1820s or 1830s, when removal and hard labour were both tried as deterrents against the Irish seeking relief. The tensions thrown up by the Irish burden on the poor rate was to be a foretaste of the wild reactions which accompanied fast-growing Irish communities in the larger industrial centres.

The Emergence of Permanent Settlements

The wandering Irish – reapers, navvies and destitute paupers – were gradually being overshadowed by urban Irish settlements in the major towns and cities. By the 1820s and 1830s, permanently settled members of the Irish population who worked as labourers, masons, factory hands, dock workers and hod carriers, and who were engaged in rough work such as tanning, glue making, chemicals and sugar refining, were far more numerically significant than their itinerant countrymen, even though the two groups lived parallel lives until the twentieth century. Fixed Irish enclaves had existed in the capital since the sixteenth century, when observers also noted their significance among the city's 'great multitude of wandering persons'.[13] By the eighteenth century distinct communities of Irish workers were noticeable in London, not least in the vicinity of the docks, where Irish workers were the most common non-native labour. They dominated workers' limited combinations in this period, and sought to control elements of the labour process in Wapping and elsewhere. By the turn of the century, London's Irish population was both sizeable and well established. A survey of 1814, for example, put at 14 000 the number of Irish who relied on charity alone, with the total population much greater.[14] The rapid growth of Irish communities in this period is shown by the changes experienced in Liverpool. In 1707 one-sixth of rate-paying families (205) in the city were Catholic; by 1800 some 5000 (six per cent) of the total population were Irish.[15]

Scotland's Irish population also grew rapidly in the eighteenth century, and was well spread throughout the central Lowlands and in the western counties by 1800. From the 1780s, Ulster Protestant weavers were beginning to colonise parts of Wigtownshire, Kirkcud-brightshire, Ayrshire, Lanarkshire and Renfrewshire, though the Lothians area, around Edinburgh, waited a little longer for a similar influx. These Irish migrants – like horses, cattle and other commodities – were part of an age-old two-way economic inter-relationship between Ulster and Scotland. The Reverend Richard Sinnot told Cornewall Lewis in 1836 that no part of Kirkcudbrightshire and Ayrshire was without Irish settlers, the majority of whom were

Protestants, while the Reverend William Thompson told him that the greatest influx to his part of Ayrshire occurred as a result of the 1798 rebellion.[16] The movement into Scotland in the late eighteenth century centred mainly on textiles and agriculture and was often temporary or transient. Yet it reached as far north as Aberdeen, where in 1836 there was an Irish-born population of between 2500 and 3000, most of whom found work in linen and cotton, with general labouring typically ubiquitous. The Catholicism of the Aberdeen-Irish was said to keep them apart from the native population, though the Reverend Charles Gordon thought they managed quite well in the face of native antipathy.[17] This movement into Scotland's weaving regions also found its parallel further south in Cumberland, especially in and around Carlisle. Iron smelting also encouraged migration between Ireland and both Scotland and the lake counties. This certainly accounted for the Irish population of the isolated north Lancashire town of Ulverston, which in 1800 had 150 (five per cent) Irish-born residents out of a total population of 3000.[18]

At the turn of the century, then, migration patterns were beginning to solidify, with growing towns attracting increasing waves of Irish. Central Scotland was rapidly developing into one of the most highly industrial regions in the world and Irish labour was consequently drawn in, with a strong desire for steady work usually met only in the most unpleasant industries. This period also witnessed the development of craft controls, which affected incoming ethnic groups, most notably in coal mining, where Irish workers were usually restricted to pit-head labouring because of a failure to break the native stranglehold on hewing. In Ayrshire the Irish found work in textiles as well as coal, as they did across northern Britain. Irish salt workers were also noted in Ayrshire as well as Cheshire. The most densely packed Irish-born populations outside Liverpool, Manchester and Glasgow, however, were to be found in textile towns such as Maybole in Ayrshire. In 1831 another Ayrshire town, Girvan, had a population of 6430, three-quarters of whom were Irish-born. Most of these were employed as hand-loom weavers, outworking for Glasgow merchants. Rapidly expanding medium-sized towns, such as Kilmarnock (which between 1831 and 1841 grew from 12 768 to 18 093), also had large numbers of Irish migrants who worked as labourers, stone breakers and weavers.[19]

The Irish in Renfrewshire were clustered mainly in the towns of Barrhead, Greenock, Paisley, Renfrew and Pollokshaws. Much of the early migration to this county was attracted to the cotton factories, with labouring also providing much work. Around half of the adult population of Paisley were workshop-based hand-loom shawl weavers fashioning the town's famous print. The population of the town was stable, but the work was subject to sometimes wild fluctuations in market demand. One Paisley cotton master, John Orr, claimed in 1834 to employ 199 Irish hands in his mill out of a total labour force of 279, and he offered a staunch defence of the free flow of Irish migrant labour into Britain. Orr's fellow cotton factory owner, Alexander Carlile, shared this view of the value of Irish labour, though his assessment was decidedly double-edged. Carlile demanded the right to use Irish labour because it was cheap and efficient, although he claimed the Irish were mainly from 'the poorest classes' and rarely were found in the middle ranks of society. He defended the payment of lower wages to the Irish on the grounds that it would be 'mischievous to give to any person wages beyond his degree of civilisation'. He explained: 'Give an increase in wages to a respectable weaver, and he will multiply his comforts; ... give a less cultivated man a considerable increase, and you, almost to a certainty, morally degrade him; it [a higher wage] is spent in mere animal enjoyment'.[20] Such conveniently twisted logic undoubtedly fuelled suspicions among native workers who were anxious about the Irish influx. In Greenock, the local Catholic priest, William Gordon, estimated his flock at 4000, mostly Irish. The wider Irish population obviously included non-attenders, but also Orangemen, as he called Protestants, although the priest had no estimate of their numbers. Labouring at poor wages of 10–12s provided many of them with work. Indeed, around half of all unskilled labour in the town was Irish, with many of these employed in the sugar refineries.

By the 1830s, the big city and the Irish migrant had become synonymous in the contemporary imagination. Conditions in these cities, and the undeniably large ethnic influxes to them, perhaps made this linkage inevitable. By 1841 Liverpool and Manchester contained the mostly densely populated areas on earth. At a time when the average population density for England and Wales was 275 persons per square mile, the figure for Liverpool was 138 224 and for Manchester 100 000. Indeed, Dr Duncan, Liverpool's Medical Officer of Health (and the country's first), claimed that in one part of Liverpool's north end people were packed in at a rate of 657 963 per square mile.[21] Although contemporaries regularly associated dirt, disease and overcrowding in the cities with the waves of Irish migrants, the root cause of the problem was the prevalence of densely packed eighteenth-century housing – court and cellar dwellings – which had been a major social problem long before the major arrivals of the Irish.[22] The cities of Liverpool and Manchester attracted particular attention for numerous reasons. With overcrowding at record levels and mortality rates which in 1840 ran at 34.4 in Liverpool and 33.3 in Manchester (compared with 27.0 in London), and average ages at death just 17 years and 20 (against 26.5 in the capital), these two great conurbations were of obvious interest to social reformers and critics.[23] Moreover, Manchester's Irish town, the dock areas of Liverpool, and a host of alleys, rookeries, and jerry-built back-to-backs, typified life, not only in these two great centres, but also in many of the mill towns of Lancashire and west Yorkshire. In such areas of tight residential clustering and inadequate social provision, Irish migrants featured prominently.

After 1815, Irish settlements in the big towns and cities, and related social problems, did indeed grow quickly. By 1831, Glasgow's Irish-born population was around 35 000, while the Irish-born of Liverpool were fast becoming the most notable ethnic community in the British Isles. In 1831 Liverpool's Irish had numbered 24 156 – many fewer than in Glasgow – but by the next census this Irish community had increased threefold.[24] The first great influx of Irish to Manchester occurred around 1800, because of a shortage of native hand-loom weavers, and permanent settlements had existed in the city since then, growing all the while.[25] By the mid-1830s the Irish in Manchester and its environs accounted for perhaps two-thirds of what was then a Catholic population totalling 30 000–40 000. The 1840s, and the Famine, would lead to further rapid increases.

Despite the commonly accepted stereotype, the Irish community of Liverpool was not simply unskilled, even though heavy dock work dominated all occupational experience there. William Dillon, a Liverpool draper, told Cornewall Lewis that, although the Irish were over-represented in heavy and unhealthy work, for example in the local soaperies, a few of the Irish in Liverpool were middle class. Samuel Holme, a prominent local builder, presented Lewis with figures that break with the conventional image of Irish labour. Holme reckoned that while one-fifth of the Irish were in the lowest sorts of work, as many as 780 Irish workers in Liverpool (10.4 per cent) were mechanics (see Table 2.2). He considered Irish labour to be beneficial

Table 2.2: Irish occupations in Liverpool in January 1834

Occupation	Number employed
Mechanics of various sorts	780
Brickmakers	270
Sugar-boilers	200
Masons' labourers	350
Bricklayers' labourers	850
Chemical works and soaperies &c.	600
Sawyers	80
Labourers employed in smithies, lime-kilns, plasterers' yards and by paviors	340
Lumpers about on the docks who discharge vessels and re-load them	1700
Porters employed in warehousing goods &c.	1900
Coal-heavers, and sundry other employment	430
Total	7500

Source: evidence of Samuel Holme, in Royal Commission on the Condition of the Poorer Classes in Ireland, Appendix G, *Report into the State of the Irish Poor in Great Britain*, Parliamentary Papers (1836), p. 29.

to the city, but believed they depressed the rate at which wages increased. He also expressed dismay at their being so 'burdensome upon the parish'; 'if they can obtain parochial relief, or subsist by mendicity', Holme claimed, 'many of them will not work at all, but live in a state of filthy contentedness'.[26]

Comments on the Irish in Manchester also reveal much about the way the Irish lived, or were presumed to live. Irish labour dominated the poorer aspects of the building trades, though migrants were also well represented as bricklayers and masons, as was common elsewhere. Once the Irish were established in these trades, moreover, they, like Durham miners or Clydeside shipwrights, fought to exclude all but their own kind from entry. While employers viewed Irish labour favourably, they also noted the propensity of the Irish to down tools in order to gain redress. Manchester commentators placed much less emphasis upon the skills element than their Liverpool counterparts, and though many Irish shifted from hand-looms to power-looms, a substantial number in the mid-1830s were working by hand, over long hours for poor pay, as spinners and weavers. As elsewhere, many in Manchester took a hostile view of the Irish influx.

The Reverend James Crook of St Austin's Catholic Church spoke somewhat contradictorily of the work of his Irish flock. He reckoned the Irish took the jobs that English workers did not want, though he still held the view that wages would have increased more rapidly had the Irish not arrived in such numbers: the Irish 'have got, and retain, the monopoly of this department of industry by offering to do their work for lower wages than the English'. A Manchester cotton manufacturer, Peter Ewart, disagreed with Crook's assessment. He argued that the Irish had no negative impact on wage rates, though he agreed that English workers had become 'assimilated to the Irish', evincing lower moral standards, drinking and living less comfortably. Another textile master, John Potter, told how he had recently discharged all but two or three of his 30 Irish power-loom weavers because they 'did their work in an untidy and slovenly manner'. Potter reckoned that Irish workers were just as quick to learn as the English, but he criticised their submission to lower living standards. Potter went on: 'they seem as content with 9s or 10s a week, as an Englishman would with 14s or 16s'. James Aspinall Turner, a cotton manufacturer, pointed to a different problem. Half of his 500 hand-looms were worked by Irishmen to make the fancy and coloured cloths which power-looms could not yet manage, and he expressed surprise that the Irish were content to earn less money than the English, which they did by working fewer hours. This attitude towards work did not matter to Turner because he paid by the piece and not by the hour.[27]

There is, then, a common theme of Irish workers clinging to pre-industrial customs and struggling against the rhythms of machino-facture which some viewed as a measure of lower civilisation. This view is endorsed by another cotton producer, James Guest, whose 800-strong workforce included some 400 Irish weavers. He explained how on one occasion Irish hand-loom weavers had complained about their low wages and had burned down a factory of power-looms which they identified as the cause of their grievance. Guest qualified his story by stating that this outburst was due to a sense of injustice and the pressure of new techniques of manufacture. He did not consider the Irish to be naturally or perpetually inclined towards such behaviour, and endorsed this assessment by reference to the work of his best overlooker, an Irishman. Guest summed up the Irish with a rather more judicious sentiment than was usually expressed by his peers:

I think the Irish are just as competent as the English to the manufacturing business of this town, if they are properly taught. The Irish appear to me to be quite as industrious as the English, and I consider that their turbulent disposition arises from their ignorance, which is corrected by education.[28]

Yet another difficulty perceived by employers was brought to light by Joseph Bell. Although Bell employed over 100 Irish hand-loom wool weavers, he kept them apart from the English, because it was 'unpleasant to have both together', presumably because of the workplace tensions that arose between them. Few employers explained the Irish effect on wages as succinctly or honestly as James Taylor, a silk mill owner from Newton Heath. For him, the Irish were used primarily to thwart the combinations and wage demands of English workers, especially in boom times when labour was scarce.[29]

As well as providing evidence of both the positive and negative aspects of Irish labour, Manchester illustrates perfectly the anxieties that were beginning to well up over the question of Irish migration in the mid-1830s, at the time Cornewall Lewis was compiling his report. Despite the exhortations from employers that Irish labour was vital to the well-being of Lancashire manufacturing, others were expressing concern at an old problem: the increasing cost of Irish pauperism. According to one Poor Law officer, while the burden of the poor in Manchester had doubled between 1823 and 1833, from £7983 16s to £14 556 4s 3½d, the cost of maintaining the Irish had grown fourfold, from £817 16s 8d to £3326 17s 8d.[30] Another local overseer, Thomas Armitt, alleged that part of the problem was the Irish pauper's willingness to lie to overseers in order to gain from either public or private charity. Armitt held the view that the Irish were deceitful pilferers, and whiskey smugglers, whose attitude to life was careless and wasteful. He chose to exemplify the attitudes of the Manchester Irish by telling Lewis of their apparent happiness to let the parish bury their friends and families while they 'have a feast, and get drunk'.[31]

By 1841, the archetypal image of the Irish in the big cities was well entrenched. In that year, the four main centres accounted for almost half of all Irish-born migrants in Britain, and the proportion was still high (almost 35 per cent) in 1871 (Table 2.3). During this period, between one-tenth and one-fifth of the Irish-born were found in London, though the proportional impact of the Irish was much

Table 2.3: The proportion of the Irish-born settlers in the four major urban centres of Britain, 1841–71

	1841	National share %	1851	National share %	1861	National share %	1871	National share %
London	75 000	18.0	108 548	14.9	106 879	13.3	91 171	11.8
Liverpool	49 639	11.9	83 813	11.5	83 949	10.4	76 761	9.9
Manchester	33 490	8.1	52 504	7.2	52 076	6.5	34 066	4.4
Glasgow	44 345	10.7	59 801	8.2	62 082	7.7	68 330	8.8
Total	202 474	48.7	304 666	41.8	304 986	37.9	270 328	34.9

'National share %': denotes the proportion of the Irish in the whole of Britain who lived in each city at each census.
Source: Census of England and Wales, 1841–71; Census of Scotland, 1841–71.

greater in the cities of Manchester, Glasgow and especially Liverpool because they had much smaller populations than the capital. Liverpool, for example, housed around ten per cent of all Irish-born residents in Britain throughout this period, and Glasgow was not far behind. Thus, it is not surprising that historians tend to focus on these centres when discussing the early- and mid-Victorian influx.

From the mid-eighteenth century these three great Irish centres (outside the capital) grew with remarkable symmetry. In all three the overall growth rates were staggering. In 1801 Liverpool's population stood at 82 000; within 50 years this had grown to 376 000. The corresponding figures for Manchester were 75 000 and 303 000; while those for Glasgow were 77 000 and 345 000. Birmingham, too, attracted migrants. By 1836 it was clearly the most important Irish centre in the Midlands, with around 6000 migrants located there. The Irish in Birmingham generally found heavy work but, according to the Reverend Edward Peach, made no effort to go into business on their own. It was claimed that every available job in the Birmingham building trade attracted 20 Irish applications to each one from an English worker. The Irish there generally worked as plasterers' or bricklayers' labourers.[32]

The commentaries offered in the Lewis report touch on almost every feature of Irish life: their work, leisure and lifestyles; the food they ate and the fluids they consumed. Most of the respondents mixed their social reflections with at times overbearing moral judgements. Peach painted a portrait of the Irish in Birmingham as earnest when sober but reckless when drunk; as hard working but without the necessary drive for self-improvement. He explained how the relative prosperity of English life encouraged them to marry earlier than in Ireland, a trait that was noted elsewhere.[33] For the observers of Irish society in Britain, women and children were targets just as were men. The fact that Irish children often went barefoot was blamed squarely on the women. They were perceived as bad household managers, as likely to indulge in excessive drinking as the men, and in some cases wilder and more difficult than their husbands. Lewis allowed his usually judicious guard to drop when explaining the unhelpful role played by Irish women:

> Another circumstance, which has a powerful influence in retarding the improvement of the Irish settlers in Great Britain, is the unthrifty and dissolute character of the women; as it is on the wife

that care of the house, and on the mother that the training of the children, chiefly depend among the poor. The Irishwomen are likewise, for the most part, not only wasteful and averse to labour, but also ignorant of the arts of domestic economy, such as sewing and cooking. Hence they are unable to make the best of the plain food which they purchase, or to keep their own and husbands' clothes in order, even when they only require mending.[34]

There was endemic disdain for the Irish family's mute acceptance of the most rudimentary sort of living conditions: a 'pallet of straw' to sleep on, and few possessions besides 'a stool, sometimes a table, an iron pot and a frying pan, a jug for water, a few plates and a leaden or pewter spoon'.[35] Their failure to improve a low diet of potatoes and 'stirrabout', and perhaps a herring or two, was contrasted with the native population, who craved better sustenance. The accusation that Irish families spent their surplus income on drink and merry-making had by the mid-1830s become something of an obsession in all towns of settlement, because it was viewed both as a cause of crime and as an explanation for the increasing burden of the Poor Law. The Irish were also widely perceived as carriers of disease, when in fact the wider physical environment in which they lived was respon-sible for incubating the microbes.

What emerges in this period, especially from Lewis's report, is a story of growing panic and antipathy in the face of ever-increasing migrant traffic. Few industrialising areas were untouched by the inflow, though even then the big four cities stood out as magnets for settlers. The Irish population in the 1830s was overwhelmingly proletarian, usually ill-housed and overcrowded, and invariably unskilled, or at least working in appalling conditions, even though there were exceptions to this depiction. Despite the bile of some of his respondents, Lewis came down against an Irish Poor Law, which he assessed would not stem the emigrant tide. Future events were to vindicate him. When the Poor Law (Ireland) Act was passed in 1838 Ireland was sending more migrants than ever before, and the country stood on the brink of an economic and social catastrophe which would create an exodus undreamed of by Lewis's mosaic of priests, constables, employers and beadles. Negative attitudes had been welling up since the 1820s and were endemic by the 1830s; yet this great migration was far from complete. In the coming decades (1841–61), Britain's Irish population would almost double.

The Famine Emigration and its Aftermath

The potato blight had dramatic consequences. Traditional Irish society was sent reeling by its horrific effects, while in Britain, aside from the great political crisis over the Corn Laws, and the split between the agrarian and industrial factions in the Tory party, which was caused by the question of how to deal with the ensuing Famine, its most obvious effect was to accelerate most dramatically the process of Irish migration. This panic emigration obscured what had been previously a purposeful and clearly directed settlement, as the voices of concern, which had already been raised about the Irish dimension of the 'Condition of England' question, became increasingly frantic and intemperate. Accusations of moral degeneracy were the stock in trade of observers of Irish settlements, but even then the awful effects of the Famine ensured that condemnations of character, living conditions and job competition became more venomous. Moreover, the views of ordinary people and local dignitaries were further worsened by the hysterical press reaction to the Irish Rising of 1848 and the much-maligned Irish dimension of what was regarded as an increasingly wild-eyed Chartist movement.[36]

At root, though, it was the sheer volume of pauper migrants, and related epidemics of disease, which dominated the Victorians' psychological landscape. Similar fears had been raised immediately after the French Wars, but the Famine bore down with such unimaginable pressure that local authorities became ever harsher in their reactions. Although Liverpool suffered the most, the effects of the Famine flight also struck most ports with Irish connections, as well as countless smaller towns across the west and into the Midlands, Yorkshire and the north. The historic market town of Ormskirk in Lancashire, for example, is not the sort of place normally associated with Irish settlement or Famine emigrants; yet in 1849 Charles Price Symonds, the local surgeon, noted that 18 per cent of the town's 6000-strong population was then Irish, a figure which included many Famine-driven Irish migrants who 'pay no attention to cleanliness nor ventilation' and who were roundly blamed for the epidemic disease that broke out.[37] It was in these years that the term 'Irish fever' became a generic epithet to describe the clutch of diseases, especially typhus, which the Irish suffered and spread.

But the history of the Irish during these years is best captured in Liverpool. Early Victorian Liverpool was a great Atlantic port, the gateway to America and Britain's main empire trade centre. The city was by far the most important element in a massive oceanic traffic in people, goods and services. Liverpool connected Ireland to both Britain and America; and though many Irish ports maintained other important links (Cork with Wales, Belfast with Glasgow), and some sent traffic directly to the Americas and the empire, no other port in Europe provided a conduit for such an epic movement of people. Indeed, Scally writes of this as the 'Liverpool system', a vast enterprise in human traffic which drew in and sent out masses of migrants. Between 1840 and 1860, 150 000 people of all nationalities annually were processed by Liverpool's shipping networks.[38] The fact that the city was the main centre through which Irish settlers passed is also reflected in the large numbers who settled there. In 1841, the city's Irish-born numbered 49 639 (18 per cent); within ten years this had grown to 83 813 (25 per cent). In this short time, therefore, the Irish population increased by 69 per cent, and the Famine flight had not even ended.

The Irish who began to trudge down the gangplanks on to the Liverpool docks in the spring of 1846 entered a city that already had a very strong Irish ambience; it was the most Irish of Britain's urban centres. By late 1846 the impact of the Famine upon Liverpool was becoming clear. After a steady increase all year, the number of Irish paupers in receipt of assistance reached a high of 13 471 by the last week of the year, as against a figure of fewer than 900 in the corresponding week in 1845. Such figures prompted the editor of one local paper to comment that 'The number of starving Irish – men, women and children – daily landed on our quays, is appalling and the parish of Liverpool has at present the painful and most costly task to encounter, of keeping them alive – if possible'.[39] So great was the social and demographic impact of the Famine emigration on Liverpool, its people and officials, that one historian has described 1847, the peak year, as 'unique in Liverpool's history'.[40] The scale of arrival between 1845 and 1849 swamped the authorities; it also built up a ground swell of anti-Irish opinion to add to that which had been a part of Liverpool life since early in the century. In 11 months of 1847, 296 000 Irish disembarked in the port, and although 130 000 went on to America and another 50 000 were classed as businessmen, over 100 000 of them were paupers. In all, between 1846 and 1852, some 600 000 Irish paupers landed in Liverpool, of whom only just over half continued on to America and Canada. In 1848, the volume of arrivals was a little less hectic, but considerable nevertheless, with something like 4800 per week entering the port, giving a total of 250 000. Of these, Neal estimates that 94 000 were paupers.[41] From 1849 to 1853, the overall pattern remained fairly stable; noticeably, though, the numbers of paupers did not drop quickly. Indeed, Neal has noticed that between 1849 and 1853 paupers accounted for between 68 000 and 80 000 arrivals each year, or from one-quarter to one-third.[42]

Such figures, useful as they are, give us no impression of the condition of the Irish who arrived in Liverpool. In fact, the story of these Irish who fled is in many ways as sad as those who died of disease and starvation in Cork, or elsewhere, for flight carried no guarantee of survival. Disease often accompanied the migrant as 'unseen lethal baggage'.[43] The portents were often very bleak from the outset. Conditions on board the Liverpool steamships were sometimes appalling for deck passengers riding on the cheapest tickets. The most notorious case involved the steamer *Londonderry*, which left Sligo with 206 deck passengers on 1 December 1848. Bad weather put those up top at risk and the crew packed all 206 into a space below deck which measured only 18 feet by 10 feet by 7 feet. More than 70 of these poor wretches died of suffocation, prompting outrage in Ireland. The fact that many died *en route* or after arrival led to widespread alarm, draconian quarantine measures and a commensurate rise in anti-Irish feelings.

For those who survived the crossing, the city of Liverpool offered little except damp cellars and soup kitchens. Estimates are that 27 000 took to illegal dwelling in filthy cellars which had been previously condemned and had often been boarded up. Many died, often starving, but usually of disease. In 1847, Dr Duncan, the Medical Officer of Health, described Liverpool as the 'city of plague'.[44] Shortly after the Famine, the pinch of poverty there was exacerbated by epidemic disease: especially cholera and typhoid, as well as dysentery. The combination of sickness, hunger and abject living conditions proved to be a poisonous phial. Witness this description of the living conditions which these Famine Irish suffered:

> among a certain number of individuals, in Bent Street, it was reported that four were lying down in one bed with fever, that twenty-four grown-up young men and their sisters were sleeping in a filthy state in one room and that fourteen persons were living in

another filthy place. Twenty-six people were found huddled together in a room elsewhere and eight had died of fever in one house.[45]

Such individuals, when massed together, placed an immense burden on the local Poor Law guardians. In one week in January 1847, 143 872 Irish paupers received relief from the increasingly be-leaguered magistrates. At the same time, private charity also provided much-needed support. The local Provident Society relieved nearly 40 000 Irish cases in the late 1840s, though this was a small fraction of total demand.[46]

Conditions were worst in Liverpool, and there some brutal answers to the 'Irish problem' were tried out. While the authorities genuinely attempted to prevent starvation (though failed to prevent hunger and disease working in tandem), their most punitive answer to the problem was to invoke the removal legislation which placed responsi-bility of the pauper upon the parish in which he or she was settled. Consequently, more than 60 000 Irish were sent back to Ireland – and possible death – during the late 1840s and early 1850s. Although it must be remembered that this high figure (it was only 4732 in Manchester) was derived partly from the fact that those who wanted to go back only had to turn up in Liverpool claiming poor relief for this to be likely, the process was nevertheless savage and unthinking.[47] Others also fell back on the removal system, as was the case in Cardiff, where authorities acted with such alacrity that ships' captains began landing Irish passengers on beaches a little way from the city. The authorities countered with a £10 reward for evidence leading to conviction.[48] Removals were carried out with the endorsement of local ratepayers, who were more terrified by the cost of relief than they were by their consciences. Those who shouldered the burden were not working class – whose anti-Irishness derived more from personal contact and religious intolerance than from the cost of relief – but members of the middle class.

Many arrivals in Liverpool simply recuperated there before moving on to other destinations in Lancashire, Cheshire, Yorkshire and the Midlands. Having set off on foot, these migrants made use of vagrant sheds, which provided impromptu staging posts between towns. Thus, someone heading for the Midlands might stop in Knutsford and Macclesfield before reaching Stafford. One couple, the Waters from Mayo, headed for Sheffield, via Dublin, Liverpool, Prescot and

Warrington before ending up in a Stockport lodging house, where they stayed for two weeks before being ejected by bailiffs. John Waters and his children went into the workhouse but left when the parish relieving officer threatened to remove them to Ireland. Waters subsequently died of starvation. In April 1850 a not dissimilar fate struck Bridget Callaghan, whose corpse was found surrounded by her crying children, lying under a Knotty Ash hedgerow which had been their bed for one rainy night.[49]

Many others made it to their desired destination, prompting newspapers as far apart as Newport and Sunderland to write of 'famishing and half-naked strangers' and the 'miserable condition' of the Irish. Words such as 'swarming' and 'herding' were commonplace, with Famine migrants increasingly portrayed as subhuman and bestial.[50] The *Glasgow Herald* described the scenes with a typical observation: 'The streets of Glasgow are at present literally swarming with poor vagrants from the sister kingdom, and the misery of these can scarcely be less than what they have fled or been driven from at home'. Religious passions were also fomenting with the age-old spectre of 'Popery' raised in explanation of the Irish influx. Indeed, the city's *Witness* newspaper went as far as to blame the very Famine itself on 'a religion of dependency and indigence'. The 33 267 Irish who landed in Glasgow between June and September 1847 were without exception either wholly dependent upon charitable help or 'in the last stages of wretchedness'. Disease, and with it death, had become common among the Glasgow migrant stream and, as else-where, this hardened public opinion, from a position of pity or sympathy to one of fear and worse. Between 1845 and 1846 there was a doubling of the death rate in Glasgow (from 1 in 39 to 1 in 18 of the population). Whereas the cholera outbreak of 1832 had claimed 3005 Glaswegian victims, the same disease carried off more 2300 in December 1847 alone. The poor rate rose in line with the increased burden of Irish paupers and the spread of disease among the poor. In 1847 the rate had been 2s 4d per head; 12 months later it was 3s 4d. Critics blamed the Irish, but the medical inspectors were more concerned about 'Those frightful abodes of human wretchedness which lie along the High Street, Saltmarket, and Bridgegate ... the bulk of that district known as the "Wynds and Closes of Glasgow" ... [where] all sanitary evils exist in perfection'.[51]

Ports of entry may have borne the brunt of the Famine migration, but the effects of such a rapid increase in arrivals were soon felt inland. Famine victims began to arrive in York soon after the potato blight first appeared in 1845. In the year to March 1846 over 2000 were assisted by the Poor Law guardians. The figure for the next 12 months increased by more than 50 per cent to 3513, and more than 2700 were aided in March and April 1847 alone. With this increase came sickness and disease, the incidence of which was highest in the poorest residential areas, such as Walmgate. Just like Liverpool, though smaller in number, the Famine refugees in York gravitated to the poorest accommodation – overcrowded and damp houses. In May 1847 the spread of disease in York was alarming and a temporary hospital was erected to house the poor Irish.

The case of York illustrates well the inadequacy of local Poor Law and charitable structures in dealing with this scale of problem. The Quakers of York, especially the Tukes, did what they could for the Irish, and the Poor Law guardians intervened in the usual way, though other authorities were criticised for not doing anything to improve the environments which fed and distributed disease. None of the authorities of Ireland, Bradford, Leeds or York helped Teddy McAndrew, whose case has been emphasised by Finnegan as typical of the cycle of Famine, flight, poverty and sickness which affected many incomers. McAndrew had left Sligo with his wife, four children and a baby in the summer of 1847. The paltry £2 they raised by selling their land was spent before they had reached Bradford, where the infant and three children died 'of hunger and measles combined'. The three remaining McAndrews made for Leeds and then York, by which time both husband and wife were ill. They were refused entry to any lodging houses and Teddy McAndrew died under a hedge where he and his wife and child had been resting. Samuel Tuke visited Mrs McAndrew in the fever hospital where she was expected to die. The remaining child, Tuke's daughter wrote, 'looked up at him so sweetly, he said, and he intends to take care of her if the mother dies'.[52] Although the piecemeal approach of the guardians was eventually effective against typhus, a host of other problems were attendant upon the massive influx of Irish migrants. Soup kitchens were needed to feed them; and locals reacted against the new arrivals when theft and other petty crime unsurprisingly increased.

The middle classes were most concerned with questions of morality and cost. Irish pauperism and vagrancy were key impetuses for Poor Law reform in the 1820s and 1830s, and, although the Irish burden exercised local authorities until the 1860s, the explosion of costs in the 1840s was unquestionably the point of greatest indigenous anxiety. Even in towns of secondary importance for Irish migrants, the costs of relieving the Celtic influx was out of proportion to their numbers. In Leeds, for example, where the Irish-born percentage of the population was in single figures, its cost in outdoor relief was immense, ranging from a high of 67.7 per cent of total expenditure on outdoor relief in 1850–1 down to 23.4 per cent in 1855–6. In the following year, long after the Famine had subsided, the Leeds Irish still accounted for around one-third of the total cost. Indeed, the 'Irish burden', Neal has shown, was a widespread problem in the north. Between 1846 and 1847 not even backwater towns and villages went untouched; every town or village seems to have been *en route* to some other place that the Irish wished to find. Chapel-en-le-Frith in Derbyshire saw cases increase from 27 in 1846 to 393 in the following year; the people of Beverley in north Yorkshire witnessed a doubling from 259 to 570; in Selby the increase was more than fivefold (40 to 230); while towns on the highways across Lancashire experienced quite staggering developments. Ormskirk, for example, went from 16 cases to 2211.[53]

When the *Morning Chronicle*'s social surveys were conducted in the north of England in 1849, its journalists were able to confirm that the Irish formed marginal communities, and that, as a people, they were existing rather than living. One of these writers was A. B. Reach, a noted anti-Irish polemicist, and though his opinions need careful scrutiny, some of his views about employment patterns support the more measured evaluations of Henry Mayhew, Reach's counterpart who investigated London's poor. Reach observed the Irish of Lancashire and Yorkshire surviving in a street economy, attracted to trades such as hawking, scavenging, rag gathering, picking oakum and making mats; or, like the Irish in Oldham, making cheap ling brushes for as little as 4s per week. Everywhere in Reach's survey, Irish families lived in 'cellars', 'haunts' and 'foulds', all of which were filthy, unswept and overcrowded.[54] The *Morning Chronicle* could not have chosen a worse time to study Irish migrants in urban Lancashire or Yorkshire, for pauperism and hardship were bound to have been visible on the streets of communities hit hard by the Famine.

Native apprehension was increased by journals such as the *Morning Chronicle*, as depictions of so many awful, sometimes tragic, Irish lives failed to dull anti-Irish antipathies. Anti-Irish stereotypes were hardened by the Famine, even though most of them had been in place long before. Taken together, the ratepayer's burden, the labourer's fear of job competition, the Briton's hatred of Catholicism and horrific effects of the Great Famine conspired to make a formidable bulwark against Irish integration. The costs of the Famine for Irish society were incalculably massive, but the same series of events also scarred British society, and with it the lives of the Irish in Britain. For the Famine unquestionably worsened the views of British and Irish towards each other. The communal violence of the 1850s and 1860s and the political wranglings over Home Rule are, in their different manifestations, evidence of the way this most tragic series of circumstances sharpened the sorts of rivalries and hatreds which had long characterised Anglo-Irish relations.

And yet we must not imagine that even a majority of the Irish lived as pauper wretches on the very fringes of human civilisation. The Famine sent forth a shock wave of pauper migrants which considerably stretched resources, but for many of those well paid Liverpool-Irish mechanics of the 1830s, the Famine, though it involved their countrymen, could be viewed from a safe distance. Moreover, though the Famine migration was marked by the social and geographical concentration or compression of the new arrivals, for most of the rest of the century diffusion and dispersal are more apposite controls for understanding Irish settlement patterns.

Beyond the Famine: the Far North of England

The period between the Famine and the 1870s provided some of the ugliest instances of anti-Irish antipathy and violence. Yet the same years also witnessed a gradual shifting of the Irish community away from the big cities and into the smaller towns, albeit still concentrated in the Midlands, Lancashire and Yorkshire, the north-east and central and western Scotland. Improving work opportunities may have come the way of second- and third-generation settlers, but in few places could the Irish in 1870 or even 1900 be described as an invisible minority, that is, ethnically and economically fully integrated. The politics of Home Rule and the stubbornness of the marketplace ensured that the Irish remained noticeable. In a fine study of the Irish in Britain in this later period, Fitzpatrick has gone as far as to say that the pressures upon Irish immigrants were sufficient to ensure that the period from 1871 to 1921 'did not witness the complete transformation of the Irish in Britain into either an expatriate community or a fully accepted ingredient of British society'.[55] The limitations on acceptance might be measured by the continued Irish over-representation in British crime figures (see Chapter 6). Equally, while 'even the most blinkered observer could no longer claim that the Irish were confined to ghettos and "Irish-towns"',[56] they still found themselves residing in the poorest and most run-down parts of towns. In the archetypal settlements – Glasgow, Liverpool, Manchester and London (which still accounted for one-third of Britain's Irish-born in 1871) – most Irishmen and Irishwomen remained proletarian, notwithstanding the inroads made by a minority of migrants into white-collar occupations. Scotland is thought to have seen more Irish upward mobility than elsewhere, with one Glasgow observer stating in 1913 that 'what were called the "low jobs" in the city are not now exclusively left to the Irish'.[57] However, in England – where Liverpool and south Lancashire dominate our perceptions – dock work, portering and general labouring were dominant. The picture in the north-east and in Cumberland was similar to that in Scotland, with an emphasis on mining, shipbuilding and metalwork, although a lack of research in these areas prevents definitive or broad-ranging statements.

Despite the horrible and seemingly chaotic image of migration derived from the Famine period, the majority of Irish settlers in Britain followed well trodden routes of entry. Long after the Famine, would-be migrants to Britain travelled south or east to the nearest port, from where boats took them to specific British destinations, as had been the case for centuries. Thus Ulster migrants departed from Belfast, Londonderry or Newry and overwhelmingly arrived on Clydeside, the Ayrshire coast or Cumbria. Those from Leinster, and many from Connacht, passed through Dublin to Liverpool; leavers from Munster and parts of Connacht entered Bristol, South Wales or London from Cork.

The pre-Famine years had seen most migrants settling in the port of entry, but the years after 1850 became marked by a greater range of settlement patterns. This change was effected by the geographical spread of industrialisation. At the same time, continuing chain migration ensured that migrants from particular families, parishes and counties were likely to head for the same regions, so that the traditional Irish centres of, for example, Liverpool and Glasgow were continually replenished. Discernible patterns of arrival and movement were thus noticeable. Hence, the Yorkshire Irish were mainly from Connacht and Leinster, with the Leeds Irish coming especially from Dublin, Mayo and Tipperary, and those in Bradford from Queen's, Mayo, Sligo and Dublin. In York, between 1851 and 1871, Mayo was the dominant Irish county of origin, while fully three-quarters hailed generally from the west of Ireland. In the same period, 40 per cent of the Irish in Stafford came from the Castlerea area, which touched three counties: Galway, Roscommon and Mayo.[58] Between 1851 and 1891, the Cumbrian Irish came overwhelmingly from Ulster, with Antrim and Down being prevalent. In the shipbuilding town of Barrow, moreover, Belfast provided more migrants in 1881 than any other recorded place. The Barrow–Belfast link was nurtured by geography, a regular steamer crossing and the traditional cyclical migration between the major shipbuilding regions.[59]

It is important that smaller settlements in areas such as the west Cumbrian iron and coal belts, which attracted large numbers of Irish settlers during this important 'take-off' phase of the Industrial Revolution, are not overlooked in favour of the great cities which dominated the 'Condition of England' and Famine periods. One of the most important towns was Dundee, which contained proportionally more Irish-born than any major centre except Liverpool. Mechanised yarn manufacture made Dundee one of Britain's most important linen centres. Between 1841 and 1851, the population increased by 25 per cent, to 80 000, with the Irish-born accounting for one-fifth in the latter census year. Linen work was particularly attractive to Irish workers from Ireland's own declining linen regions. Dundee's linen industry drew in far more women than men and they dominated community life there, mixing hard work and a robust leisure culture with a grim determination to be highly unionised.

The major 'Irish' regions of Britain in 1851 are indicated in Table 2.4. While the importance of the north-west dimension is evident, a noticeable feature of these figures is the important development in the far northern English counties of Durham and Northumberland. The Irish in these counties were generally much later arrivals than in the north-west, so the 1851 figure significantly underplays the growing importance of the migration to these mining, shipbuilding and heavy engineering regions. It was to regions with such industries, rather than to mill towns, that most Irish came in the second half of the nineteenth century. If cotton was 'king' in the generations before 1850, coal, iron and ships most definitely shared the crown for a

Table 2.4: The Irish-born in the four English regions with the largest Irish settlement, 1851

	Total	Irish-born	%
North-west	2 490 827	214 318	8.6
London	2 362 236	108 548	4.6
Yorkshire	1 789 047	57 266	3.2
Durham and Northumberland	715 247	31 167	4.4
Monmouthshire and Wales	1 188 914	20 738	1.7

Source: Census of England and Wales, 1851.

century thereafter. Unsurprisingly, then, Irish migration reflected this fact. By 1861 Durham alone had nearly as many Irish-born residents as had the two counties together ten years earlier. By 1871, the combined total had reached more than 50 000 (see Table 2.5). What is also apparent is the importance of another under-studied county, Cumberland, which had long-established Irish communities, dating to the early seventeenth century and the growth of Whitehaven (see Table 2.5). The mid-nineteenth century onwards, however, witnessed a much more significant influx, much of which, like that to the north-east, was promoted by developments in iron and coal.

With the Irish-born in these three northern counties hovering around the five per cent mark, each contained substantial and important settlements. Most of the urban populations from which the Irish-born were drawn clustered into distinct geographical sectors. In Cumberland, this occurred around Carlisle, Workington, Whitehaven

Table 2.5: The Irish-born populations of three northern counties, 1851–91

	Cumberland: Number	%	Northumberland: Number	%	Durham: Number	%
1851	9866	5.1	12 666	4.2	18 501	4.7
1861	10 529	5.1	15 034	4.4	27 729	5.5
1871	11 870	5.4	14 506	3.8	37 515	5.5
1881	11 826	4.7	10 414	2.7	27 663	3.2
1891	6 371	2.4	9 613	2.0	22 496	2.2

Source: Census of England and Wales, 1851–91.

and the surrounding iron and coal belts; in County Durham, the majority were found north of Durham city itself – especially in towns such as Sunderland, South Shields, East and West Boldon and Gateshead, Felling and Pelaw. In the south, the Hartlepools and Darlington had important Irish communities, and Teesside, Middlesbrough and the surrounding Cleveland hills provided work for Irishmen in iron mining and quarrying.[60]

Iron-making seems to have been a particularly important outlet for Irish migrants in the far north of England. This was especially the case in west Durham and in Cumbria. Such opportunities could be noticed in Bishop Auckland, Shotley Bridge, Consett and Tow Law, where mining and relatively small iron- or steel-making processes occupied many Irish workers. Many of these iron colonies, such as Tow Law, were small, with Irish populations that numbered only in the hundreds. Tow Law, which grew around mid-century with investment from the Weardale Iron Company, had an Irish population of 189 (9.8 per cent) in 1851 and 519 (10.5 per cent) in 1871. An important observation to be made of Tow Law is that Irish migrants seem to have been able to obtain work as miners, which was vigorously resisted in older established pits, for example, those collieries owned by Lord Londonderry around Durham and Seaham. Yet, among the Irish-born of Tow Law the number of miners was exceeded only by those who worked in the ironworks. In Cumbria, coal mining was mostly controlled by non-Irish workers while the mining of iron ore was strongly Irish. In a similar vein, Campbell has shown, the pits of Lanarkshire were either very Irish or anti-Irish.[61] Research is still needed into the north-east dimension, but it is likely that by the 1860s and 1870s the Irish were beginning to break into the most strongly protected sectors of the economy: even strongholds such as the mines of the great northern coalfield. Perhaps this penetration can be explained by the fact that new mines in this area were opening and were thus more difficult for native miners to control. It is plausible to argue that traditional pitmen were simply unable to police the labour intake of such a rapidly expanding mining region.

Rather like the iron-ore towns of west Cumbria (Cleator Moor, Frizington, Arlecdon), Tow Law was isolated and rough hewn, but, though its Irish cohort was small, it must be regarded as part of a chain of similar places dotted around on either side of the Pennines. In Cumberland, Cleator Moor, which had a peak population of

10 420 in 1881, was between one-fifth and one-third Irish-born in the
30 years before that date.[62] This town may have been small compared
with the large centres of industrial south Lancashire, but its robust
and tightly knit Irish community, like many of those in Durham and
on the north-west coast, was able to exert considerable pressure in the
town's cultural life. Irish miners dominated the local cooperative
movement, as they did in similar iron colonies like Askam and Dalton,
in north Lancashire, and Irish groups like the Orange Order and
the various Home Rule groups made a lasting impression on local
life.

In Northumberland, a number of towns such as Morpeth, Ashington,
Bedlington, Gosforth and Tynemouth provided further opportunities
for Irish migrants in general labouring and mining, iron-making and
engineering, fishing and many small-scale trades. By the 1870s both
banks of the river Tyne were well developed, both highly industrial
and densely populated. The north side, from North Shields and
Howdon to Wallsend and Newcastle, presented work for a steady
stream of incomers, Irish included, with opportunities in boat- and
shipbuilding, fishing and dock work, engineering and metalwork, as
well as all the ancillary trades, from warehouse work and transport to
food processing, that had long marked out the riverside economies of
the Clyde and the Mersey. By the 1870s, with Irish workers flowing
steadily into towns as far afield as Plymouth and Aberdeen, most
British workers had a day-to-day experience of living side by side
with Irish workers.[63]

The classic perception of the Irish as labourers in the poorest
grades of work is borne out by the realities of many lives in this
period; nevertheless, there are indications that a significant proportion of these arrivals found better sorts of work. According to
Pooley, semiskilled jobs were held by 50 per cent of Irish males,
although this figure could be higher in certain places, as in Cardiff,
where 80 per cent of the Irish-born were thus employed. There was
also a significant semiskilled Irish labour force, totalling between 17
and 40 per cent. This skill factor can be demonstrated for the Irish
populations in a range of towns. Even in York, where work was often
of menial character, there was a substantial skilled element, averaging
around 25 per cent among the Irish-born male workforce.[64] In the
iron-ore centres of Cleator Moor, semiskilled or skilled work accounted for upwards of 90 per cent of Irish-born males.[65] In towns
such as Birkenhead, Barrow, Sunderland, Jarrow, Wallsend, Greenock

and many others on the Tyne and Clyde the Irish workforce also included skilled males, some of whom were Protestants. In Greenock, however, many of the Irish were sugar workers in the 1890s, as they had been in the 1830s; and the proportion of dockers among the Greenock Irish fell by only ten per cent, from 60 to 50, between 1851 and 1891.[66] Nevertheless, an increasing proportion of Irish in industrial towns found work in shipbuilding, iron and steel manufacturing and engineering, in trades such as boilermakers, smiths, fitters, riveters, mechanics, tin-makers, iron moulders, platers, and a host of other well paid and skilled or semiskilled occupations which were noted for their offering of regular and reliable work and high levels of unionisation.

For many of the Irish in Britain, as with other ethnic or regional groups, occupational profiles were a generational matter, though no research has been carried out which might allow an assessment of the extent to which sons improved on their fathers' occupations. Burchell's study of occupational mobility among the Irish of San Francisco is instructive as to how we might use British censuses to a similar end. In most cases, by the 1880s the offspring of the San Francisco Irish-born were almost twice as likely as their parents to be in skilled or white-collar occupations; and whereas around one-third of Irish-born males were unskilled, the figure for their male offspring was nearer one-tenth.[67] Lancashire, where the Famine impacted heavily upon what had been a well established and cohesive community, suggests a very different experience from San Francisco. Here, Lowe has indicated a decline among the Irish-born (though an increase for the non-Irish-born) in the areas of small business (from 7.9 to 5.3 per cent) and skilled work (from 21.5 to 15.4 per cent), whereas the generic category labourer increased from 30.9 to 52.3 per cent.[68]

In 1872 the *Nation* sent forth 'Our Special Correspondent', the journalist Hugh Heinrick, to gather information about the size of the Irish community in Britain and to see how it was placed to influence elections in the towns and cities of England. Heinrick's letters, which the *Nation* published in instalments, were meant to be a clarion call for would-be Irish voters to support the quest for Home Rule. Heinrick's writings are shot through with disappointments about low levels of enfranchisement among the Irish, and the extent of drunkenness among certain elements of the community, but his surveys provide a useful insight into the way the migrants were

adapting to the new country. Heinrick's was also the first national
survey to include reference to what was the most important Irish
community to have developed since the Famine, that of the far north
of England, on both sides of the Pennines.

By the 1870s, the Irish settlements in Cumbria and the north-east
were mixed communities, with mining and related services providing more jobs than any other sector. There were plenty of echoes of
earlier days, with most Irish working men in Newcastle, labouring on
the docks, in iron foundries, on public works or in the mines – work,
remarked Heinrick, that required the 'greatest strength, energy, and
endurance'. Although Irish workers remained over-represented in
the heavy and dirty aspects of most trades, Heinrick also noted strong
suggestions of social improvement among certain classes. On the one
hand, Carlisle's 6000-strong Irish population mainly comprised
'unskilled labourers and factory hands' and 'a large number of
huxters [sic] and shopkeepers', but in Newcastle some of the Irish
had 'worked their way to competence, a few to independence,
while the great bulk of them find constant employment at good
wages, and are in a condition of comparative prosperity'. Overall,
Heinrick noticed in Newcastle more signs of social and economic
achievement – the emergence of a genuine Irish middle class – that
might be bettered only in Liverpool, Glasgow or Manchester. The city
had some 400 Irish businessmen in 1872, and around 4000 skilled
artisans. Thus, one-sixth of the entire community had pulled themselves up from 'the severest drudgery to a condition of comparative
prosperity'.

The living conditions of the Irish in the north-east corresponded
with these signs of improved rank. Heinrick, in fact, noticed that the
Irish in Newcastle generally lived in better conditions than their
English counterparts. Similar observations were made of the Irish in
Walker, Wallsend and Howdon, where they accounted for 10 000 out
of a total population of 23 000. Further downstream, in North
Shields, the Irish accounted for ten per cent of the town's total of
40 000 and were, Heinrick wrote (in an attempt to contrast native
perception with migrant realities), 'favourable socially, and morally
even more favourable still'. Some of the Irish communities which
Heinrick visited in South Tyneside were even more impressive.
Gateshead, which had a population of around 64 000, and both
Jarrow and Hebburn, which between them totalled 30 000, had Irish
communities totalling one-third of the whole population. In South

Shields, more than ten per cent of the 45 000-strong population was Irish. Throughout the region that Heinrick called the 'Vale of Tyne' he estimated there was were some 83 000 Irish settlers.[69]

Another survey, similar to Heinrick's, was conducted in 1891 by John Denvir, the prominent Liverpool Irish nationalist organiser. Denvir's efforts were also meant to be a census and a rallying cry for the Home Rule cause. His findings for the north, drawn from eyewitness accounts and extensive first-hand experiences acquired by travelling and campaigning throughout the British Isles, offer a similar impression to that of Heinrick. The usual places – Newcastle, Sunderland, Carlisle, Workington and Whitehaven – were singled out as important Irish centres in the north, and similar conclusions as to social status and political power were drawn. Denvir thought the Irish in Whitehaven and Carlisle, as in Newcastle earlier, were beginning to show signs of upward mobility. And he said of Newcastle: many had 'attained to good social and public positions', adding that 'several of those who came here as packmen are now among the foremost citizens of the place'. Although the Irish across the region continued to cluster in labouring jobs in often disagreeable sectors such as chemicals, there were also continuing signs that they were managing to attain artisan status. The healthy state of this community is indicated by the fact that for several generations after the Restoration of the Catholic Hierarchy in 1850 (see Chapter 3), the diocese of Hexham and Newcastle had Irish bishops. Dr Chadwick, the second incumbent, a native of Drogheda, and the fourth, Dr O'Callaghan, was of London Irish extraction.[70]

Right down to 1914, across the north-east, in towns such as Sunderland and Newcastle, the Irish – like the majority of working men – were occupied as waterfront labourers or shipbuilders; in engine shops, ironworks and blast furnaces; in and around the pits; and anywhere else that employers needed that ubiquitous rank of worker known as the 'general labourer'.[71] Such profiles were also apparent in west Cumbria, with towns such as Barrow, Millom, Maryport, Whitehaven and Workington providing remarkably similar opportunities. The main difference was that in west Cumbria, iron-stone, and not coal, was the major mineral to be extracted, and though there were coal seams under the Irish Sea too, these remained in the control of native workers until the twentieth century, whereas iron-ore extraction had been a largely Irish endeavour since the 1840s.

Conclusions

The classical perception of the Irish as crammed into cellars, dwelling in what amounted to compressed 'ethnic villages', might have been a reality in the 1830s and 1840s, in certain archetypal places – for instance, the classic slums of the big cities – but the picture began to change by the 1870s. By then, though the Irish often remained unskilled and still dwelt in the poorest areas, they were also 'widely distributed throughout the urban hierarchy'. Many found better classes of work, and some 'lived in widely scattered, middle-class residential suburbs'. The ethnic barriers that were being erected in the 1830s and 1840s had for the most part been broken down by the later period and this meant 'the poor Irish living in Irish-dominated residential areas would have had extensive opportunity to interact with their non-Irish neighbours'.[72] This often promoted violence in Lancashire, Scotland and elsewhere, but it could also result in growing toleration and a reaffirmation of pre-Famine modes of cooperation through such conduits as the unskilled unions of the 1880s and 1890s. However, elements of communal cohesion among the Irish, particularly through religious networks, were sometimes able to mask the integrating influence that might be expected in a social and economic world which was moving, during the mid-Victorian years, from concentration to dispersal and from spatial segregation to physical homogeneity.

3

SPIRITUAL AND SOCIAL BONDS: THE CULTURE OF IRISH CATHOLICISM

Introduction

In 1836 Father Ignatius Collingridge, the English priest of St Chad's Catholic Church in Birmingham, paid the Irish a loaded compliment. Although he argued that they were 'much more charitable to one another in sickness, and in all distress, than the English', he went on to say that this character trait was 'the natural effect of the general obloquy and wretchedness in which they all find themselves equally involved'.[1] While Collingridge's view aligns with what was often written about migrants during the 'Condition of England' crisis, it is surprising that he did not emphasise the role played by *his* religion in forging such bonds within the Irish flock, for the intimate character of Irish Catholicism was clearly enforced by the shared experience of migration and settlement. Can it be denied that such shared backgrounds would have been influential in the kindness which one migrant might show to another?

The history of the Irish communities of Victorian Britain would be incomplete without reference to the migrant's spiritual and social attachments to Catholicism. Evidence abounds to demonstrate the vital function performed by the Catholic Church, parish and priest in helping new arrivals to settle and adjust. Each provided a connection between the old country and new communities, and the priest was particularly important, guaranteeing a friendly face at the end of an

75

often difficult journey. Catholicism implied a sense of communal cohesion and mutual identity, and in an often hostile social environment the Church became a beacon of hope. The huge size of Irish migration in the nineteenth century, moreover, led the once small and isolated English Catholic Church increasingly to become an Irish mission.

After the Reformation, and before mass Irish settlement, Catholicism in the British Isles had been marginal and, in many respects, a downtrodden denomination. Before 1815, apart from a few upper-class 'old Catholics' and a level of popular support in parts of Lancashire, north Yorkshire and the north-east, Catholicism's greatest security was among the clansmen of the western seaboard of Scotland, even though the latter were quite small in number. Indeed, Irish migration utterly transformed the demographic profile of Catholicism in Britain. By 1851, when Irish migration was flowing freely in the wake of the Great Famine, the religious census recorded a total of 252 783 Catholic churchgoers in England and Wales. This snapshot is a crude measure of the Catholic faith and hides as much as it reveals. Although Catholicism accounted for only around four per cent of worshippers at this time, the census revealed Catholicism to be at its strongest since the Reformation; moreover, as Irish Catholics clustered together in urban areas, their significance was much greater in London, the industrial Midlands, the north of England and western and central Scotland. Furthermore, because not everyone went to church on a weekly basis, there would have been many more Catholics than the figures suggest, and the majority were, we know, Irish by birth or parentage. While some completely rejected their Catholic religion, many others would have viewed the taking of just Easter communion as a sign of healthy religious practice. Such people missed the census enumerators. Catholic attendance the world over was challenged by the logistical pressures of mass Irish migration. Until the 1860s at least there was an acute shortage churches and of pew space. The Church simply could not cope with the demands placed upon it by the Famine inrush, and many Catholics had to make do with home visits, impromptu gatherings in people's front rooms or personal devotion. If we make an adjustment for all these problems, a more reasonable estimate of Irish Catholics in Britain in 1851, which accounts for second-generation Irish Catholics as well as the first, might be between 500 000 and 750 000.[2] Thus, by the 1850s the Catholic Church in Britain *was* an Irish church.

Much writing on migrant settlement thus echoes this fact, and the view of the Victorians themselves, by implying that Irishness and Catholicism were synonymous. While this position has some basis in fact, because a majority of Irish settlers in Britain *were* Catholic, it is also partly a function of the anti-Catholicism and anti-Irishness of Victorian society, for non-Catholics did not always view the spread of Catholic churches as a positive development, even though Lord John Russell, the Prime Minister who openly criticised the 'Papal Aggression' of 1850 (see below), acknowledged the important socialising aspect of all religions. Within the Anglo-Catholic tradition, in which religious practice was strong, the pre-Famine Irish, with their low levels of attendance, were something of an embarrassment. The fact that the majority of Catholic settlers were poor sharpened tensions, though the fact that the poverty, disease and poor living conditions of many Irish Catholics were offset to some degree by the heroic work of parish priests and lay Catholics seems to have been lost on contemporary critics. When the Famine compounded the marginal economic status of so many Irish Catholics in Britain, one of the few coherent responses, aside from the sometimes grudging provision of the Poor Law guardians, was a quite inordinate degree of Catholic mutualism. Amidst this gloom, and against the widespread enmity of contemporary society, a sentimentalised picture of the Catholic Church sometimes emerges; yet there remains more than a grain of truth in it.

Our task here is to examine the relationship between Irish Catholics and their religious/cultural life, for the link between the people and their faith is a vital aspect of this great migration.

Catholicism Renewed

The revitalisation of British Catholicism has important wider contexts. The Roman Catholic Church had been exposed to a fiercely anti-clerical onslaught during the French Revolution; and in the nineteenth century the growing traditions of liberalism and nationalism were often secular in tenor, and this presented a threat to Catholicism as it did to religion more generally. In post-Reformation Britain, the Roman Catholic faith had been held up as medieval, alien and anti-libertarian, a superstitious and vulgar creed which was fundamentally at odds with Protestant views of their own religion as progressive, democratic and conducive to free government and individual liberty. The fact that the established church was Protestant gave a political significance to such views, with the consequence that anti-Catholicism had long been, and remained throughout the Victorian years, a key feature of British popular identity.

In this age of great flux, therefore, the Vatican was faced by a key question: how to maintain a basically conservative and autocratic faith in an age of increasing individualism. This became one of the key concerns of Catholicism during the nineteenth century. Despite a previous period of retreat, however, and a degree of enforced introspection, the years after 1815 witnessed a defiant Catholicism struggling to reassert its powers, with Gallicanism, which tolerated semi-autonomous local customs and practices, outpaced by an evangelical form of Catholicism, ultramontanism, which enforced strict Catholic practices and reaffirmed papal authority, taking on militant Protestants at their own crusading game. In the nineteenth century numerous attempts were made to press home a centralised, Romanised vision of the Church. The classic examples were the Syllabus of Errors (1864), in which Pope Pius IX condemned 'progress, liberalism and modern civilisation', and the Vatican Decrees (1870) which included the famous 'doctrine of papal infallibility'. The general mood and direction of the Catholic Church between 1790 and the 1870s clearly influenced the nature of the spiritual and social role it performed, for example causing problems for Catholics wishing to join popular organisations, such as trade unions, which their Church proscribed as part of its conservative dogma. Only in 1891, with the issuing of the *Rerum Novarum*, which was part of a large number of encyclicals issued by Pope Leo XIII, was there a liberalisation of the Church's position over social issues, such as welfare reform and trade unionism. In this publication, the Pope accepted limited rights of combination, upheld property as sacred and, importantly, rejected both *laissez-faire* capitalism and secular socialism.

It would be misleading to claim that all papal edicts were carried out to the letter at all levels of the Church. With branches as far apart as San Francisco, Melbourne and Liverpool, the scale of Famine emigration meant that by 1860 the Catholic Church was a large-scale concern, with all the problems of liturgical policing this implies. Catholic activity at the parish level frequently ran against the letter of the law as issued by primates and popes. This certainly was the case in Ireland, especially in the traditional western counties. Priests ministering to the Irish in Britain employed many different approaches, including flexible religious practice, in their efforts hold on to the faithful or to defend them against the opprobrium of militant Protestants. This latter threat had an important galvanising effect. In the Victorian period, when renascent Catholicism was considered a threat to the Church of England from *within* (through Anglo-Catholic ritualism and the apostasy of some Anglicans who went over to Rome), as well presenting an independently revitalised force in its own right, opposition to what were regarded as Romanising tendencies, fierce denunciations of the Pope, as well as physical attacks upon Catholics and their priests were common in the generation after the Famine. The portrayal of Catholicism as evil was a common theme of the period, and British Protestants remained deeply suspicious.

Although measures of Catholic relief had been granted in 1778 and 1791, before the Catholic Emancipation Act of 1829, Catholics in Britain and Ireland had been legally defined as second-class citizens. They were not permitted to build churches with spires and their priests risked prosecution if caught wearing ceremonial garb; Catholics could not hold high office, and were prevented from becoming Members of Parliament. William Pitt the Younger, who masterminded the Act of Union (1801), had promised to abolish the remaining restrictions on Catholics, but the threat to the English constitution that this concession allegedly posed produced a mighty backlash in Pitt's own party among ultra-Tories. For nearly 30 years, until emancipation, a political war was waged over the tension between Catholic and Protestant liberties.[3] The Catholic question also gave the United Kingdom its first example of the power of massive, peaceful protest in the form of the Catholic Association, formed in 1823 and led by Daniel O'Connell, the brilliant and charismatic moral force reformer. The movement for emancipation also demonstrated the growing importance of the Irish Diaspora. Though O'Connell, a fierce opponent of slavery, refused to go to America while that institution remained in place, his Catholic Association spawned branches in, and drew financial support from, Irish communities of Britain and America and from the peasants of Ireland.[4]

As well as appreciating the size of Irish Catholicism and the range of its influence, there is a need to acknowledge its nature. During the nineteenth century, Roman Catholicism in Ireland grew in strength and organisation, with a new uniformity evident in its practice, even though the population of the island halved between 1845 and 1900. Pre-Famine Ireland was marked by considerable geographical and cultural differences in the character of the commitment to Catholicism. Catholics in the west were committed, but in a different way. The confiscation of property from Catholics during the colonial period worked against the maintenance of strict Catholic practices, financially constraining the spread of churches and the training of priests. The rapid growth of population between 1750 and 1845 increased the Church's problems, with the result that far-flung communities, most notably in the west, were able to maintain semi-Christian forms of Catholic worship.

It has been argued that post-Famine Ireland experienced a 'devotional revolution', whereby the spread of modern communications, the penetration of the English language and, most importantly, the destruction of traditional peasant society paved the way for an assertion of liturgical practice and a richer visual symbolism under the tutelage of the ultramontane cardinal Paul Cullen.[5] While older ideas of religious practice, from a belief in holy wells and fairies to the practice of penitence, were dying out before the Famine, the demise of traditional society and the contraction of the Gaelic language undoubtedly encouraged this trend and pressed home the ultramontane advantage. The Famine, rather ironically, therefore, facilitated a process of religious modernisation. The falling population of Ireland increased the Church's ability to send more priests among the people and was crucial to the process of renewal. From 1845 to 1900 the numbers of priests and nuns in Ireland rose consistently. Before the Famine there had been one priest to every 3000 parishioners; by 1900, the ratio stood at one to 900.[6] The advantages enjoyed by the Church in Ireland were absent in Britain, where social change, based on rapid industrial and urban growth, was immense.

Gilley has argued that the concept of 'devotional revolution' must not be overplayed; not just because Cullen's predecessors included reformers, but primarily because the combination of low levels of industrial and urban development, allied to sharp population decline, meant 'the Church in post-Famine Ireland was batting on an easy wicket'. He continued: 'A further stimulus to Catholic pride and renaissance was provided by the development, particularly in Ulster, of a rabid no-popery mentality'.[7] It should also be noted that there was a link between religious renewal and the rise of Irish nationalism in the period.[8] Too often religion is seen as incompatible with expressions of a secular nature; yet as the century wore on there was in grass-roots Irish Catholicism an increasing coming together of both priests and people around the twin symbols of flag and cross.

While bearing in mind Gilley's reservation, it is necessary to acknowledge that post-Famine migrants *were* entering Britain with an increasingly modern notion of religious practice, based upon regular attendance at mass and a stricter conformity to the Church's teachings. In other words, they had a more organised, socially holistic idea of the role of the Church, as well as of the associationalism that was an increasing part of the urban mission of most denominations. At just the time when the Catholic hierarchy was recognising the need to provide economic guidance and leisure facilities for the faithful, the parish communities were becoming more disposed towards accepting such developments. At root, the demographic changes effected by mass Irish settlement meant that by the 1840s it was increasingly clear which of the Church's twin missions had become dominant: the role of Catholicism in Britain as 'national church to the Irish poor' far outweighed its 'proselytising work' aimed to convert the 'well-born and rich'.[9]

The Catholic Church and the Irish in Britain

In general, the spiritual dimension of Irish Catholicism in Britain has been played down by social historians, for example Thompson, Lees and Lowe, and emphasised by the historians of religion, such as Gilley and Connolly. The former group stresses the sociocultural dimension of the Irish Church, likening the growth of new religious networks to a broad-based 'reforging of Catholic identity in the new communities of Britain',[10] but the latter have challenged this emphasis upon the social dimension of the Church, arguing that it under-estimates the spirituality of religion. Connolly, for example, has suggested that 'Catholicism was not primarily or simply an agent of modernisation, or worse, urbanisation, or perhaps even christian-isation; but will possibly be better understood as gathering its momentum as a holy enterprise'.[11] Gilley, too, has questioned historians who 'only understand an institution if it discharges a secular function and who reduce religion to an odd form of collective behaviour'. This 'secular mentality', he has argued, is 'unhistorical, for it cannot grasp the self-understanding of a religious people who live not only for this life but for another'.[12] Although this perspective offers an understanding of the religious mind, the social function of the Catholic Church needs to be recognised as a notable feature of Irish community life. Perhaps, therefore, a useful accommodation can be achieved between what we might term 'religious' and 'social' perspectives on the Catholic Church and Irish migration by asserting that the social function of the Church was meant to support, not diminish or secularise, the spiritual. The priest, through whom so much religious activity flowed, was both a religious missionary and a social being, but the two spheres were not completely distinct.

By the late 1840s, successive waves of migrants had overwhelmed the well disciplined structures of the Roman Catholic Church in England and Wales. Since 1688 the Catholic Church in Britain had been governed by four vicars apostolic, who oversaw four vicariates or unions (London, Northern, Midland and Western). Although migration prompted the Pope in 1840 to double the number of vicars apostolic to eight, the Famine influx pressured these structures still further. In 1850, therefore, further reform was initiated with the re-establishment of a parish and diocese system modelled on that of the established Church, with the vicars apostolic being replaced by archbishops. The Restoration of the Catholic Hierarchy prompted a wild backlash of popular opposition against what Protestants tendentiously termed 'the Papal Aggression'. This signal of Catholic renewal dovetailed neatly with the flood of Famine arrival to take anti-Irish and no-popery sentiments – in what was already a fiercely anti-Catholic country – to a new high.

Despite this native hostility, Irish settlement ensured that by the mid-Victorian period Roman Catholicism in Britain was *the* major growth denomination, as what had once been pockets of Catholicism expanded across the major industrial regions. Catholic chapels and churches became a common feature all urban skylines. From as early as 1821 the Irish Catholics of Manchester outnumbered their English co-religionists, and between 1800 and 1850 there was a 1300 per cent increase in recorded Catholic baptisms in Birmingham, and the numbers of known Catholic families grew by 1700 per cent. In 1841 the city had been home to around 9000 Catholics; within ten years Irish Catholics alone recorded more than that number.[13] Even in London, where Catholicism remained small in proportional terms, the actual size of the denominational body became considerable.

Although Catholics in the capital were seldom more than a small percentage of the population, reaching 8.4 per cent in Holborn, where the Irish and Italians lived side by side, there were still somewhere near 200 000 of that faith in inner London in the 1890s.[14]

These increases were matched eventually by the growth of church provision, though meeting such need was a struggle. In the 1840s there had been just five Catholic chapels or churches throughout western Scotland; by 1854 the number of churches had increased to 49, with priests numbering 63. In 1846 there were 99 Catholic religious houses in Lancashire and 21 priests in Liverpool and 14 priests in Manchester and Salford. By 1870 the figures for these cities had increased to 64 and 39 priests, respectively, while the county rate for Lancashire had mushroomed to 225 churches and 338 priests. The rates of growth were equally spectacular in other Lancashire towns, such as Preston, St Helens and Oldham.[15]

Numbers do not necessarily equate with degrees of devotion. One of the problems posed by census takers and subsequently by historians of religion has been how to measure the degree to which the faithful maintained their allegiances. Historians have suggested that the levels of attendance among the Irish in Britain were lower than those in Ireland. Evidence presented for Ireland prior to the Great Famine shows that there were sharply differentiated attendance rates between Gaelic (western) and English-speaking (eastern) Ireland. The former averaged from one-fifth to two-fifths; the latter from one-third to three-fifths. In Lancashire in the 1830s somewhere near 40 per cent of Irish people were regular churchgoers, which compared favourably with the 25–30 per cent estimated for London throughout the century.[16]

Despite poverty and hardship, the lure of non-religious affiliations, the alienation of English Catholics from the Irish working class, and the more secular nature of urban life, there is much evidence to suggest the continued piety and devotion of Irish migrants in Britain. In Liverpool, the 1851 religious census revealed that 32.5 per cent of Catholics were regularly attending mass. While the Anglican figure was 40.7 per cent, the predominantly Irish nature of Liverpool Catholicism, and the proximity of the census taking to the Famine influx, meant fewer Catholic Church places were available than was the case with other denominations. The degree of religious devotion in Liverpool underpins the common belief that Catholicism was the strongest faith in the city. In February 1853 neither Anglicans nor

Nonconformists could attract as many worshippers as they had seats, whereas some 43 380 Catholics attended churches with only 15 300 seats. Two years later the contrasts were more marked, when a survey found that only 44 842 of 63 009 Anglican seats were occupied, while Catholic attendances of 46 130 remained, due to several services each Sunday, around three times higher than seats available (15 900). This figure represented something near 50 per cent of all Catholics in the city and Catholics were particularly proud of their record, given the 'thousands of homeless, moneyless, rainmentless, foodless creatures that call the Catholic church their mother in Liverpool'.[17]

Despite their devotion, Irish Catholics were not universally welcomed inside their churches. Mass Irish settlement often brought well heeled English Catholics into contact with a largely proletarian community of Irish labourers and their families, and there was something akin to religious apartheid between the groups in terms of where they worshipped and who ministered to their needs. There is evidence of such division between the two groups – better-off English Catholics and the poor Irish – in Birmingham. In that city, St Chad's Church was for a long time taken to be the poor Irish chapel, with St Peter's providing for the other sort of Catholic. In the 1840s, however, A. W. N. Pugin, the famous church architect, preferred the site of St Chad's to build Birmingham's Catholic cathedral; neither St Peter's nor a neutral third site was deemed suitable. Following the decision a striking cross-migration occurred, with the Irish moving across to colonise St Peter's while the English Catholics crossed to the site of St Chad's and to the new cathedral.[18]

Irish migrants were also viewed with disdain within the Catholic Church because of their putative political aspirations. From the 1830s bishops and priests in the Northern Union were becoming increasingly edgy about the clandestine activities of many in their working-class constituencies, with oath-bound trade unions and Ribbon societies (see Chapter 5) presenting what the Church viewed as a serious threat. While greater accommodation was made by the Church after the Fenian episodes of the late 1860s, especially in the 1870s when Parnellite moderation began to dominate the nationalist agenda, the increasing political role of Irish priests often led to criticism or punishment from bishops. The complexities of religion and politics in later Victorian society are illustrated clearly by mixed reactions to groups such as the Ancient Order of Hibernians (AOH). The Catholic clergy in Ireland viewed the AOH as a secret society and the movement enjoyed a stormy relationship with the Church there, even though it gained respectability and Church approval in the United States. Before Joe Devlin, the Belfast nationalist leader, revamped the AOH in the 1900s, and it gained much greater religious support, it was viewed with suspicion and fear. In 1896 the police described it as 'a very low class' organisation that 'no respectable nationalist appears to sympathise with', and many bishops proscribed the AOH, instructing priests to withhold the sacraments from members.[19]

The bonds of Irish Catholicism nevertheless remained strong, with many tales of the hard work and sacrifices of ordinary Irish people. Indeed, the heroic image of a poor Irish Catholic church, forged anew by the poorest elements of Victorian society, was seized upon by Catholic propagandists as an example of the positive role of the Church and of the responsible attitudes of God-fearing Irish Catholics. One of these writers, M. C. Bishop, relayed a particularly striking story of communal strength and spiritual fortitude. His words capture the tenor of contemporary Catholic views:

> a priest belonging to the order bearing the 'un-English' name, 'Oblates of Mary Immaculate', got together some fifty labourers of Whitechapel [London] and preached to them under a railway arch. The fifty increased to five hundred before long, and the congregation migrated from the railway arch to a garret, and then to a temporary iron church. Meantime by much begging, by the help of a few benefactors of the upper world, but chiefly by the pence and farthings of the Romish roughs thereabouts, schools were built.

So popular were these early provisions that the priest had to hold six masses on Sundays, three on weekdays, and sermons each evening. Finally, on 22 June 1876, these Irish labourers witnessed the opening of a grand Catholic church with 'no stint of beautiful materials'.[20] Despite exaggerations, their achievements, and those of the priest, were real.

Less well known stories of adaptation and self-improvement can also be noticed in the annals of less famous Irish centres than London, Liverpool, Manchester or Glasgow. Barrow-in-Furness, a Victorian boom town on the north Lancashire coast, provides us with a useful example of this. For years Barrow Catholics had no proper place of worship. From 1858 till 1865, mass was heard at the house of Joseph Walmsley, or above his paint shop, by a priest who travelled nine miles from Ulverston. In 1865, with the population escalating rapidly, Father John Bilsborrow established a mission in Barrow and two years later E. W. Pugin's impressive Catholic Church of St Mary of Furness was consecrated. Although local priests regularly complained that fewer than 50 per cent of Barrow Catholics attended Sunday mass, rates of between 36 per cent (1880) and 47 per cent (1887) suggest the degree of devotion in this small industrial town compared well with major centres.[21]

The Power of the Priest

The relationship between priests and people in the pre-Famine era was sometimes tense. English bishops often viewed the Irish flock with disdain, and English priests, who were dominant in the pre-Famine days, tended not to strike up the same close relationship with Irish Catholics as did Irish priests. Part of the problem was sheer numbers, though cultural and political differences also distanced Irish parishes from an English hierarchy. The English priest was often very upper class in his ideas and aspirations; he was accustomed to aristocratic converts, well-to-do Catholic families or prosperous middle rankers, not slum-dwelling, sometimes boisterous, Irish migrants. Likewise, the English Catholic Church, with its often intellectual and elitist attitudes, was not readily identifiable to the Irish. It was not until after 1850 that the numbers of Irish priests became sufficient to deal with the needs of their expatriate brethren. Where Irish priests ministered to Irish Catholics, there was a noticeable improvement in relations.

There is no doubt that in peasant Ireland Catholic priests were invested with an authority which combined cultural mores and spirituality. Priests were said to have an almost mystical hold over their flock. In nineteenth-century Britain, Irish settlers experienced a generally more secular world than was experienced at home. If this transition meant some Irish Catholics drifted away from the Church, it did not necessarily diminish the day-to-day religious and secular power of the priesthood. Although the average Irish Catholic did not believe that priests had magical powers, the sense of respect which surrounded the priest – especially the Irish priest – was palpable.

The problems faced by priests were numerous, though each of these provided opportunities for the priest to consolidate his hold on the parish. He was purse holder, fund raiser, building site manager and clerk of works to the church. In his more usual capacity, the priest also had to deal with the settlement of a heavy flow of often dislocated and distressed newcomers to the parish, which was especially the case in the Famine years, on both sides of the Atlantic. The priest arbitrated between the bishop's purist definition of a 'good Catholic' and his parishioners' rather looser idea of faith. So what was a priest to do with a congregation who liked a drink, sometimes fought, but who remained God-fearing and devoutly Catholic? Priests were skilled mediators, not least between a vulnerable migrant population and its hostile enemies in the community at large. While priests in Wales sometimes struggled to find land for church building, because anti-Catholicism often restrained the philanthropic urges of some landowners, as in Britain generally, they did not face the additional challenges which faced their counterparts in the ethnically diverse United States. Father Whelan, the first resident priest in New York, complained that 'In this country it is necessary for a priest to know at least the Irish, English, French and Dutch languages, because our congregation is composed of these nationalities as well also as Portuguese and Spaniards'.[22] And each of these national groups struggled to impose its own identity on the American Catholic Church.

In return for their hard work, Irish priests could expect devotion and respect from their co-religionist fellow countrymen. Henry Mayhew offered this well known description of one priest's passage through the streets of his parish:

> Everywhere the people ran out to meet him ... women crowded to their door-steps, and came creeping up from the cellars through the trap-doors, merely to curtsey to him. One old crone, as he passed, cried 'You're a good father, Heaven comfort you', and boys playing about stood still to watch him. A lad ... was fortunate enough to be noticed, and his eyes sparkled, as he touched his hair at each word he spoke in answer. At a conversation that took place between the priest and a woman who kept a dry fish-stall, the dame excused herself for not having been up to take tea 'with his rivirince's mother lately, for thrade had been so busy, and night was the fullest time.' Even as the priest walked along the street, boys running at full speed would pull up to touch their hair and the stall-women would rise from their baskets; while all noise – even a quarrel – ceased until he had passed by.[23]

This sense of respect, even awe, is not difficult to explain. Among the poor Irish of London, Liverpool and the other big settlements, the Irish priest was a reminder of a past life; he was a vestige of culture so important to most migrants in an alien and inhospitable new community. Irish priests lived frugal lives in the same environs as their parishioners, often in dwellings that little bettered those of the poor members of the community. They had no salaries and drew what they needed from the church collection boxes; their financial position was thus a long way short of that of the Anglican clergy, and certainly did not include the use of a vast rectory and a string of servants. Census evidence, in fact, suggests that in the new Victorian towns it was common to find four or five priests living together with perhaps one servant or a housekeeper to meet their domestic needs. These priests went among the new Irish communities like missionaries, devoting their entire lives to their ministries. As Raphael Samuel noted, the priest's 'daily transactions were conducted as those of a familiar, ... who at the same time enjoyed a peculiar and esoteric power, a figure at once accessible and remote'.[24] Priests were placed in a position of reverence; and their blessings and counsel were eagerly awaited on all manner of issues. In Liverpool, as the city reeled under the effects of the Famine influx, many of the poor Irish, living in cellars, cold and hungry, saw few outsiders other than their priest. And it did not go unnoticed that a number of priests died in Ireland during the Famine as they attended the sick and dying. This degree of devoted attendance was often marked by great sacrifice among priests ministering to the Irish poor in Britain. One such man, Father Billington of York, died in late 1847, having contracted typhus fever from his parishioners.[25] The same fate also awaited priests visiting the Famine Irish of Liverpool, or the migrant ships and quarantine hospitals of Ellis Island, New York. The priest was not supposed to fear death, which is just as well, for his most important work, whether reclaiming lapsed Catholics, offering words of comfort or granting the last rites, involved daily passage among the desperately ill and dying.

It was not just social intimacy which conferred a sense of gravitas, of patriarchy, upon the priest and his office. Nor was it his shared experience of a new world, though all these matters cemented relations. The nature of Catholicism was itself sacerdotal in a way that Protestantism was not, though priests such as Father Todd argued that the Irish attachment to the priest was actually theological, not sacerdotal: 'To them the priest is the "man of God", as the prophets were to the devout Israelites of old', though Todd acknowledged that:

It is natural, indeed, that some personal feeling should be mingled with this theological perception of the Sacerdotal character. The priest is the father and the friend to whom they naturally turn in all their cares and sorrows. He is a friend long tried and never found wanting.... For their sakes he has not hesitated to brave sickness or death, and what is often much harder to be borne – the scorn, contempt, and hatred of the world. [26]

Indeed, anti-sacerdotalism was commonly aimed by English Protestants against the Roman Catholic Church. Anti-Catholics loathed the priesthood as something which held an incomprehensible mystical control over parishioners. The confessional, for example, was lambasted as a forum in which unmarried men could pry into the intimate lives of their female charges. Yet for tight-knit Irish Catholic communities, the confessional was very important, with priests commonly spending four hours daily listening to their parishioners.[27] In general, Catholic priests were kept busy by a very full religious calendar as well as by a wide range of day-to-day parish duties.[28] During marriage ceremonies priests exerted considerable pressure upon any non-Catholic partners in mixed marriages to become Catholic and to undertake to raise their children in accordance with Catholic doctrine. Thus, at the same time as a priest might turn a sympathetic ear, he could also wave a big stick. Whichever method he employed, would-be waverers were often easily brought back into line by a personal visit from the 'holy father'.

In this way, too, the priest's influence stretched beyond the spiritual world. Some priests, for example, defied the hierarchy of the Church and supported political initiatives like Home Rule and Fenianism. In a less demonstrable way, if an Irish priest was hostile to a political leader, or to some form of ideas, then the prospects for gaining grassroots support, if not removed, were certainly reduced. Catholic writers also stressed the role which the priest played in curtailing Irish excesses, some of them potentially serious, it was thought. As M. C. Bishop wrote in 1877:

By every political and social law, the million of the Irish settled wherever the roughest and worst paid labour has to be done, ought to be the least manageable and the most explosive of the dangerous classes.... That the Irish do not figure yet more largely than they do in the criminal statistics of our great cities, that this alien million is not an advanced cancer in the English body politic, is due not to policemen, but to priests; not to 'necessary progress', but to the agents of Catholic charity.[29]

There was also a much more mundane aspect to the priest's role as mediator. This power was regularly demonstrated on a Saturday night. One of his most important social functions was to quell the Irish disorder, which he did with a stern word or a swirling cape and a flailing cane. As well as stepping into smoke-filled tap-rooms to break up drunken brawls, Irish priests (although the English as well) encouraged self-improving pastimes, such as outings, teas and balls, music-hall-style evenings and lectures. None of these functions, however, obscured the spiritual presence of the Church in the culture and history of Ireland.

Although he wielded considerable power, the Irish priest was not, by and large, a martinet. Generally, Samuel reckoned, his actions were 'tempered by a realistic appreciation of the nature of the flock, their hereditary weaknesses and strengths'. Charles Booth, in his survey of the East End of London, in the 1890s, viewed priests as 'lenient judges of the frailties that are not sins, and of disorder that is not crime'.[30] This is perhaps why adverse reaction to Irish intemperance or pugilism was forthcoming most regularly not from Irish priests but from temperance-orientated Protestants, or from within the Catholic hierarchy. In many ways, the Irish priest was more Irish than his flock, and was, as a result, as alien from the upper reaches of his own Church as those over whom he enjoyed absolute authority. Although Owen Dudley Edwards has argued that priests in Britain or America could not expect as of right the same very special role they had at home in Ireland, he considered they could work themselves into a very special position: in the wilds of Canada, for example, the Irish priest gained great respect because he 'followed his people wherever they went, and had, sometimes, preceded them into the wilderness as missionaries to the Indians'.[31] While the environs of Manchester and Liverpool were not quite so wild, there was also a frontier sense to the work of priests there.

Whatever the pressures built up against his success, the priest remained a key individual. Ordinary Irish migrants rarely met their bishop and never saw the Pope, except in icon. Yet they saw the priest daily. He alone offered them absolution: he married them, baptised them and buried them. The priest was friend, protector and sage.

Associationalism and Social Catholicism

The seemingly secular nature of modern, urban society worried religious leaders throughout the Victorian period. Attempts were made to modernise the Catholic Church, and to mould the devotional practices of the faithful into something uniform and long lasting. In promoting proper training of priests, or by encouraging community-wide dedication to church building, the Catholic Church in Britain was little different from its counterpart across the Diaspora. Within such construction programmes, the erection of schools was seen as vitally important, and it was common for church and school to be built in rapid succession. The levels of delinquency among Irish Catholic children, and their general reputation for wild and un-educated ways, emphasised the need for schools in the wake of large-scale migration.[32]

Great importance was also attached to the Church's seemingly secular initiatives, from the promotion of temperance and self-education, to the creation and extension of Church-based friendly societies, and the promotion of positive leisure-time activities. In developing such a broad prospectus of alternatives to drink, poverty and vice, the Catholic Church was again much like its Nonconformist counterparts; moreover, both were set against what they believed was the contagious spread of secular forms of associational culture. From trade unionism in the 1820s and 1830s, to Fenianism and Home Rule nationalism in the 1870s and 1880s, the Catholic Church felt constantly threatened by movements which allegedly undermined the function of the Church and which, under certain circumstances, might have destroyed religion altogether. A hangover from the revolutions of 1789, 1830 and 1848 bore heavily upon religious elites; the fact that they had escaped French-style turmoil did not prevent them, or the churches, from fearing the levelling tendencies of the secular world.

In the period before the 1860s, the Catholic Church employed a very conservative notion of social welfare. When Catholic clergymen preached intervention, they had in mind charitable works, and missions of mercy for the poor, hungry or infirm, not social equality or a welfare state. The economic emphasis of the Church was, in fact, classically liberal and individualist. The clergy emphasised ways to improve the individual's lot, and were guided in their teachings by the principle of soul salvation, while the Catholic view of the soul was inimical to reform. According to the Catholic liturgy, one American priest argued, 'Social evils which afflict mankind are the result of Adam's sin ... [and] all reform, properly understood, should begin with a return to religion and the Church'. If we add to this belief the commonly held assumption that Irish Catholics came from a land where the peasantry was idealised and revered, not despised, we can glimpse the powerful brake on radical or political interventionism. Irish peasants had long been encouraged to look to afterlife salvation, not for earthly reforms. 'Poverty, self-denial, and resignation to God's will', according to Dolan, 'were Christian ideals aptly suited for a peasant society, and Irish clergy were trained to reinforce this world view'. Irish priests taught that 'it was God's plan to have rich and poor live together so that one could practice alms-giving and the other patience and resignation'.[33] In Catholic literature, and in newspapers, poverty continued to be explained as a virtuous state, as otherworldly. In this formulation, charity was a requirement for good Catholics who were themselves better off.

Catholics in Britain also involved themselves in the act of supporting the poor in this way. As Gilley has demonstrated, the Victorian period witnessed a rekindling of the 'ancient Catholic virtue of Holy Poverty'. This development resulted in much greater toleration of the poor Irish and improved dedication to them. Thus the Catholic response to industrial poverty foreshadowed the backward-looking, romantic language of English ethical socialists such as William Morris and R. H. Tawney.[34] This philosophy rested on the idea that the morality and communal cohesion of medieval monastic society (by definition Catholic) had been destroyed by Protestantism and had replaced community mindedness with the individualistic greed of capitalism and, by implication, the debased, wretched immorality of industrialism and urban life. Therefore, 'the Catholic mission to the Irish in London was ... "to revive the true glories of the happy ages of England's greatness, when the Priests of God ... shelter[ed] ... the needy and oppressed"'.[35]

While priests worked tirelessly to this end, among the fever dens and slums of the industrialising world, laymen also acted in the spirit of their faith, through conduits such as the Ladies' Charitable Society and the St Vincent de Paul Society (SVP), which were dedicated to charitable dispensation and social and spiritual improvement. Branches of the SVP sprang up across the Diaspora, providing a charitable safety net for the Catholic communities that were covered. In Glasgow it owed much to the exertions of Hugh Margey, a Donegal-born school superintendent who was also active in the temperance movement and in promoting the Christian Doctrine Society and St John's Catholic Library. The SVP came to Glasgow and New York in 1848. In the first four years in Glasgow it dispensed alms to an average of 746 people per week. By 1864 branches of the SVP had been established in all 20 of New York's Catholic parishes. Protestants in England and Scotland regarded the SVP as a Jesuit front – fanatical, Romanist and alien. Allthough some commentators have emphasised the SVP's role in playing down Irish allegiances to many political groups, from Chartism to Fenianism, Aspinwall has asserted that the Glasgow SVP was far from an instrument of conservatism, acting instead to promote both class and ethnic awareness among an overwhelmingly poor Irish population.[36]

In New York, Liverpool, Manchester, Glasgow, and indeed in every other major centre of the Diaspora, the Catholic Church promoted a network of charitable institutions and associational networks. By the late 1830s there were Catholic benevolent societies throughout all the centres of Irish Catholic settlement, especially in the north of England. These networks became stronger and more important in the second half of the century, when the scale of migration made the experience more impersonal. Cullen's leadership of the 'devotional revolution' in Ireland was, moreover, matched by the works of his counterparts in both England and Scotland, where Cardinal Manning and Archbishop Eyre became active participants in the development of social Catholicism. Eyre, for example, was an active supporter of all manner of social initiatives, especially education and the acquisition of useful knowledge.

Schools were crucial for the faith to prosper, for which reason there was an immense denominational battle in the later Victorian period over the kind of religious instruction which state schools should provide. The number of schools within the growing Catholic parish network expanded remarkably quickly, a sure sign of the priorities established by the clergy. When Abraham Hume in 1846 surveyed Liverpool's Vauxhall ward, where 40 per cent of residents were Irish, he found that two-thirds of children received no schooling. This was during the Famine period, after which provision and services were rapidly improved. By 1853 there were 8000 day places for Liverpool's Catholic children; within five years a further 2000 had been added; and by 1871 the total figure was 15 000. In Glasgow in the 1830s five day schools serviced the needs of 1400 children, while 11 Sunday schools catered for more than twice that number. By 1851 there were almost 3500 day places provided, although some of this number went to Protestant schools. At the same time, day, Sunday and evening schools were springing up in Glasgow – as they were elsewhere – providing education from the likes of the Jesuits, the Sisters of Mercy or the Franciscans.[37] At this time, therefore, the Catholic Church, with the priest at the helm, was making very deliberate attempts to provide adequate schooling and thus to produce 'useful citizens, loyal subjects, decent members of the working population and good Catholics'.[38]

Not all places were sufficiently large or dynamic to attract members of the various Catholic orders which played so important a role in developing such networks in the major centres. In Barrow-in-Furness impressive efforts were made to build up church and school provision from a base of zero, primarily on the initiative of local priests and parishioners. By 1871, just four years after the consecration of St Mary of Furness, the town's Catholics had raised £1200 to build an adjacent school with accommodation for 600 children. In 1877, the Furness Railway Company provided some of the funds for the Catholics to erect an outpost school 'among the grim huts' of Barrow Island. This location quickly became the nub of Catholic community life on the island and led in 1885 to the planting of a separate church dedicated to St Patrick. Between 1880 and 1887 such developments within the local Catholic community were enforced by steady increases in the provision of schooling, marked by a rise in available places from 660 to 1076.[39]

If education provided a way of socialising the young so that they understood their religious and social responsibilities, the crusade against drink was meant to rescue the adult working class. With alcohol playing such a pivotal role in the Irish celebrations of life and of death, the problems associated with excessive indulgence in usquebaugh, the 'water of life', were considerable.[40] Father Theobald Mathew was the personification of the Catholic temperance crusade, although he made common cause with non-Catholics too in his quest to staunch the flow of alcohol. Nor was he simply an anti-drink temperance campaigner: for him, intoxicating liquor was but one evil that prevented the attainment of a worthier life. During the 1840s Mathew visited many of the major communities of the Diaspora, issuing pledges to thousands, and prompting the establishment of anti-drink campaigns from New York to Lancashire and Glasgow. In London in 1843 Mathew's week-long temperance crusade had a marvellous if (as was common) short-term effect. Although there were several Irish temperance clubs in the capital at this time, Mathew's efforts were quite remarkable, with between 60 000 and 100 000 turning out to see him, with 20 000 allegedly taking the pledge in the first three days.[41]

Each part of the Diaspora seems to have had a local temperance figurehead. In Lancashire in the 1860s, for example, Bishop Goss of Liverpool continually enjoined the Catholics of his diocese to avoid drink. In the same city, Father Nugent was responsible for establishing a branch of the Catholic Total Abstinence League. The efforts of such as Mathew had a largely temporary effect, although Catholic temperance organisations enjoyed a certain rate of success. Drunkenness, in particular, was a problem, and its incidence seems not to have declined by the 1860s, from which time Cardinal Henry Manning of London began to organise numerous rallies up and down the country to turn Catholics from drink. He founded the League of the Cross (1872), which borrowed symbols and a system of rankings from the Salvation Army, and it is claimed that 28 000 joined this organisation. Enthusiastic supporters of the Mathew and Manning initiatives included Archbishop Eyre of Glasgow, who established branches of the League of the Cross throughout his city.[42]

The social dimension of Catholicism was not simply about the pronouncement of spiritual virtue or self-improvement; it also had a genuinely mutualist, associational aspect. In the light of the offerings of trade unions during what the Church perceived as the dark and unsettling days of the 1830s and 1840s, Catholic priests were often at the forefront of movements to provide financial support to the community. By the late 1830s, the Catholic Church was associated with benevolent dispensations in most major centres of Irish settlement in the north-west. Covering such eventualities as sickness and death, these organisations pooled funds that were distributed in the common interests of members: such was the case with Preston's United Order of Catholic Brethren, which functioned under Church guidance. As time went by, the Catholic Church (like other churches in the Victorian period) was beginning to provide a full service to the flock, covering roughly the same ground as movements such as the Oddfellows or the Foresters. In the country's primary Irish centre, Liverpool, there were in the 1860s at least three Catholic building societies, a not uncommon development at this time.

Associationalism also reached into the members' leisure time. From the 1860s, Church-inspired organisations increasingly became a mainstay of the community's social life, organising teas, balls and dances; putting on lectures, readings and theatre; building reading rooms and libraries; organising day trips and excursions. A typical example was that of the Catholic Young Men's Society (CYMS), an organisation established for 'mutual improvement in the extension of the spirit of religion and brotherly love'. It provided reading rooms, lecture programmes, educational opportunities, (non-alcoholic) refreshments and the opportunity to meet fellow Catholics and to engage in promoting the welfare of the parish. The CYMS had in fact been active in Glasgow before the Famine, organising trips and picnics.[43]

One of the best examples of the interweaving of religion with community strength and pride in the nation occurred in the celebration of St Patrick's night. During times of trouble – such as 1848, for example, or when the Fenian panic erupted in 1867 and 1868 – St Patrick's night was held up by nervous authorities as a potential point of trouble. From the end of the 1860s, however, the Church tried to quell the usual drunken rowdiness of St Patrick's celebrations by encouraging gatherings which were self-improving in tenor. Indeed, the Irish Catholic propensity to gather for stories of the homeland, to applaud Irish singers, or to raise money for, say, Catholic school rooms was never more apparent than at the increasingly grand, clerically inspired gatherings of 17 March. Splendid balls and banquets were held in most centres of Irish settlement – whether in the archetypal cities of Glasgow or Liverpool or in the smaller outposts such as Whitehaven.

A variety of Hibernian societies also sprung up in our period, some with Church blessing, others without. Until much later in the nineteenth century, the Church avoided organised marches and galas, and any Catholic indulgence in shows of Orange-style territorialism were usually proscribed or criticised by the hierarchy. When Church 'walks' were organised, which happened in most parishes in the later Victorian period, the aim was, as Fielding has shown, to demonstrate religious pride, not national identity.[44]

The role of nationhood in Irish Catholic celebrations, such as St Patrick's day, is rather ambiguous. On the one hand, it is possible to consider the Church's seizure of St Patrick's day as a deliberate ploy to divert support from nationalist groups; on the other hand, not all clergymen were as bitterly opposed to nationalist celebrations, or calls for Irish freedom, as their diocesan superiors. In Barrow-in-Furness in 1903 there was uproar in the Irish community when the Bishop of Liverpool, Dr Whiteside, removed Fathers Barry and Motherway from the town because of their alleged anti-English, pro-nationalist sympathies. The Irish Catholics of the town berated the Bishop throughout the year, defending the honour of the priests, and in fact exerted far more energy in this cause than they ever did for Isaac Butt, Charles Stewart Parnell or John Redmond, the three main constitutional nationalist leaders of this period. The Catholic parishioners defended their priests' usage of national symbols as a way of preventing the loss of young Irish Catholics to apathy, apostasy or intermarriage, but the Bishop was unmoved and the two men never returned to their posts in Barrow.[45]

Another measure of the growing communal confidence of the Irish and Catholics of Britain was their promotion of a great range of partisan newspapers. The spread of such written communication was mirrored throughout the Diaspora, with New York being one of the most important producers of Catholic and Irish publications. In Britain, not only were nationalist publications, such as the *Freeman's Journal* and the *Nation*, part of the potential reading in these times, there was also a corpus of specifically religious publications which could nevertheless display remarkable clarity over Irish issues, such as the *Tablet*, and a chain of regional or local *Catholic Heralds* founded in the 1880s by Charles Diamond. In Lancashire, this genre was best represented by the *Lancashire Free Press*, the *Northern Press* and the *Catholic Times*.[46]

There was also a rather more militant aspect to official expressions of Catholicism. This development was inevitable given the vehement anti-Catholic tenor of religious life in the Protestant worlds of Britain, Canada and the United States. Aside from the various papal utterances of the Victorian period, there were many more localised examples of both Catholic pride and self-defence. One of the most outstanding was the Catholic Truth Society, founded in Salford in

1885, which was intended to teach Catholics a form of intellectual self-defence, by justifying those aspects of Catholicism – such as the Latin service and papal authority – which Protestants were inclined to attack. This development was in part a consolidation of early changes in the training of priests. In the early part of the century, the Church felt the need for Catholic clergymen to counter Protestant opprobrium, though it acknowledged that these priests were often ill-prepared for such combative roles. Later in the century, efforts were made to consolidate such self-defence mechanisms by offering similar training to laymen. The Catholic Truth Society was organised at parish level to instruct lay Catholics, and its members were used to provide supplementary religious services, such as Sunday benediction and evening devotions.[47] As a sharp counterpoint to the popular Protestant lecturing tradition of this period, the Catholic Truth Society was a sign of both the confidence and the militancy of popular religion at this time.

Conclusions

Irish migration provided the Victorian Catholic Church with a stark choice: either to provide spiritual and social support for the Irish influx, or to fall into terminal decline. The need to minister to the thousands of Irish Catholics settling in Britain was made more acute by the increasingly secular imprint of the world they entered. When compared with the experience of other churches, denominations or groups, the record of Catholicism in the Victorian century was manifestly a success. Whether by outflanking early trade unions, by displaying communal cohesion in the building of churches and schools, or by organising grand concerts of Irish singers and players, by the 1850s the Catholic networks were focused and strong, yet still growing and improving. While it is often pointed out that many thousands of Irish failed the litmus tests of good Catholic practice by not making an appearance at Sunday mass or performing Easter duties, it is important to counter with a question: how many of these non-attenders still participated in Catholic balls, or joined with their countrymen in toasting St Patrick? While numbers of worshippers in Lancashire or London in the 1830s or 1840s were similar to the rates uncovered for pre-Famine Ireland, it seems unlikely that this situation remained the case once Cullen's 'devotional revolution' or the demographic transformation of the post-1850 period had taken place. It is unsatisfactory, moreover, to imply that church attendances wholly equated to levels of belief, even if we have little of statistical significance with which to organise a contrary position.

In assessing the balance between the spiritual and social bonds of Catholicism, the last word probably must go to the historians of religion, who claim that spirituality provided the context for all else. Let us remember Gilley's words: 'at the heart of Catholicism, indeed of Christianity, is the claim that all men are exiles, poor banished children of Eve, shut out of the garden from the beginning'.[48] If this comment is considered against the remarkable physical and social growth of the Catholic Church in this age of industrialisation and mass Irish migration, then the point becomes even more noteworthy.

4

THE PROTESTANT IRISH

Introduction

Despite Akenson's assertion that 'from 1815 onwards the migration out of Ireland attracted Protestants and Catholics proportionately, in approximately equal numbers',[1] we still know very little about Irish Protestant migrants to Britain. This gap becomes even more apparent when the strength of the Scotch Irish traditions in the New World is acknowledged. The Canadians, for example, have long recognised the importance of Protestant migrants in their national past. The American aspect has also attracted much attention from historians. Indeed, the impact of the Protestant Irish on the development of early American culture has been greatly exaggerated. From as early as the nineteenth century, descendants of the colonial Scotch Irish were perpetuating an heroic image of their ancestors as among the foremost founders of white America – 'rugged frontiersmen' and 'Indian fighters', true Jeffersonian Democrats and the first republicans.[2] The same descendants also pronounced shared Ulster roots with all manner of famous Americans, including Daniel Boone (who was descended partly from Devon Quakers) and Andrew Jackson. This Scotch Irish myth has a clearly sectarian dimension in that these early colonial settlers were especially celebrated for being so different from their Catholic counterparts, the 'wild Irish'. Furthermore, the myth is said to have gained particular currency as American Irish Protestants reacted against the Home Rule agitation of their Catholic countrymen.

When compared with the sentimental image of the Scotch Irish as the 'nation builders' of American history, little of substance is known about the more mundane story of ordinary Protestants in later American life.[4] Aside from the dominant filio-pietist hero worship, just outlined, the reasons for this oversight are several. In broader terms, the historiography of Irish migration tends to concentrate on the poor Catholic migration, which dominated the generations between the Famine and the Free State. This concentration in turn is partly promoted by the powerful message conveyed by the social lives of these poorer migrants as they struggled to exist in the new communities; but it is also to do with the alleged ease of Protestant assimilation. Writings on the Protestant dimension – particularly that in America – tend to stress the similarities between Protestant migrants and the receiving country, emphasising their smooth passage into the mainstream of life in the new communities. Unlike the Irish Catholics, one historian has remarked, the Scotch Irish were 'full Americans almost from the moment they took up their farms in the back country'.[5] Perhaps similar assumptions influenced W. J. Lowe's claim that 'Very little is known about Irish Protestants in Lancashire ... because they simply do not emerge from the available sources as distinctive. Some Protestants were probably part of the Catholic-dominated Irish community life, but their significance cannot be assessed'.[6]

Our ignorance of these Protestants stems also from the long-run and relatively steady nature of the migration that sent them out of Ireland. With roots deep in the late seventeenth and eighteenth centuries, the Protestant exodus simply does not have the shock value of the Catholic emigrations of the nineteenth century, especially that of the Famine generation. Yet the nature of this exodus is vital to our understanding of the wider picture. Between 1717 and 1776 some 200 000 to 250 000 Presbyterians (70 per cent of all leavers) journeyed from one of several Ulster ports to Philadelphia and New York, at a time when the entire Presbyterian population of the northern Irish province was perhaps half a million. Ulster continued to send migrants at a rate of 5000 per annum in the 1780s and 1790s. The French Wars, the Anglo-American War of 1812, legislation aimed to prevent the loss of human capital to the former colonies, and to protect the Protestant Ascendancy (the dominance of economic and institutional life by Anglo-Irish Protestants) in Ireland, each stemmed the tide of emigration at various times in the period of the late eighteenth and early nineteenth centuries, but still 100 000 to 150 000 managed to leave Ulster for America in the 30 years after 1783.

Between 1803 and 1805, 70 per cent of all Irish emigrants departed for the United States from the key Ulster ports, providing further evidence of the importance of the Scotch Irish in this phase of emigration.

In the nineteenth century, Protestant migrations were over-shadowed by the large-scale Catholic exodus which helped to people the cities of the English-speaking world. Yet, Protestant migration continued to be important. There was a fairly continuous inflow to Scotland and northern England in this period, and people of the same origin played a fundamental part in the emerging culture of Irishness in Canada, Australia and New Zealand. The majority of Irish emigrants to Canada were, like their eighteenth-century American counterparts, Protestants. Settling first on the eastern seaboard – in the Maritime provinces and Nova Scotia – they gradually moved inland to Ontario. As late as 1871, 850 000 (25 per cent) of the Canadian population was Irish-born. In the provinces of Ontario and New Brunswick the figure was even higher, with the Irish-born accounting for between 30 and 40 per cent. Furthermore, it has been estimated that some 55 per cent of the Irish who went to Canada were Protestants.[7] The importance of the Orange Order as a frontier organisation, spreading wherever the migrants went – including the prairie states in the 1870s, though especially around the Great Lakes region, on the border between Quebec and Ontario, and further east and west – attests to the pervasiveness of Protestant Irish settlement from the earliest colonial times till the later nineteenth century.

There were also important Protestant migrations elsewhere in the expanding British empire. In pre-Famine Australia, for example, at a time when assisted passages were limited, the majority of Irish arrivals were either convicts or wealthier Ulster farmers. The latter group was akin to that which peopled America in the colonial days; few were poor, and some had notable means. Henry Osborne, for example, left Tyrone for New South Wales in 1828, carrying with him a gift of £1000 from his father, which he exchanged for Irish linen. He then applied for and received land grants worth £2560 each. On arrival he sold the linen at a handsome profit, for such commodities were still very scarce and expensive in Australia, and took up an option on 30 convict labourers to work his first grant of land. The land, near Wollongong, in the Illawarra district south of Sydney, turned out to be good dairy pasture land, and by 1854 Osborne held 261 000 acres of land. On his death in 1857, he was described as one of the richest men in Australia.[8] Although it is difficult to quantify the importance of Protestant Irish settlement in Victorian Australia, it is reasonable to assume that only in Canada and New Zealand was this group more important. Ulster settlement in Australia became especially marked in the later decades of the century, so that in 1911 (which is the only date for which we have comprehensive Australian census data on religion) some 26 per cent of the Irish-born professed Anglicanism (14 per cent), Presbyterianism (9 per cent) or Methodism (3 per cent) as their religion.[9]

No Irish migration to Britain – Protestant or otherwise – reached the level of that to eighteenth-century America, nor matched that to New Zealand or Canada in the nineteenth century. Yet Irish Protestants in Britain require our attention. The history of Irish settlement in Britain is coloured, often vividly, by explosions of sectarian violence, which themselves bear testament to the emergence of both Protestant and Catholic factions in the towns of Lancashire, Cumbria and western Scotland (see Chapter 6). However, this intra-Irish aggression – what the Victorians called 'party strife' – is only part of the migrants' story of settlement and adjustment. Take, for example, the Orange Order, which features prominently in the rest of this study. Although Orangeism typified the militant religious dimension of Irish life, and was often very localised, it also fostered among Irish and indigenous Protestants an associational culture that echoed certain aspects of the impressive parish-level organisations of working-class Irish Catholics.

Patterns of Protestant Migration to Britain

The most important Protestant Irish migration to Britain passed from eastern Ulster to the west of Scotland, as the two regions are closely linked in geographical and cultural terms. Ulster and Scotland share a Calvinist religious tradition and for centuries Ulster scholars preferred Scottish universities to English. Migration between them has gone on for centuries and remains a notable feature of both northern Irish and Scottish life. The two regions were drawn close by cultural exchanges, then, but closer still in the eighteenth and nineteenth centuries by parallel and complementary economic developments, not least in textiles and shipbuilding. It is no surprise that labour migrants during the Industrial Revolution should retrace the den by their ancestors to a country separated from Ulster by miles of water at the closest point. Indeed, many of the Irish who settled in Scotland can be described, in cultural ter, at least, as return emigrants. Those who peopled the Protestant plantations – which were designed to curtail Catholic powers in the early modern period – had been overwhelmingly from Scotland.[10]

During the earliest phases of the Industrial Revolution, economic transformations further encouraged the close links of Scotland and Ulster.[11] From the 1770s, and especially during the 1790s, the Ulster linen industry was struck by recession, as competition from British cotton goods began to bite. Simultaneous developments in the Scottish textile industry expedited a demand for skilled weavers and bleachers from Ulster. Between the 1780s and the 1820s, 'cotton rather than linen was the "glamour" industry of Belfast'.[12] The growth of the city's textile factories encouraged a steady migration in from its hinterland. The majority of the workers who arrived in Scotland at this time were from Antrim, Down, Armagh and Londonderry – the Protestant heartlands of Ulster – and this development, added to the lack of Catholic participation in the better linen trades, meant the majority moving east to Scotland at this time were Protestants.[13] The pressure upon outworkers during the French Revolutionary period in Ireland, which also affected silk and cotton at times, precipitated migration to a broad arc of British destinations – from west Yorkshire, Cheshire, Lancashire to Cumberland and south-west Scotland – with migrant communities sprouting up wherever the emergent textile industry demanded it.[14]

Many of the followers of Robert Emmet (who led a rising in 1803 and was executed) fled to America, whereas others crossed the narrower stretch of water to England and Scotland. Indeed, Cornewall Lewis wrote in the 1830s that the 'first powerful impulse to the Irish immigration to Great Britain was given by the Rebellion of 1798' because 'Many persons who had been implicated in the events of that unhappy period were naturally ready to seek an asylum ... where they were not known, and where they could, as it were, begin a new life'. This migration in the aftermath of the rebellion impacted upon the politics of the Irish in Britain. The political agitations of the 1790s also coincided with the introduction of new technologies into British textiles, and arrivals from Ulster found work with relative ease in these new environs primarily because 'there existed among the native working classes of both sexes ... a strong objection to factory labour'.[15]

These Ulster-born workers in Scotland mostly settled in Dumfriesshire, Wigtownshire, Ayrshire, Renfrewshire and Glasgow and other places where textiles predominated. Towns like Girvan, Ayr, Maybole, Pollokshaw, Paisley, Port Glasgow and Greenock – all of which harboured trademark Orange lodges – were key attractions for Ulster Protestants.[16] Estimates suggest that by 1838 up to 30 per cent of the weavers in Scotland were Irish; in Girvan, the Ayrshire weaving centre, the figure was much higher, at around 90 per cent.[17] Given what we know of weaving in Ulster, it is likely that Irish Protestants dominated this trade, a fact born out by the Catholic priest for Wigtownshire and West Kirkcudbrightshire, Richard Sinnot, who claimed 'a large number of the Irish in this county are not Catholics', and that 'almost all the Irish in this part of Scotland are from Ulster, a few from Connaught, and scarcely any from the other two provinces'.[18] Between 1876 and 1881, it has been shown, 35 194 (83.2 per cent) of all Irish migrants to Scotland came from the nine counties of Ulster; of these, some 24 811 (58.7 per cent) originated in the north's most Protestant counties.[19] Overall, in this period, it has been estimated that Protestants accounted for around one-quarter of the Irish in Scotland.[20]

The economic climate of northern England also proved attractive to Irish Protestant labour. Carlisle, for example, experienced a textiles boom in the mid-eighteenth century and between 1763 and 1780 the city's population doubled. By the late eighteenth century Carlisle was attracting migrants who were 'mostly "industrious Scots" from Dumfriesshire and families from northern Ireland, some of whom found work in spinning mills and calico printing, although the majority worked hand-looms'.[21] By the 1830s Carlisle's textile trades had become concentrated around factory production, although the largest example, Peter Dixon's Shaddongate mill, still relied on the domestic output of 3500 workers. Elsewhere, Cumbrian textile workers were spread wide, as might be expected of a sparsely populated rural region. Domestic weaving was an important part of the local economies of a number of villages and small towns, from the Scottish borders to the river Lune, including Longtown, Penrith, Kirkby Lonsdale, Cockermouth, Kendal and Ulverston.[22] Although the Cumbrian textile trade was much less impressive than Lancashire's, it was nevertheless important to local workers and provided an inlet for small numbers of Irish weavers.[23] In fact, the nature of the Irish migration which this work encouraged and the continuance of rather primitive outworking practices, based on the hand-loom, meant Cumbria had more in common with south-western Scotland than with Lancashire.

Very little research has been undertaken to compare the residential and occupational stratification of Catholic and Protestant Irish communities in Britain. Hepburn's detailed quantitative studies of Belfast have shown that members of the Catholic working class usually experienced much worse living conditions and poorer employment prospects than their Protestant equivalents, but did these patterns also emerge among migrant populations?[24] Much anecdotal evidence exists to suggest that Protestants enjoyed significantly higher status in the shipbuilding industries of the Clyde, and this state of affairs was probably duplicated on Tyneside and elsewhere, though what we lack are detailed studies of the impact of religious affiliation upon residential and occupational structures such as Letford and Pooley's rigorous examination of women's experience in Liverpool's communities in 1851. Their work makes many important points about the impact of religion upon economic status. By cross-examining the census and burial records of the city centre's main Irish wards, Letford and Pooley suggest that while Protestants and Catholics – Irish and non-Irish – shared the same wider neighbourhood environments, there was significant localised clustering, with, for example, Irish Protestant households often ringing, but rarely penetrating, the main Catholic enclaves. Furthermore, their study also shows how Irish Protestant women enjoyed significantly better social status than their Catholic Irish counterparts: for example, 61.5 per cent of Irish Catholic women married unskilled males while the corresponding figure for Irish Protestant women was only 36 per cent. These Protestants were also much less likely to live in multiple-occupancy dwellings.[25]

The demise, if not disappearance, of hand-loom weaving, which occurred in the 1830s, broke the chain of connection between Protestant Irish migration and the northern textile industry. Although hand-loom weaving offered a meagre living for a shrinking workforce until after the Famine, and though the Irish continued to work in the cotton factories of Scotland and Lancashire, the most noticeable development of this later period was the rapid emergence of iron-ore and coal mining, metal manufacture and shipbuilding. All of these industries seem to have attracted Irish Protestant labour, which in

turn perpetuated many noticeable features of earlier Irish Protestantism, for example the local Orange lodge. Even outside these
skilled trades, Ulster migration encouraged sectarian tensions in the
workplace, as was the case in both Greenock and Port Glasgow, where
unskilled work predominated and 'Catholic and Protestant workers
from Ireland worked in uneasy proximity in the sugar refineries and
quays'.[26]

Following the Famine, migration from Ulster (in a spectacular
reversal of eighteenth- and early-nineteenth-century trends) slowed
down and constituted only five per cent of all Ireland's loss by
migration in the period from 1881 to 1901.[27] The few who did leave,
however, tended to head for the traditional destinations of western
Scotland and Cumbria, doing so via the usual routes. New work
opportunities, especially in heavy engineering, explain the maintenance of this trend. In Scotland, the iron and coal industries
offered opportunities for skilled workers, and this situation attracted
Irish migrants to numerous towns in the counties of Ayr, Renfrew,
Stirling, Dumbarton, Lanark and parts of the Lothians. In Coatbridge, Protestant Irish settlers exceeded Catholic by about two to
one, while the overall number of Irish colliers and miners at times
outnumbered the native-born. In 1841, 13.3 per cent of mineral
miners in Coatbridge were Irish-born; ten years later the figure had
grown to 49.1 per cent, before falling back to 44.9 and 35.9 in the
subsequent two decades. In Larkhall in 1861 the Irish-born accounted
for a more modest, but still significant, 17.4 per cent of all miners;
moreover, between 1855 and 1875 only 3.4 per cent of this Irish-born
community married according to the rites of the Catholic Church.
This evidence suggests that an overwhelming majority were Protestants.[28]

To the south, settlement patterns and workplace opportunities in
the Cumbrian iron-ore and coal mining districts seem to have been
similar to those in Coatbridge and Larkhall. The mining colony at
Cleator Moor, for example, comprised upwards of 35 per cent Irish-
born in the mid-Victorian years, with Irishmen utterly dominating
the iron mines, ironworks and flax and jute factory. In Cumbria, like
Scotland, the emergence of a bellicose Orange Order suggests that
Protestants were present among the migrant population. Furthermore, census samples for the west Cumbrian towns of Whitehaven
and Workington suggest that Irish migrants were overwhelmingly
from Ulster. In Whitehaven (1871) and Workington (1881), for

example, 100 per cent of those Irish-born who were sampled hailed from the northern province, with Down the dominant county.[29]

Meanwhile, on the Clyde the development of large-scale steel shipbuilding further enforced the cross-cultural links between Scotland and Ulster. Pollard and Robertson have shown that cyclical migrations between the big shipbuilding centres – the Clyde, Belfast, Tyne and Wear, and Barrow – brought both Catholic and Protestants to Scotland and England. In fact the majority of skilled men in British ship-building were trained on the Clyde, and a large element of the unskilled labour requirement was met by Irish Catholics. McFarland argued that these links, with labour migration often organised through employers' agents and newspaper advertising, enabled many Protestant workers to enter the Scottish workplace on a fundamentally higher level than their Catholic countrymen. Many, for example, secured skilled or semiskilled labour in Clydeside towns and, though many Irish Protestants undoubtedly worked as labourers, a significant proportion also entered trades such as boilermaking, riveting and engineering.[30] In Govan and Partick, the extent of Orange–Green animosity suggests both Protestant and Catholic Irish were present in populations which, as late as 1911, comprised, respectively, 11.5 per cent and 12 per cent Irish-born. In Barrow-in-Furness, north Lancashire, patterns of settlement were similar; the emergence of shipbuilding in the early 1870s fostered large-scale Ulster migration, so that by 1881 the Irish-born accounted for around ten per cent of the town's population. In this same year, over 50 per cent of the Barrow Irish came from the easternmost counties of Down and Antrim, with 20 per cent from Belfast alone. The advent of the shipyard, coupled to the large steelworks, created a large core of skilled trades. In 1871 the shipbuilding employed 600 men and steel about 2000; by 1874 ships accounted for around 2000 workers. Consequently, by 1881 over one-quarter of Irish-born males were involved in skilled occupations, including 167 boilermakers, fitters, blacksmiths and riveters.[31]

These employment structures and patterns of migration continued to impact upon the culture of western Scotland, coastal Cumberland and north Lancashire into the twentieth century. Apart from patterns of migration and certain workplace opportunities, these north-western regions were also united by a common element – the presence of a vocal, vociferous and increasingly obvious Orange presence. It is this to which we now turn.

The Orange Order

In many respects, Irish Protestants were just like their Catholic counterparts. Churches played a significant role in their lives, and their communities comprised a complicated web of sociability and mutualism. Pubs, clubs and personal networks were important across the Irish Diaspora, irrespective of sectarian affiliations, while the rigours of migration tended to exaggerate both Protestant and Catholic senses of identity. As migration reached epic proportions in the 1830s, moreover, formal institutional developments became as important as individual and family networks in encouraging group coalescence and ethnic identification.[32]

No other vehicle of Irish Protestantism, indeed of plebeian Protestantism more generally, made such an impression as the Orange Order. In the 1820s and 1830s the Order had been very similar to Ribbonism: both movements had been tainted by their traditions of secrecy and intrigue; each was marginalised by a potential for violence or uprising. By the 1870s, however, the Order had repackaged itself as a more respectable and more overtly public medium for expressing popular loyalist sentiments. Like numerous Irish Catholic groups, the Orange Order provided close attachments for individuals; the local lodge became a drinking club as well as offering friendly-society-type benefits, a centre of Masonic ritual and a vehicle for public expressions of group unity. Although it became one of the most strident and widespread groups, a mixture of sociability and politics, it was matched in many ways by Catholic groups, such as the Ancient Order of Hibernians, and should be viewed accordingly.

Although the Orange Order changed many times during the course of the nineteenth century, it continued to provide incoming Irish Protestants with a forum through which to express their identity and, in many cases, to mix with native Protestants. It is misleading to dismiss Orangeism as nothing but a bellicose parading movement, a once-a-year gathering of drunken bigots or as a vehicle to align working-class voters to the Tory Unionist cause. The Order could be each of these things; but it was also more besides. The Order's broader utility can be measured by its geographical spread. By the mid-Victorian years it had reached into all countries of the empire.

The history of the Orange Order is hazy. It is known that, as early as the seventeenth century, groups of well-to-do men who gathered together to celebrate the Williamite settlement used the Orange name, although these early expressions were rather different from the robust, working-class movement that Orangeism became from the late eighteenth century. In Britain and Ireland, organisations dedicated to upholding the Protestant constitution were numerous; some had been formed by aristocratic gentlemen; others by merchants and well-to-do traders; still others by lowlier men from the trades. Groups such as the Society of the Blue and Orange (1727) were common in eighteenth-century Ireland, while looser affiliation was denoted by the adoption of the prefix 'Orange' by some Ulster Masonic lodges. As McFarland shows, the term Orange simply denoted the formalisation of deeply felt Protestant patriotism.[33]

In the mid-eighteenth century, at a time when it had been waning, Orangeism gained renewed vigour by opposing growing peasant violence among redresser groups such as the Oakboys, Steelboys and Whiteboys, whose main concerns were rents, wages and tithes. The potential for unrest was increased in the 1780s by Catholic incursions into the traditionally Protestant arena of linen weaving, although given that these were times of rapid expansion, with work enough for everyone, this threat alone is not enough to explain the increasingly sectarian dimension of these movements or of a new group, the 'Peep o' Day' Boys, which has been seen as a direct precursor of nineteenth-century Orangeism. Miller and Gibbon agree that initially Protestant violence stemmed from a general fear that long-held status privilege was being undermined rather than because of any particularly acute economic grievances against Catholics,[34] though it was a combination of the two which gave rise to the Armagh Troubles of the 1780s and 1790s, and the violent clashes between Protestants and Catholics. In the aftermath of the French Revolution, developments had been so speedy that the organisation was formalised in 1797 with the formation of a Grand Lodge. The Irish Rising of 1798 cemented such developments by bringing more members into the fold.

Irish Orangeism was perceived as a threat to social stability much more than was the case in British towns and cities. As a result, the authorities sought to suppress Orange activities through numerous restrictions on public processions, such as the Unlawful Oaths Act (1823) and the Unlawful Associations Act (1825). In England, the Order very quickly internalised a wider, more mainstream and politically conservative ideology, avowedly defending the principles of the established church and the Tory Party, denouncing Catholicism, popery, ritualism and, later, the growing agitation for Home Rule.

From the 1870s, Fenianism and Irish nationalism spurred an Orange renaissance in the north of England, while the adoption of a central position in English political and religious consciousness made the Orange Order one of the largest and most prominent single expressions of national identity in the period.

The ease with which Orangeism passed into the heartlands of industrial Britain illustrates clearly the wider sense of Protestant identity that came to link elements of northern Irish society with what Ulster Unionists today call the 'mainland'. In the early 1800s a number of socio-economic and political factors eased this transfer – the vagaries of industrialisation, the revolutionary threat from France and the historic strength of anti-Catholicism – and each initially played a part in creating social tensions conducive to the reception of Orange ideas. The growth of Irish migration to Britain at this time and the return of British troops and militiamen who had participated in the savage suppression of the 1798 Irish rebellion provided channels through which these ideas flowed. Middle-class opinion in northern England was also receptive at this time. The threats arising from Jacobin ideas and the social problems caused by economic change led northern employers to view the Orange Order in quite instrumental terms. They reckoned that, like earlier 'Church and King' mobs, the bellicose patriotism of Orangeism could be employed to divert working-class activities from Luddism, or general political insurrection, through anti-Catholicism and popular Protestantism towards patriotism and loyalism. For these reasons, the British dimension sprang up to follow its forebears in Ireland. By the late 1790s, the first lodges had emerged in Manchester; from the early 1800s gatherings had been recorded in Wigan, Rochdale and Ashton-under-Lyne. Elsewhere in Lancashire, Yorkshire and Cumberland, most growing centres of industrial development also happened to be places of Irish immigration, and this encouraged the formation of lodges. The prospects were enhanced for a permanent role in England when in 1807 a central body, the English Orange Institution, was formed.

The Scottish dimension was also noteworthy in these early years. The first lodge north of the border appeared in the Ayrshire weaving town of Maybole in 1799 or 1800. Many of the early Scottish lodges were also the work of militiamen returning from Ireland, while the heavy passage of Ulster weavers to Glasgow and the west coast provided a civilian population that was highly receptive to its tenets.

Important Orange appearances in Wigtown and Tarbolton enforced the link between early Protestant migrations and the weaving centres of south-western Scotland. Ulster migrants also established the Order in Airdrie, Beith, Kilbirnie, Ardrossan, Port Glasgow and other places on the Clyde.

Even though lodges were known to occur as far afield as Exeter, Norwich and Dundee, the main geographical range of Orangeism was to the north of an imaginary line drawn between the Humber and the Dee rivers. In 1830 there were three main centres of Orange organisation: Lancashire led the way with 77 lodges, followed by central Scotland with 39 and Yorkshire with 36. These together represented 66 per cent of Britain's 230 lodges.[35] There were also areas that registered little Orange activity in 1830 but would become key centres later on. One of these was the Lake counties, which in 1830 had only five lodges: one in Kendal and two in both Carlisle and Whitehaven. The north-east recorded a total of seven, with two lodges in Newcastle, and one each in Darlington, Durham, Sunderland, Wallsend and Morpeth. Yet, by the 1870s these regions in the far north of England would contain dozens of lodges. Despite the claims of one prominent Orangeman, Colonel William Blennerhasset Fairman, that by the 1830s the northern English lodges had become more English than Irish, it is clear that the timing of Irish arrivals clearly had much to do with these initial patterns of emergence.[36]

The early years of the British Orange Order were markedly turbulent. Efforts were made to centralise its organisational structure in the 1820s and 1830s. The main movers behind this plan, the Dukes of York and Cumberland, were roguish figures who saw the Orangemen as a useful lever for their own political ends, rumours of which alarmed the authorities. As a result there was a Select Committee investigation (1835) into the clandestine activities of the Orange Order. There then followed a wave of negative publicity and the leadership dissolved the Order's official structures. The movement continued to thrive in the north of England and Scotland, especially in Liverpool and the Glasgow area, drawing renewed strength from the increased pace of Irish migration. The efforts at centralisation may have compromised the Order's key constituencies in the 1830s, but the northern movement continued to attract a lower-middle-class leadership and a solid working-class support.[37]

The Orange march or 'walk' has long been a key symbol of the Order's collective identity. The first recorded Orange parade occurred on 12 July 1797 in Ireland. Precisely when the British lodgemen followed suit is not known, although there was trouble at a Manchester parade as early as 1807. From then, the marching tradition seems to have become ingrained in the big northern centres. Until the 1830s, however, Orange parades attracted only a few hundred participants, with little suggestion of the enormous event that the 'Glorious Twelfth' was to become after the Famine. It was during the 1840s that the size and influence of Orangeism began to grow. Still, though, public expressions of Orangeism were smaller than they would be later. Estimates for Scotland in 1848 suggest that the total number of Orangemen was no more than 700. From the 1860s most regions of northern England and Scotland could boast more members than this Scottish figure. In that decade, one demonstration in the key Clydeside towns of Airdrie or Paisley could attract a four-figure turnout, while Glasgow itself witnessed the largest crowds.

From well before the Famine years, however, Liverpool led the way for British Orangeism. No other town or city could match either its unique Irish composition or the great weight of its Orange tradition. As early as 1843, for example, a procession of 2000 gathered in the city to celebrate Orange Day. In 1849, at the height of Famine settlement in Liverpool, the longest ever Orange parade to that date evoked great violence and one fatality. In the aftermath of the 'Papal Aggression', in 1851, another 2000 gathered to march through the Liverpool streets. The continuation of considerable Irish migration to Lancashire, growing middle- and working-class fears about the burden that this entailed, and the generally heightened sense of Protestant militancy meant that by 1859 the 'Glorious Twelfth' in Liverpool saw a parade of around 20 000 marchers.[38]

Although Liverpool Orangeism grew quickly in the 1840s and 1850s, the boom years in Scotland and Cumbria came after 1870, when the size of demonstrations increased markedly and outdoor jamborees replaced traditional indoor dinners. In Liverpool in 1876 between 60 000 and 80 000 turned out to cheer 7000 to 8000 processors in what Neal describes as 'the biggest Orange turnout in English history'.[39] In 1872 in Glasgow 32 lodges and 1500 lodgemen were present on the 'Twelfth' and in the following year between 15 000 and 50 000 demonstrated their support.[40] Throughout the 1870s and 1880s, other Scottish towns – such as Kilmarnock, Dumbarton and Port Glasgow – held their own impressive demonstrations, with an average attendance of 8000, and it is estimated that

90 000 Scottish Orangemen celebrated the 'Glorious Twelfth' in 1878, with 14 000 to 15 000 Protestants marching in Glasgow alone.[41]

While native members were always important in Liverpool Orange lodges, the Irish Protestant dimension dominated in Glasgow. Irish Protestants had been the lifeblood of Irish settlement in Scotland since the 1780s and, though Catholic elements increased in the 1830s and 1840s, Protestants featured strongly until after World War I. Even in the 1920s the Scottish Order continued to attract a disproportionate support from second- and third-generation Irish settlers. McFarland and Walker explained the failure of indigenous Protestants to support the Orange Order in several ways, alluding particularly to distractions caused by the schism in Scottish Presbyterianism (between 'Old' and 'New' Light varieties), as well as the Scots' general suspicion of aggressive party loyalties.[42] To such issues can be added the long Liberal traditions of Glasgow and the city's development of strong municipal socialism. Furthermore, Irish immigrants in Glasgow tended to be unskilled workers in what was a skilled city, which separated the local populace from the migrants, a context which partly explains the marginalism which restricted Irish political influence in the city and prevented the development of an immigrant political machine such as was apparent in Liverpool.[43]

While general factors such as industrial development and Ulster immigration clearly created a suitable environment for Orangeism to prosper, specific events also sparked life into the movement. Orangemen were freed to some extent by the repeal in 1870 of the Party Processions Act, which had been passed in the 1820s to limit, with only partial success, public demonstrations by Orange societies, especially in Ireland, but other factors were important. The Fenian panic of 1867 and 1868 and the inflammatory tours of William Murphy, perhaps the most famous of the popular Protestant demagogues, whipped up Orange and Green feelings with rabble-rousing displays. With temperatures running high over Fenianism, Murphy was able to strike a raw nerve with his fiery mixture of obscene anti-Catholic vitriol and stoutly Protestant outpourings.

When Murphy was beaten almost to death by a gathering of 300 Cleator Moor Irish miners, as he prepared to address Whitehaven Orangemen in the Oddfellows Hall, the same local Orangemen responded by building up their movement on a scale previously unknown. In July 1871 some 500 county brethren met in the town; in the following year, following Murphy's death from his injuries, they held an 'imposing procession'. Never before had 'the well-known regalia of orange and purple ... headed by the recently purchased banner' been part of the working-class culture of Cumbrian society.[44] To the south, in the Furness area of north Lancashire, Orange developments in the 1870s also progressed with considerable speed, on account of the large influx of Irish workers coming to find employment in the local iron mines and to work the iron- and steelworks of the region. From 1872 to 1874 between five and ten lodges emerged in the Barrow district.[45] With much short-hop migration from the wider north-west, especially Lancashire, and a steady inflow of Scottish shipbuilders, it is perhaps unsurprising that these Furness Orangemen included non-Irish Protestants, as well as Irish, among their number.

The movement continued to spread in the Lakes region. From an organisation which attracted only a few hundred in the 1860s, the Orange Order had within several years become a major regional affair, with Cumbrian celebrations of the 'Glorious Twelfth' coming to attract thousands of participants. Many of these people came from far and wide, gathering together at provincial jamborees to celebrate King Billy's victory at the Battle of the Boyne (1690) and to denounce the alien Catholic religion. By the early 1880s even the small pit villages of the Cumbrian coal and iron fields had at least one lodge, while the bigger coastal centres of population, such as Workington, Whitehaven and Barrow, often had four or five separate branches at any one time.

The mid-1870s witnessed the continued momentum of the Order in Cumbria. In 1874, a crowd of approximately 1500 attended the 'Glorious Twelfth' celebration.[46] The procession travelled about five miles from Whitehaven to Cleator Moor and the nearby pit villages, and sympathetic press reporters enthused about the power and prestige of the local lodges of the Order. On the occasion of the 1874 parade, one writer expressed amazement that, although the Order had been virtually unknown before the 1870s, it had grown with such great purpose in such a very short time that the Whitehaven district was 'as regards financial contributions to the Grand Lodge, the largest district lodge in the world'.[47]

This spirit is clearly an exaggeration, especially when it is considered that Liverpool and Glasgow alone regularly hosted Orange attractions which were ten times the size of Cumbria's largest gatherings. Cumbria's Orange tradition, though important to its members, was further dwarfed by the global expanse of the movement.

In Canada, for example, it was considered that up to 30 per cent of the male population joined the Order at various times. In 1833 Ogle Gowan, Canada's top Orangeman, reckoned there were 11 000 members in Ontario alone, and 13 000 within two years. By the 1860s, J. H. Cameron, the Canadian Grand Master, reckoned on 100 000 members in 1860. By 1889, when similar Orange sources claimed there to be one million Orangemen throughout the British empire, the Canadian lodgemen were estimated to number 250 000. Although Houston and Smyth suggest a figure of nearer 70 000 is appropriate for Orange support in turn-of-the-century Canada, we must remember that an exaggeration of their strength was part of the Order's confrontational make-up.[48]

The fact that the Cumbrian Order claimed that its rebirth was a direct result of the beating which Cleator Moor miners dished out to William Murphy while he was in Whitehaven, strengthens the sense of persecution, combined with vigilance, that typified the Orange-man's standpoint, while individual episodes such as the beating of Murphy were underpinned by increasing industrial development and Ulster migration to regions such as west Cumbria. As a result, the ritual 'Glorious Twelfth' celebrations were able to draw increased support from most of the towns and villages around the region. During these times, participant lodges mustered an average of around 1500 to 2000 for the annual Orange Day outing, with large crowds of onlookers lining the route of their marches. A similar number descended on Barrow in 1882, when 50 lodges visited the town from as far afield as Whitehaven and Burnley.[49] The celebrations of 12 July 1877, which were hosted in the small iron colony of Askam (some five miles or so from Barrow), illustrated the continued and growing support for Orangeism, with a turnout of between 5000 and 6000, drawn from all across west Cumbria.[50]

The 1880s and 1890s revealed, if anything, further interest in the Orange Order's activities. Levels of support, which remained high throughout, were undoubtedly spurred by the Home Rule crisis. In Liverpool and other parts of Lancashire, there were numerous divisions between Orange and Green sections of the Irish community, and this pattern was repeated throughout the major industrial areas of Cumbria and Scotland. Sometimes the war was conducted in the pages of the press; on other occasions, violence and street disorder provided the readiest outlet for one side's view or another's. At the same time, the language of empire loyalism and unionism which dominated Orange thinking was also linked into wider streams of thought concerning the inferiority of Celts and the natural leadership qualities of allegedly more advanced Anglo-Saxons. Home Rule was dismissed because it threatened the logic of empire; but it was also attacked because the Celts of Ireland were considered to be unfit to govern themselves, much as were tribesmen in Africa.[51]

In the early twentieth century, Orangeism maintained a significant, though perhaps reduced, presence in Cumbria. Lodges continued to meet and march, but attendances in the hundreds, rather than thousands, pale next to the Liverpudlian or Scottish experience. During the Edwardian years, for example, around 50 lodges existed in Liverpool. Even the Men's Bible Classes of George Wise, the militant Protestant demagogue who dominated municipal political and religious life in the city in the 1890s and 1900s, attracted over 1500 Protestants. The Orange calendar in Liverpool was marked by marches, processions and jamborees, over 30 in all, culminating in the celebration of the 'Glorious Twelfth'. Meanwhile, on the eve of World War I in Scotland, the Orange Order counted somewhere around 40 000 members allied to around 400 lodges. Even in this later period, Ulster Protestants and their offspring were the mainstay of the Scottish Order. After the war, industrial militancy, workplace unrest and the rise of Labour prompted the Orange Order to redouble campaigns around the loyalist–Tory axis. In 1919, when 4151 new recruits (including 806 women and 1757 juveniles) joined the movement, 15 000 attended the annual July gathering at Ruther-glen outside Glasgow. In the following year between 25 000 and 30 000 were mustered in Govan, with a further 5000 meeting in Motherwell at the same time. Throughout the 1920s, attendances seem to have averaged around 40 000–50 000. The movement maintained this renewed purpose in Scotland till the 1930s, when the harsh economic climate and the rise of even more militant move-ments, like John Cormack's Protestant Action in Edinburgh and Alexander Ratcliffe's Scottish Protestant League in Glasgow, precipi-tated the decline of Orangeism north of the border.[52]

The Meaning and Scope of Orangeism

Explaining the purpose of Orangeism is fraught with difficulties and ambiguities. Traditionally, historians have treated the movement as a marginal and proletarian Irish affair, in much the same way as did many Victorians. Yet the Order achieved more than marginal status in later Victorian society. It assumed an important role in uniting Tory Unionists and working-class voters against the fiercely contested Home Rule issue in the 1880s and 1890s. Orangemen in the north of England at this time combined Anglo-Saxonist and anti-Home-Rule rhetoric to articulate the otherwise inchoate values of native and Irish working-class Protestants. The movement's most important functions, however, were clearly socio-economic, and promoted on a mundane, day-to-day basis. The utility of Orangeism to employers has led Labour historians to regard the movement as an example of false consciousness, the fracturing of potential economically determined allegiances along ethnic lines. Others have discussed the Order as a vehicle of 'marginal privilege' (members of the same class separated by perceived or real privilege), and as an expression of sectional interests conforming to Hobsbawm's 'labour aristocracy' thesis. Yet Orangeism was not simply the refuge of Ulster Protestants; it was not unambiguously an upper-working-class or petit-bourgeois movement; nor is there evidence that poorer or unskilled workers were excluded. Moreover, if Orangeism represented the sectional interests of its members, then they had to be skilled in the first place. The movement attracted skilled shipbuilders in Barrow, and both labourers and miners in Whitehaven and Cleator Moor; while key employers and an array of disingenuous Tory clerics influenced the movement across the region. In Scotland, Orangeism's membership depended on the nature of local economies: thus, in Paisley, skilled trades were dominant; in Greenock, the unskilled were more important; and in Glasgow, both skilled and unskilled members played a part.[53]

Just as the Order does not fit any simply class-based model of explanation, so too individual members were attracted to the Order by a number of its features. Primarily, Orangeism was a movement of common expression: members subscribed to a unifying, glorious history of Protestant success and a shared religious/national identity which focused upon expressions of 'Church and King' loyalism, political unionism and vigilant anti-Catholicism. In a general sense, too, the lodges provided a sphere of sociability. Most were convivial; some were bibulous; others were self-improving and promoted temperance; while all were genuinely associational, providing benefits for members. Although lodgemen were close-knit and secretive, the most obvious face of Orangeism was the very public, ritualistic July demonstrations, which embodied what McFarland calls 'the pathetic dignity of Orange "speechifying"'.[54]

From the earliest times, Orangeman have taken to the streets to declare publicly their admiration for King William of Orange.[55] The utility of the parades stretched beyond the self-acclaimed right to express one or other view concerning an event of distant history. Parading was (and is) about shared tradition and collective strength. The assertion of territorial ascendancy marked out the Orangemen from their Catholic 'enemies' and instilled confidence, pride and courage in their own group. Pugnacity and tribalism were the key elements in the decision to parade; the pageantry and entertainment, the chance to dress up and promote the group, came second. The development of the marching tradition is explained by Hempton's observation that Orangemen believed that 'where you could "walk" you could control'.[56] The marches were meant to symbolise power and authority but also gravity. The decision of Orangemen to wear bowler hats, sashes and Orange lilies was to mix carnival with military dignity. The detailed painted banners were symbols of wealth and further evidence of military gravitas. Marching around local towns, fife and drum bands playing and members singing, was meant to excite and undoubtedly to incite. The tone of the songs was either heart-swelling or gut-wrenching, depending upon the hearer's creed. To march past a Catholic church playing 'Kick the Pope', 'Croppies Lie Down' or 'The Sash Me Father Wore' may have promoted a sense of well-being in Orange minds, but it created an altogether different emotion among Catholics. With integration and shared Protestantism came alienation and isolation for Catholics. As Colls rightly asserted, '"No Surrender" meant no change and no change meant continued unfreedom of Catholics'.[57]

Throughout the Victorian era and beyond, the sound and sight of the loud and at times uncouth Orange gatherings prompted many responses, some positive, others negative, but few of them ambivalent. There were few organised working-class movements that so clearly expressed the divergence between what the Victorians viewed as 'rough' and 'respectable' culture. Many of these images arose from the Order's perceived Irishness, while the drinking and violence which accompanied the marching tradition added to this sense of difference. The processions provided middle-class observers, usually Liberals, with the main focus of their criticism. The raucous pageantry annoyed and frightened peace-loving citizens; but it also exercised

their very Victorian belief in individual freedom of speech. Banning
the Order might threaten liberty; allowing it to proceed might
threaten lives. This was, therefore, a key paradox for viewers of the
'Glorious Twelfth' and it perhaps explains why pressmen, priests and
others preferred to criticise from afar than to press seriously for any
nationwide curtailment of the lodgemen.

The Orange marches themselves attracted a ragged mixture of
supporters and onlookers. Some were there for the public display, the
entertainment, and preferred drinking and fighting to sober reflection
on what Orangemen held as the deeply historic importance of
William of Orange and the Protestant settlement. At the same time,
many of the lodgemen, the members themselves, preferred the latter
course, even if they pursued it with a devilish eye to the incendiary
effects of anti-Catholic rhetoric. Not all drank, however, and the
number of lodges which had the word 'temperance' in their titles
suggests it might be simplistic to dismiss Orangeism as a drinking
club and a hothouse for the flora of violence. It is likely that drinkers
and fighters joined the lodges but that many more simply spilled on
to the streets once a year to bait an often volatile Irish Catholic
population that was adept at defending itself.

The 'Glorious Twelfth' neither begins nor ends the story of Orange
collectivism. There were other aspects of the Order which made it
appear much more like a Catholic club than the Ribbonmen or
Ancient Order of Hibernians. The ritual parades of 12 July hid a
multitude of subtleties; they may have been male-dominated affairs,
with women and children precluded from marching, but the family
aspect was often emphasised by the press, even if wives and children
seemed only to occupy places in the crowd. Women had their own
lodges, such as the Queen Victoria lodge (number 9) of Whitehaven,
which was formed in 1873. This lodge counted 60 members, who
paid 1s to enrol and weekly dues of 6d, and this money was accrued
to pay friendly benefits, thus highlighting another important function
of the Order.[58] Children in west Cumberland also had their own
'juvenile' lodges, which also involved paying dues and receiving
benefits.

These occasional snippets of evidence demonstrate that Orangeism
was as much about the members' genuine associationalism as it was
about their unquestionable pugnacity. Orangeism was originally as
much a kind of ex-servicemen's club and benefit society. In 1843, for
example, the secretary of the Liverpool Protestant Benevolent Society

was Ambrose Byeford, who was later Deputy Grand Master of the Liverpool Orange Order. Even in the Edwardian years, the Orange lodges of Liverpool remained 'social centres, and provided funeral and illness insurance benefits, as well as the hope of mixing with potential employers'.[59] The Scottish dimension was also much the same. McFarland summarises the ethos of Orangeism well with these words: 'The network of lodges seems to have retained its original informal benevolent functions paralleling the provision of the plethora of benefit and friendly societies in the nineteenth century such as Foresters, Gardeners and Ancient Shepherds'.[60] In 1883 Glasgow Ulstermen formed the Glasgow Antrim and Down Benevolent Society, which aimed 'to cultivate and maintain a friendly intercourse between natives of Antrim and Down in Glasgow and the neighbourhood and raise funds for temporary relief'. In the early twentieth century its name was changed to the Glasgow Ulster Association, but Walker claims that this organisation and others, like the Orange Order and the Protestant Friendly Associations, remained crucial to the maintenance of an expatriate Ulster identity in the years up to World War II.[61] As late as 1912, in recognition of the movement's wider purpose, the Imperial Orange Council in Scotland was trying to standardise Order's friendly-society dimension under the terms of the Insurance Act of 1911.[62]

As well as providing benefits to members out of work, Orangeism also provided a potential route into employment. The Order, in addition to its social and religious functions, Walker tells us, 'advanced a strong paternalistic employer–worker ethic which might well have made an appeal to workers who feared job insecurity in economically troubled times' like the inter-war years. The Orangemen of Scotland, for example, appealed directly to employers at times of crisis to employ loyal Protestants. Some, like Edward Douglas, the Ulster-born partner in the shipping firm Spencer and Co., did just that. His links to Glasgow Orangeism were recognised in 1921 when a presentation was made on behalf of 50 of his foremen.[63] Close liaison of this type went on throughout the strongholds of Orangeism. In Barrow, for example, employers like James Kennedy and William Gradwell were responsible for much organisational work. Kennedy, a local iron mine-owner, described in 1877 as 'The Master of Barrow', had his own lodge, Kennedy's True Blues, and was a prominent figure in the wider south Furness scene, though little else is known of him. Although Kennedy rarely missed a 'Glorious Twelfth' outing in all the years before the mid-1890s, Gradwell was altogether a more notable and controversial character. In the 1870s, he and his partner, Andrew Woodhouse, employed perhaps 750 men in their brickworks and construction business. In 1881, Gradwell became Mayor of Barrow, and local Irish nationalists claimed he used the post to favour Orangemen. While we know that Orangeism was persistently adjudged to be a proletarian movement, there is more than a suggestion that the Orange Order drew a significant part of its support from the more prosperous working class, from whose ranks were drawn eager but little-known lieutenants who provided a link between the lodges and their clerical and lay superiors. One such man, John Bawden, who was arrested after the 1884 Orange Day riot in Cleator Moor, we do know something about. He was simultaneously master of Cleator Moor lodge, a foreman iron miner and an official of the local cooperative society.[64] Bawden clearly lacked the power of a pit or shipyard owner, but the combined ranks of foreman and Orange lodge master must have impressed men whose job prospects, whose future, lay in his hands.

Conclusions

The Orange Order served a social purpose for Irish Protestants and their like-minded native peers that went beyond the Catholic-baiting and rough street culture pervading many northern towns. The Orange lodge was, like many Catholic organisations, a unifying and galvanising social organism that grew and changed as time and circumstances dictated. It was like the local Catholic club, the Knights of St Columba or the Ancient Order of Hibernians rolled into one – except that Catholics were excluded from membership by statute. At the same time, the movement also played a prominent part in opposing Catholics, nationalists and socialists; in defending their monarch and country; and in protecting the Protestant Ascendancy.

5

POLITICS, LABOUR AND PARTICIPATION

Introduction

Between the outbreak of the French Revolution in 1789 and the creation of the Irish Free State in 1922, a bewildering array of social and political movements drew support from the Irish in Britain.[1] Indeed, the number and range of indigenous and Irish organisations that at various times reached out to the Irish suggests that the migrants' often-cited marginality obscures their considerable political potential. Despite a record of wide participation, however, Irish migrants are often viewed as a people isolated by their culture and nationality. Labour historians in particular blame the iron grip of the Catholic Church, or the distraction of Home Rule politics, when arguing that ordinary Irish migrants were largely unmoved by the economic and social imperatives of class-based organisations. However, more recent research has questioned the formulation of 'ethnicity' and 'class' as distinct phenomena. Fielding, for example, considered that Irish migrants in Britain were subject to influences of both ethnic and class types. 'That this produced what, from the outside, appeared a confusing, incoherent cultural amalgam is', he added perceptively, 'due to the preconception of the observer and not the culture itself'.[2]

The range of these influences is personified by numerous Irishmen who played important roles in radical and labour politics in the nineteenth century. The O'Connor family alone produced three activists (Roger, Arthur and Feargus) who were involved in British and Irish radicalism, ethnic and class politics, from the United Irish phase of the 1790s to the Chartist period of the 1830s and 1840s. And many years later, the sort of flexibility demonstrated by Feargus O'Connor was still noticeable in the work of a new generation of Irish agitators. Michael Davitt, for example, began his career as a Fenian in the 1860s, and finished up as a supporter of Labour's parliamentary candidates in the Edwardian period. John Wheatley mixed Catholicism and socialism and was easily able to link his support for Irish reforms with the demands of the British working class. Indeed, there is a strong element of intellectual and ideological connection between Irish and British radical ideas. 'Justice for Ireland' was a common epithet in the generation of 'Orator' Hunt and Daniel O'Connell, as it was among Labour candidates 100 years later.

There are, however, numerous problems affecting any examination of the political culture of the Irish in Britain. Irish and British radical traditions may have been connected by personalities and by social philosophies, but to what extent did ordinary Irish labourers join their British counterparts in demanding change? The fact is we do not know the answer to this question, because early political records (the few that exist) reveal so little about ordinary members. Despite problems with the sources, however, an attempt is made here to present a sense of the wide-ranging and dynamic involvement of Irish migrants in both British and Irish political and labour organisations. This chapter demonstrates that, despite key rivalries and animosities, or the weaknesses of certain aspects of their political culture, the Irish in Britain were important participants in the movements that shaped both Irish and British working-class political culture over the nineteenth century.

The United Irishmen and the Jacobite Tradition

It was during the eighteenth century, with migration growing steadily, that the oath-bound clandestine culture of the Irish countryside began to influence labour in Britain. In the 1760s the most turbulent of the dockers of Wapping in London were thought to be former Irish Whiteboys or workers under their influence. Following one particular strike, the authorities described the Irish dock workers thus: 'a few of them [are] quiet laborious men, [but] the rest are of a riotous disposition and ready to join in any kind of disorder, and from 70 to 100 are the very dregs of mankind, capable of any kind of mischief'.[3]

Much deeper and more political bonds were developed later in the eighteenth century with the migration to Britain of Ulster radicals. Presbyterians from the province were at the forefront of the United Irishmen's Society, which was formed in 1791 in the Dissenting heartland of County Down. Republicanism was also adhered to in America by Irish Presbyterians, who expressed anti-English and pro-French sentiments during the revolutionary period, while similar views were noted among weavers in Scotland in the 1770s, many of whom were Irish.[4] The United Irishmen were instrumental in developing the United Scotsmen, which in turn gave rise to a 'shadowy offshoot, the United Englishmen'. When the Irish rebellion came in 1798, it was fought most fiercely in the Protestant centres of Ulster – places like Saintfield and Ballynahinch – and 'was as much an assertion of the Ulster-Scot community identity as of the wider issues of the "Rights of Man"'. Marianne Elliot describes the connections forged between republicanism in Ireland and Britain as 'an inevitable by-product of the efflorescence of the Ulster movement in 1797'.[5]

The United Englishmen had been founded by James Coigley, a refugee Irish priest, and other Ulster and Leinster activists. Most writers view the Irish role as rejuvenating and revivifying an English radical movement weakened by repression, uncertainty and internecine differences. Coigley worked with other expatriates, including the Binns brothers, John and Benjamin, two radical republicans and members of the London Corresponding Society (LCS). The Binns, who were part of the murky underground tradition of Spencean revolutionaries, believed that the LCS needed to link up with restive Irish communities in Manchester, which had become a meeting place for English radicals, Irish workers and United Irishmen.[6] By 1798 the authorities had learned of hundreds of oaths being administered in the north, not least among Irish textile workers, although United Irishmen were only just being mustered in London by Irish republicans. In fact, the capital, unlike the north and Scotland, witnessed little cooperation between English and Irish workers over the issue of revolution.

During the tempestuous years of 1797 and 1798 the twin threats of Jacobinism and Irish nationalism appeared very real. In 1797, as Irish activists worked to establish the United tradition in Britain, a wave of mutinies crippled the navy. The Irish were blamed for the events, though the causes of the mutinies were numerous. Moreover,

Elliot argues that the United Irishmen's policy of systematic infiltration began only after the mutineers had struck. Once they had begun, however, Irish sailors and United Irishmen were at the forefront. The exigencies of war meant 100 000 of the navy's 130 000 sailors had been pressed in just three years. This rapid and involuntary growth was accompanied by generally poor conditions of service and by a turbulent political climate. Estimates of the time suggest that the navy had 15 000 Irish sailors, though the mutinied ships had crews that were nearer to 50 per cent Irish. The problem for the naval commanders was not so much the proportion of Irish as the type of Irish who had been recruited. One feature of wartime enlistment was the tendency to press criminals who were awaiting trial, many of whom were Defenders (a secret society of Catholics, opponents of the Orange tradition) or United Irishmen. The crew of the most troublesome ship, HMS *Defiance*, produced 25 Irishmen for trial, of whom 19 were executed. A majority of those transported for their part in the mutinies were Irish.[7]

At the same time as the mutinies, Roger O'Connor, the father of Feargus, was campaigning in London for an Irish uprising. Father Coigley also spent the winter of 1797–8 pursuing the same ends, as did Colonel Despard, the Binns brothers and other LCS members and Irish activists. In February 1798 Arthur O'Connor, Coigley and John Binns were arrested at Margate on their way to France to seek military assistance for the rising. Documents in Coigley's possession confirmed the accusations of government spies. Binns, who Thompson said 'bore a charmed life', was acquitted of high treason, and, before any other charge could be preferred, in his own words took off for 'the counties of Derby and Nottingham, where I had many friends'. Coigley refused to give up his colleagues and was executed. O'Connor was acquitted, after repeatedly putting the blame on to Coigley, and was despatched to Ireland to face further charges.[8]

The failure of the United Irish rebellion of 1798 marked a turning point in radical activity and popular attitudes.[9] The Irish leader Wolfe Tone had wanted a war, but the United Irishmen failed to harness the sporadic risings which did occur. Indeed, one of the greatest legacies of this phase was the galvanisation of Irish Orangeism. Another product of the failed rising was the flight of many United Irishmen to Scotland and England. In the coming decade, these men and their ideas came to be employed in organisations among the Irish expatriate population and in planning further risings in Ireland. The years after 1798 also saw the emergence of more economic grievances.

Economic hardship in the winter of 1801 presented Irish activists with further opportunities. There were food riots in many northern towns, including Stockport, Blackburn and Manchester, and fugitive United Irishmen plied their trade among the disaffected. Oppression in Ireland, and the collapse of moderate English reformers, meant that in the years after the failed rising of 1798, the Irish in Britain controlled the most active republican networks. The Irish of Lancashire, Nottinghamshire and Derbyshire were clearly involved in preparations for an Irish revolution, but the arrest and execution of Colonel Despard (whose expenses had been raised by the Irish in Britain) in 1802, and the failure of Robert Emmet's premature and badly planned rising of 1803, effectively ended the revolutionary threat of the wartime period. Emmet undid the good work of Irish agents among the Irish of Lancashire, Yorkshire and the north Midlands, who had been primed for a series of diversionary risings.[10] However, the United Irish tradition did not die with Wolfe Tone or Robert Emmet, and the Irish continued to agitate. Moreover, veterans of this momentous period of Irish history continued to crop up in British radical circles up to the Chartist period of the late 1830s and 1840s.

Trade Unionism and Radicalism in
the Age of Repeal and Reform

The years from 1815 to 1848 are dotted with examples of Irish participation in the radical movement, while migrants also maintained their own organisations. Although Irish trade unionism and radical political movements were particularly noticeable in the textile centres of Scotland and north-west England, the two most influential Irish movements – one Catholic, the other Protestant – were Orangeism and Ribbonism, formed in 1795 and 1811, respectively. Each was the sworn enemy of the other. The Ribbon movement grew out of the eighteenth-century redresser movements such as the Whiteboys and the Defenders, of which Orangeism was the main Protestant opponent. Ribbonism was not simply the continuation of early forms of collective action. It was a hybrid organisation with many different functions: in the countryside Ribbonmen sought to redress traditional peasant grievances, such as rent rises and evictions; yet in the towns, they acted like members of a trade society. Unlike the United Irishmen and the later Young Ireland movement, both Orangeism and Ribbonism were overwhelmingly proletarian, and both were welcomed into the growing Irish migrant communities.

The political importance of these two movements is unclear. It seems likely that Ribbonism's geographical presence was broadly similar to that of the Orange movement, reaching into most northern and Scottish towns with sizeable Irish communities. Although less extensively researched than Orangeism, it is known that Ribbonism was an important part of migrant political and associational culture in Liverpool, while branches were also apparent at various times in Manchester, Preston and Whitehaven – each of which was also an important Orange centre. Dublin Castle, the seat of the Irish administration, knew of the importance of these expatriate networks: the Liverpool police, for example, were often called on to look out for particular characters in their city's pubs, where publicans sometimes dished out rather more than 'legally-approved convivial forms of associational culture'.[11] JOHN BELCHEM (1994)

Belchem contends that Ribbonism, as well as being a vehicle for radical nationalism, also served as a functional instrument of settlement. After 1815 the traditional elements of chain migration – family, friends and neighbourhood – were increasingly unable to cope with the migrant tide, so that alternative, formalised aids were needed by settlers. Orangeism provided a similar pathway into jobs, housing and communal networks, though, before the Tory elite took hold of Liverpool Orangeism and turned it into a well oiled political machine, Ribbonism was much the more effective movement. Indeed, Belchem considers it to have been the foundation stone of an ethnic consciousness that came to dominate the city's Irish Catholic communities for over a century. On the waterfront, Ribbonism acted as a primitive trade union. Its 'goods', signs and passwords were vital if newly arriving migrants were to obtain work, and by the mid-1830s the city had 30 branches and 1350 members. It is further suggested that clerical opposition to Ribbonism strengthened, rather than diminished, its radical appeal.[12] JOHN BELCHEM (1994)

There was also much organisational movement among textile workers at this time, assuming particular prominence among weavers. In Scotland working-class activism was most marked in those weaving districts which also had high concentrations of Irish labour. In

Lancashire, Irish participation rates in cotton workers' organisations were also considerable. John Doherty, the founder of the General Union of Spinners (1829), was just one of the thousands of Irish who made the journey from Ireland's waning textile centres, and like his less famous countrymen became similarly involved in labour disputes. Doherty became, in E. P. Thompson's assessment, 'the greatest of the leaders of the Lancashire cotton workers'.[13] He valued education for workers, preaching their dignity and honour, and was an active proponent of factory reform for 20 years after cessation of hostilities with France.

Grass-roots activity among the Irish is difficult to ascertain, though Treble has argued that in the 1820s and 1830s they were major players in the union activities of northern textile workers. He argued that from 1808, in the Lancashire cotton belt, 'immigrants played their part ... in virtually every major trial of strength between cotton hand-loom weavers and their employers'. They were also prominent among the linen and stuff weavers of Barnsley and Leeds, on the Liverpool waterfront, and among the building operatives of Manchester.[14] As one priest told Cornwall Lewis's commission in 1836, the Irish are 'more prone to take part in trades unions, combinations and secret societies than the English'; moreover, 'they are the talkers and ringleaders on all occasions'.[15] Included among these 'talkers' and 'ringleaders' were men such as John Allison and Christopher Doyle of the power-loom weavers, and the Barnsley-based linen workers Peter Hoey, Arthur Collins and William Ashton.

The combination of official trade unionism and shadowy Ribbonism caused consternation in official circles, and from 1833 the Catholic Church subjected the Irish 'to a clergy-inspired offensive against almost every form of industrial or trade society'. In Whitehaven, in 1833, for example, the Catholic Reverend Gregory Holden settled a miners' dispute in favour of the employers, and was rewarded with a tract of land upon which build a new chapel. There is also a question mark over the Irish workers' commitment to their compatriot Doherty's trade organisations, while Robert Owen's Grand National Consolidated Trades Union (GNCTU) of the 1830s attracted few Lancashire workers, Irish or otherwise. Treble explains how priests regarded trade unionism and the taking of 'illegal, unjust and profane oaths', as Bishops Briggs of the Northern Union called them, as threats to the 'working man's eternal welfare'. Thus few Irish would countenance maintaining links with British trade unionism, especially when the Church's teachings were endorsed by Daniel O'Connell, who was a fierce opponent of clandestine societies.[16] Both he and the Church worried about the trade unions' possible infringement upon third-party rights, and believed working men should be free to accept whatever wages they could get. Neither the Church nor O'Connell, however, opposed all facets of unionism, with the 'friendly' dimension in particular being seen in a favourable light. The provision of sickness and burial benefits sounded a sober and rational note and by 1839 barely a single town in northern England was without a Catholic association offering a range of these benefits.[17]

Connolly makes more of the social function of Catholicism by claiming that, although the Church proscribed trade union member-ship in the early 1830s, there was increased tolerance in later years, particularly after 1836, when Bishop Briggs replaced Penswick. Penswick had maintained a fairly continuous correspondence with Rome on the subject of secret societies and followed to the letter a Solemn Interdict of 1831 which censured membership of such organisations and withheld the sacraments from participants. But Briggs was more moderate. Nevertheless, even he would have been shocked when one of his Manchester priests, Father Gillow, likened trade unionists' oaths to the vows taken by the trainee priests of Rome and Lisbon. Such radical views, Connolly asserts, were part of a growing clerical acceptance of the moral and social justice associated with the claims of their parishioners for fair wages and a decent standard of living, in a period when even priests could be sucked into the clandestine worlds of radical politics. This association can be found in the case of one of Gillow's former supporters, Father Hearne, who had been a respectable respondent to Cornewall Lewis's enquiry in the mid-1830s, but moved from O'Connellism to a more extreme position by the 1840s, when even his flock was alleged to have been wary of his views.[18]

Irish participation in the Reform movement of the 1820s and 1830s was as impressive – though much less revolutionary – as it had been under the influence of the United Irishmen. In the run-up to the Great Reform Act and during the Chartist agitations of the late 1830s, a strand of Irish English radicalism emerged which was much less shadowy than that of the 1790s and 1800s. At the same time, many of the key Irish figures had either learned their radical trade from United Irish activists, or had themselves been participants in the 1798 rebellion. The post-Napoleonic years saw English radicals adopting

Irish grievances as part of their reform platforms. The mass platform agitation leading up to Peterloo, for example, had been characterised by the attempts of men such as John Gast, the radical and trade unionist, as well as veteran reformers like Henry 'Orator' Hunt, Arthur Thistlewood and Major Cartwright, to gain Irish support for parliamentary reform. Even the moderate reformers Sir Francis Burdett and William Cobbett campaigned to ameliorate Irish religious and economic grievances. On the eve of Peterloo (1819), Hunt issued an appeal for a British–Irish radical compact which was later published as *Address From the People of Great Britain to the People Ireland*, 4000 copies of which were distributed in Ireland alone. The title explains Hunt's intentions. Although the appeal was derived from a genuine desire for natural justice, it was also shaped by expediency and self-interest. English radicals hoped that Home Rule might result in the voluntary repatriation of thousands of migrant labourers – 'temporary sojourners' in Britain – to the enormous benefit of the native working class. This view also hinted at the growing tensions between Irish and native workers which would become endemic in the 1830s and after. Nevertheless, as Prothero has shown, the Irish propensity to violence was not lost on English organisers, such as Arthur Thistlewood, who planned the foiled attack on the Cabinet which became known as the Cato Street Conspiracy (1820), and was in league with a group of Irishmen who were to have helped use the explosives.[19]

Irish Migrants and Chartism

The period from the 1820s to the 1840s was marked by two major political issues: repeal and reform. O'Connell's repeal movement, which aimed to secure equality before the law for Catholics, was one of the great popular organisations of the nineteenth century. Because O'Connell was a moral force promoter of Catholic rights and moderate Home Rule, he gained clerical support, which strengthened his support base. By 1825–6 there were branches of his Catholic Association in many cities, including in America, where the Irish of New York, Washington and elsewhere were raising money for the cause.[20] O'Connell also moved in London's radical circles, and by the early 1830s, when the Reform crisis was building, he came down in favour of universal suffrage, annual parliaments and the secret ballot.

In fact, until 1837 O'Connell remained broadly aligned with British radicalism, and chaired the meeting which established the Metropolitan Political Union in March 1830.

Irish radical politics in these years was racked by O'Connell's enmity towards Feargus O'Connor, the former O'Connellite MP, radical activist and future Chartist leader. While O'Connell was a cautious and somewhat devious moral force reformer, O'Connor possessed a passionate, intemperate and radical character, closely associated in Chartist historiography with physical force and the ultimately divisive contribution of Irish workers. Although this inaccurate assessment reflects the anti-Irish stance of many early historians of Chartism, it can be advanced that O'Connor was a robust, demagogic leader. He was also an intelligent man, whose journalism and writings were more important than his revolutionary stance.[21] Like him, Bronterre O'Brien is another Irish Chartist who suffered at the hands of subsequent writers. The London-based O'Brien was more militant than O'Connor, but less so than the Spencean Irish of an earlier period. He was heavily influenced by French socialism and Owenism, and his intellectual powers were such that he translated works from the French. An argumentative nature and alcoholic tendencies, however, prevented O'Brien forging any long-lasting alliance, and his best work was done, it has been said, before Chartism, not least as editor of the *Poor Man's Guardian*, 1831–5.[22]

Though O'Connor and O'Connell were allies in the 1820s and 1830s, they parted company because the latter supported the Whigs in the 1830s. O'Connell had wanted to keep out the Tories at any cost, not least because of the threat of coercion in Ireland, but O'Connor was sceptical of doing any deal with British politicians who had conceded only limited electoral reform in 1832. O'Connell was castigated for supporting a ministry which resisted factory reform and pushed through the Poor Law Amendment Act, which O'Connor called the 'starvation law'. The failure of the 1832 Reform Act to realise a more popular franchise broke the alliance of middle-class reformers and working-class radicals, which had been predicated on the case for reform in the first place. Although O'Connor and O'Connell became sworn and bitter enemies because of their differences over tactics, their fracture also reflected a wider separation of moral force and physical force philosophies. In 1837, when the split finally came, O'Connell proved to be ambivalent to the Poor Law and openly hostile to trade unionism. When British labour rallied round a group of Glasgow spinners who had been arrested on conspiracy charges, O'Connell pointedly stood aloof and strengthened his party's alliance with the Whigs. The conflict between these two Irish leviathans has obscured the role of ordinary Irish workers in the various reform movements of the period. Most historians see O'Connell's moderate nationalism and O'Connor's Chartism as mutually exclusive, with the two coming together only in 1848, when O'Connell was already dead. The extent to which working-class Irish men and women defied O'Connell's entreaties and joined up with the early Chartist organisation in the late 1830s remains a matter for debate, though it must be remembered that more was involved than simply the personalities of the two leaders.[23]

Working-class support for Chartism came mainly from three groups of workers, each of which included Irish labour: traditional craftsmen, factory operatives and domestic outworkers, including hand-loom weavers, wool-combers and nail-makers. Each group was a victim of industrialism: craftsmen's independence was threatened by newer skilled trades; the working conditions of factory labour were taken by reformers to epitomise the evils of new modes of production; and the pay and prospects of domestic outworkers diminished greatly because of new production methods. The geography of Chartism reflected the concerns of these groups; its activities were greatest in Barnsley, Bradford and Ashton-under-Lyne, where the Irish-born totalled around 10 per cent of the local populations and textiles were dominant. The range of support means that no single definition of Chartism suffices to explain the movement. For most of these workers, the six points of the Charter were simply political means of achieving economic ends. It is important to note, as Dorothy Thompson has, that in the regions where Chartism was strongest, 'the Irish were not, as they may have been after the Famine in some districts, a single outgroup facing a stable local population. They were one such group among many.'[24] The economistic argument, however, undoubtedly underplays the moral and political philosophy of many Chartist activists; what proportion of the rank and file genuinely shared these wider political motives is not known, but it is likely that some, including the Irish, did. The Irish in Britain have been presented, somewhat paradoxically, as either more extreme or more conservative than the bulk of Chartism – Irish leaders more radical because they were often revolutionary republicans (as seen in 1798 and 1848); the rank and file more moderate because of their commitment, first and foremost, to O'Connellite reform. We are left, therefore, with a conundrum.

There were many middle-ranking Irish radicals, even in an age dominated by O'Connell and O'Connor. The career of one man, John Cleave, serves as a useful indication of Irish participation in the array of radical organisations which sprung up in these years. Cleave, an Irish-born ex-seaman, coffee house proprietor and publisher, was one of the most influential radicals in London during the late 1820s and 1830s. He was leader of London's largest cooperative society, based in Westminster, and an Owenite utopian socialist and republican revolutionary. He played a prominent part in many of the organisations which led to Chartism, including the National Union of the Working Classes and also the Irish Anti-Union. As a journalist, Cleave was heavily involved in the struggle of the unstamped press (newspapers published without payment of duties) and this activity brought him into conflict with the authorities. As well as supporting Catholic emancipation and Home Rule for Ireland, Cleave was also a follower of Feargus O'Connor. In 1836, along with a Catholic coal merchant, Thomas Murphy, he joined O'Connor's Great Radical Association and the London Working Men's Association. Cleave was also one of seven London representatives at the Chartist Convention in 1839, and he remained part of the movement for suffrage Home Rule till his death in 1850.[25] There were numerous other such activists. The Donegal-born migrant Thomas Denvyr, who became secretary to the Chartists' Northern Political Union, was the son of a United Irishman, and a London Irish tailor, Philip McGrath, was president of the National Charter Association for many years. As well, the link between O'Connellism and O'Connorism was personified by two Irish brothers, Daniel and Charles McCarthy, who were variously members of the Chartists and the Repeal Association, even though O'Connell forbade such dual activity. Similarly, Robert Crowe, who was imprisoned in 1845 for his radical activities, and joined the republican Irish Confederates (a radical breakaway from O'Connell's pacific repeal movement, led by the Young Irelanders) later in the decade, recalled in his memoirs how he split his time between temperance, repeal and Chartism.[26]

Rank-and-file links between British and Irish radicalism are hidden by the nature of the sources. Not all Irish Chartists stand out because of their nationality. Many expressed overt hostility to the Catholic religion that was considered by contemporaries to be the main badge of Irishness. As a result, key operators such as Peter Brophy of the Irish Universal Suffrage Union (IUSA), which was castigated by both O'Connell and the Catholic Church, who was active in England during the great strikes of 1842 and imprisoned during the great conspiracy trials of 1843, was famed as a radical, not as an Irishman. When questioned by police, Timothy Higgins of the Ashton Working Men's Association 'gave as his religion "no sect or persuasion"'. Even among the obviously religious, for example Irish priests, involvement with Chartism was not impossible, as is illustrated in the case of Father Patrick Ryan of Barnsley, who was a friend of the Dublin Chartist leader Patrick O'Higgins, and a member of the IUSA.[27]

Still the evidence of Irish participation remains fragmentary and sometimes contradictory. While Treble is able to argue that no 'ordinary' Irish participated in Chartism until 1848, when cooperation between Chartism and the Irish Confederates made revolution a real possibility, Dorothy Thompson is able to counter with evidence of the continuous importance of regional Chartist organisers. This contradiction is not easily resolved. For example, even though no Irishman was arrested after John Frost's 'Newport Rising' in 1839, migrants from Ireland numbered 17 among those arrested for Chartist offences in other areas during the same winter. The real question is, it would seem, whether O'Connell carried the Irish in Britain with him until his death in 1847. By 1842 his relations with O'Connor had soured to such an extent that, when in the same year O'Connell inaugurated the Loyal National Repeal Association (LNRA), he forbade links with Chartism, returning subscriptions to those who joined both groups.

While O'Connell spoke virulently against Chartism, there is a question mark over his repeal movement, which paled next to the successful campaign for Catholic emancipation. Indeed, a number of related issues ensured a gradual shift away from O'Connellite moderation. Dorothy Thompson has argued that the failure of his monster demonstration at Clontarf in October 1843, which he called off in the face of official pressure, broke O'Connell's spell and signalled a move towards Chartism by the Irish in Britain. The Young Ireland movement – led by the journalists who formed the *Nation* newspaper, Thomas Davis, Charles Gavan Duffy and John Blake Dillon – split from the LNRA in 1847. A more radical agrarian agenda was also promoted in the influential writings of James Finton Lalor. The Young Irelanders employed the sort of physical force rhetoric which O'Connell abhorred. The 'Great Liberator' had a much-weakened grip on his Irish empire by the mid-1840s, and there were moves to link the Irish and Chartist movements at the time of his death. While the Famine occupied the minds of ordinary Irish people, it had a radicalising effect on middle-class reformers. Thus, while in 1847 W. H. Dyott of the IUSA had expressed suspicion of the 'literary adventurers' of Young Ireland, the claim of John Mitchel, the Irish republican leader, in 1848 that 'Every Chartist is a *Repealer*', opened the way for an Irish–Chartist alliance.

1848

The momentous year 1848 saw Chartism and the Young Irelanders' newly formed Irish Confederates come together with a twin programme of repeal and democratic reform.[28] The 'year of revolutions' illustrates the extent of Irish participation in Chartism, despite O'Connell's opposition or the much-vaunted economic differences between them and native workers. Only the desperate victims of the Famine were beyond the scope of Chartism; their 'daily struggle for survival necessitated "political" engagement with philanthropic and relief agencies' rather than with a radical political movement.[29] Yet even in Liverpool, which was being swamped by a huge and desperate migration, and where the Irish had been resolutely O'Connellite and anti-Chartist, the year 1848 witnessed a huge proliferation in radical activity. The authorities feared the port would be used as a staging post by Irish brigades trained in New York, and the explosion of republican Confederate clubs in Liverpool and Birkenhead strengthened these fears, as the formerly moderate Irish middle class in Liverpool began to recruit supporters for a repeal of the Act of Union through the Ribbon networks.[30]

The same year also witnessed the emergence of an ugly and vituperative anti-Irishness, whipped up by the press and the government. Although Chartism was a bridge between migrants and hosts, the political mobilisation of 1848, fostered through migrant networks and associational culture, should not hide the fact that, as Belchem reminds us, the Confederates were 'impatient repealers' not 'ideological republicans'. The Irish were, however, more extreme than the British Chartists; they were also equally redundant in the context of a reordered political culture. Belchem argues persuasively that the nature of popular politics was changing at mid-century in way which reduced the utility of spontaneous public displays and mass platform demagoguery. Formalised political organisation would be a key feature of British political culture from the mid-Victorian period, at a time when notions of public and private space and the limits of acceptability and respectability were being redrawn.[31] The reformism of the state also drew the teeth of popular radical movements. However, with the European climate of 1848 promising much for radical agitators, and with the British state employing considerable violence in maintaining civic authority, it would be hasty to dismiss the ultimately counter-productive Chartist–Irish alliance as doomed from the start. These movements undoutedly offered some prospect of class-centred co-operation, but the links between them were weak, planning was poor, and there was little evidence of close communication between William Smith O'Brien, the Dublin-based leader of the Confederates, and Feargus O'Connor.[32]

Despite the widespread panic in the manufacturing districts of Lancashire and Yorkshire, in Liverpool and Manchester, and in the surrounding towns, Chartism was ultimately marked by constitutionalism and discipline. Physical force was regarded as a last resort. The meeting planned for 10 April 1848 on Kennington Common, London, which was suspected by moderates such as O'Brien, drew the opprobrium of the press and was veiled in tight security. *The Times* on that day damned the Irish dimension of Chartism in a deliberate attempt to rouse public opinion against the movement: 'the Repealers wish to make as great a hell of this island as they have made of their own'. Moreover, as Belchem argues:

> it was the spectre of the Irish, quite as much as the dread of the revolutionary contagion spreading across from the continent, which brought about such an accretion of strength to the forces of order in 1848, allowing the ruling class to mount a massive display of its monopoly of legitimate violence.[33]

As well as being pressed by military muscle, the Chartists were outmanoeuvred by the weight of anti-Irish opinion, their poor organisation further exposed in the embarrassing withdrawal of a huge petition on the grounds that it contained obscene and fictitious names.

The fizzling out of Chartism was underlined by Irish responses to the arrest, in May 1848, of John Mitchel and other Young Irelanders

rges of sedition. In June, Mitchel's sentencing became a focal
.t for radical agitation: 14 years' transportation was seen as wholly
.ijust and caused outrage. Although in Bradford a Chartist national
guard, 50 per cent of which was Irish, began to drill openly in the
streets, Lowe argues that the reaction to Mitchel's punishment marked
the end rather than the beginning of public cooperation between
Chartists and Confederates. Increasing pressure from the authorities
drove the expatriate Confederates in Lancashire back into the secret
networks which had marked their earlier organisations.[34] At the same
time, while Irish politics were being radicalised, the anti-Irish stance
of the press was hardening.

The association of English radicalism with wild Irishness was a
skilful piece of propaganda. Mitchel was repeatedly represented by
Punch as an Irish monkey in what was the most significant pictorial
development since the Irish peasantry was first represented as the
monster of O'Connell's Frankenstein. Throughout the course of this
turbulent year, the idea of Britain's cultural superiority and of
Ireland's difference was sharpened. The month of August saw some
clandestine cooperation between northern Chartists and Confederates, and though there was nothing to suggest a revolution, the press
still made the connection. For them, the insurrectionary conspirators
were easily identified: 'MOONEY, ROONEY, HOOLAN, DOOLAN'
were their names.[35] The vitriol of the newspapers, the assiduity of the
state and the inherent constitutionalism of Chartism made a rising
unlikely. In the event, as Foster has noted, 'Britain's "1848 Revolution"
happened in Ireland',[36] when in July of that year William Smith
O'Brien's ill-planned and unsupported rising ended ignominiously in
widow McCormack's cabbage patch. No credible network of communication had been established between Ireland and Britain,
although arms had been collected. In the end there was no rising in
Lancashire, or elsewhere in Britain, to support Smith O'Brien.

Fenianism

The Great Exhibition of 1851 seemed to mark a new dawn for
Victorian society: the inherently stable British constitution had resisted
the revolutionary potential of mass Chartist demonstrations. Moreover, the repeal of the Corn Laws, and with it cheaper food, and a
generation of economic prosperity seemed likely to ensure that
Continental-style revolution remained no more than an alien threat.

The Irish scene, however, could hardly have been less tranquil, with the threat of Fenian terrorism shaping the popular view of Irish nationalism, and with the emergence of a genuinely transatlantic political movement aimed at Home Rule by peaceable methods, under the aegis of Isaac Butt, Charles Stewart Parnell and John Redmond. The Irish response to each of these organisations was very different. The Fenian movement, with its emphasis upon oath-bound and clandestine operation, was part of a long tradition dating back to the eighteenth century,[37] though it grew most directly from the Young Ireland movement. The Famine transformed radical attitudes in Ireland, with the spectre of starvation and emigration fostering a sense of outrage at England's wrongful treatment of the sister isle. Once the day-to-day exigencies of the Famine had passed, and the deep psychological blows had transformed numbness to anger and hatred, a certain portion of Irish society was moved to declare that British influence must be removed from Erin's shores. The political repercussions of Irish disillusionment were considerable. The Fenian movement was to be the precursor of the modern-day IRA, with its effective strikes at 'mainland' Britain.

The Irish Republican Brotherhood, as the Fenians were originally known, was founded in New York in 1858 by veterans of the Confederate movement. It was initially an undoctrinaire liberation movement, attracting support from Irish Americans. In the 1860s, moreover, 'Irish Yankees' – veterans of the American Civil War – were to play a vital role in its British campaigns of disruption. With around 150 000 Irishmen having served with the Union forces, many in 'Irish-only' regiments, the pool of resources was deep, and by the late 1860s the American brotherhood counted a membership of up to 50 000, with many more sympathisers.[38] During the same decade the movement took root in Dublin and then spread quickly to Britain, gaining footholds in the new communities. Fenianism first appeared in Lancashire, for example, under a front organisation, the National Brotherhood of St Patrick. By 1863, 15 branches of this organisation could be counted in London alone. The movement spread among all substantial migrant communities in England and Scotland, and its organ, the *Irish People*, was said to have almost destroyed the circulation of the *Nation* among expatriate Irishmen 'in many places north and south of the Tweed'.[39] The Brotherhood in 1865 claimed 80 000 members in the United Kingdom. Although the Catholic Church vehemently opposed Fenianism, the Church's networks of close-knit parish-level organisations were regularly infiltrated by activists, not least because not all priests followed the official line. Father Lavelle, for example, who became well known in the west of Scotland, was condemned in the press during 1867 for his 'semi-seditious language', which, it was suggested, aimed to 'fenianise the lower orders of Irish'.[40]

During 1867 and 1868, the main years of the Fenian threat, Britain was racked by reports, most of them bogus, of Fenian activities, including imminent insurrection. Public opinion reached fever pitch, and the press became hysterical, even though the police had little difficulty infiltrating the Fenians' bibulous bar-room culture and were clearly well apprised of their major movements. Fenianism was riddled with informers, who led authorities to numerous stockpiles of weapons and ammunition. However, the Fenian threat gained a particularly sinister resonance from the publicity surrounding four incidents in 1867: the abortive raid on Chester Castle (February); the failed Irish rising (March); the Manchester raid (September); and the Clerkenwell bombing (December).

The attempt to seize the arsenal of Chester Castle, although something of a non-event, was nevertheless astonishing. On the day of the planned raid, local and national newspapers noted the arrival of large numbers of young Irishmen from Liverpool, Manchester, Preston and Halifax. In this sense, planning was good. The Chester authorities called out the militia and the town was gripped by panic. The chief organiser was John McCafferty, a Civil War veteran, whose order was to seize arms and take them to Holyhead and then by steamer to Ireland. As was typical, the plan was scuppered by an informant. In addition, many volunteers were arrested in Warrington, Leeds, Dublin and elsewhere, before they could make it to Chester, while those who did arrive in the town were met by police and army patrols. The raid ended without bloodshed or even a single shot; however, the fact that 1200 Fenians could be mustered in one place was a cause for considerable alarm. Meanwhile, McCafferty fled to Dublin via Whitehaven. The local press in west Cumberland spread the rumour that he had visited Cleator Moor, a small iron-ore colony with a turbulent Irish population, to raise money for the Fenians. The authorities monitored McCafferty's departure on the *New Draper* and he was picked up on arrival in Dublin, where he was sentenced to death. The sentence was commuted, however, and McCafferty joined a growing band of Fenians serving long spells in prison.[41]

In many ways the Manchester rescue of September 1867 was even more remarkable. Here the Fenians launched a daring raid on a police van to rescue two prominent Fenian prisoners, Thomas J. Kelly, the chief executive of the Irish Republican Brotherhood, and his aide Timothy Deasy, as they were moved across Manchester. Unfortunately there was a scuffle, shots were fired and a police officer, Sergeant Brett, was killed. Amidst scenes of pandemonium, Kelly and Deasy escaped. As the police combed the Irish quarters of Manchester searching for them, Kelly was hidden in a water cistern and had to swap clothes with a priest to avoid detection. The two eventually made it to New York.[42] Back in Manchester, 28 men were charged to face magistrates, and the veteran Chartist leader and lawyer Ernest Jones defended some of them. After a highly publicised trial, seven men were sentenced to penal servitude, while three – Larkin, Allen and O'Brien – were sentenced to death. The evidence for their conviction was dubious and the public outcry was considerable. John Bright and Charles Bradlaugh lambasted the cowardice of the government and there were disturbances in Birmingham and rallies elsewhere in the lead-up to the hangings. However, the next episode, an attack on Clerkenwell gaol, rocked the nation and alienated sympathisers.

This further attempt to free Fenian inmates by blowing a hole in the prison wall was not officially planned or promoted by the Fenian command. The explosion was bungled, and instead of freeing anyone it killed 20 people in nearby houses. Within three weeks, with temperatures running high over Clerkenwell, Larkin, Allen and O'Brien were hanged, and in mid-1868 a Glasgow Irishman, Michael Barrat, was tried and hanged for the Clerkenwell explosion.[43] Public sympathy for the Fenians evaporated. However, the fate of the 'Manchester Martyrs' had steeled many Irish migrants. As a result, when Michael Langan, an Irish resident of Barrow-in-Furness, was hauled before magistrates for assaulting a police officer, he told the arresting officer: 'yes you bloody thing, there might be plenty of people shot or robbed in the street while you are here, I shall shoot some of you constables some time. You hung those Fenians at Manchester did you?'[44] Many Irish communities, however, chose to issue ameliorative statements during early 1868, denouncing the atrocities at Manchester and Clerkenwell. In February, for example, a petition of loyalty, containing 22 000 Irish signatures, was sent to the Queen by the London Irish.[45]

Fenianism shook the British public. A further effect of the move-ment's activities was to propagate a common view that the Irish community was characterised by webs of intrigue and double-dealing. Episodes like those of 1867 altered the pitch of anti-Irish and anti-Catholic hostilities and strengthened the 'insider versus outsider' mentality of migrant life. There were also political repercussions, for the Fenian panic accentuated the lurch to Conservatism which marked Lancashire politics in the 1868 and 1874 elections. On a more positive level, however, Fenianism projected the Irish problem to a wider audience than ever before. It has been said that Fenianism was the reason why Gladstone, on hearing of his election victory in 1868, announced his mission to 'pacify Ireland', a Herculean task at which he worked for three decades. The Fenian arrests also gave rise to Isaac Butt's Amnesty Association, an organisation dedicated to freeing the imprisoned political campaigners, which in turn spawned the Home Rule organisations which played such a major part in later Victorian and Edwardian politics.

Home Rule and Unionism

The transatlantic nature of Irish politics, which Fenianism en-gendered, was also emphasised in the 1870s with the emergence of the constitutional Home Rule movement. Led by the Irish MPs in Westminster, and funded by the Irish communities in America, Australia and Britain, as well as at home, the various organisations of the Home Tule tradition were the most successful expression of Irish nationality among the Irish Diaspora. The constitutional nationalist movement also threw up a number of heroes, old and new. By the 1880s it had produced men of the stature of Charles Stewart Parnell and T. P. O'Connor, and was able to draw in support from ex-Fenian activists, such as Michael Davitt and John Devoy. At the grass-roots level, a number of prominent regional figures grew to national prominence during the quest for Home Rule. John Denvir, the Liverpool Fenian, historian and writer, was one of the most notable; others included Dr Andrew Commins, who worked tirelessly in the 1870s to establish a viable political organisation among Britain's Irish community, and John Ferguson, the Belfast-born Glasgow business-man, who became the most prominent organiser north of the border. The extent to which these men attracted and held the support of their Irish compatriots has been the subject of some debate. Despite early optimism, however, Irish nationalism in Britain never achieved its full potential, except perhaps in Liverpool.

The late 1860s witnessed the first stirrings of formal and consti-tutional political organisation among the Irish in Britain, through Butt's Amnesty Association. By 1870 the campaign to free the Fenian prisoners had formal branches in London, Birmingham, Liverpool and elsewhere. The Home Rule Confederation of Great Britain (HRCGB) was formed in May 1870 by Butt and spread quickly, especially throughout northern England and Scotland. His plan was to channel Irish national aspirations into modest proposals for home government without alienating the migrants from their adoptive towns. A. M. Sullivan, the editor of the *Nation*, the newspaper founded by the Young Irelanders, was among the worthies who addressed a meeting held in Liverpool in 1872 attended by 2500 delegates from across Britain. Bradford alone claimed six branches and 670 members. In the same year, though, perhaps only the Glasgow organisation of the HRCGB was genuinely solvent. With 1500 members in the 1880s, Glasgow's 'Home Government' and 'William O'Brien' branches were two of the most important in Britain.[46] The nationalist cause was additionally promoted by a range of newspapers, from the *Free Press* to the *Glasgow Observer*, and the *Nation* and the *United Irishman* to many local examples of Charles Diamond's *Catholic Herald*.[47] O'Day has written of these heady developments as part of a plan to 'Americanise the political influence of the Irish in Britain'.[48]

From its earliest days, the Home Rule movement was dogged by tales of drunkenness and violence, and Butt was anxious that priests should be attracted into the movement to give it respectability. Although there were 14 in attendance at the 200-strong first annual convention in Manchester in August 1873, the extent of clerical support has been debated. Walker's examination of the Dundee Irish suggests priests remained aloof from nationalist politics, and that when they did become involved it was usually so as to tighten the Church's grip on the parish rather than to forward the cause of Ireland.[49] Nevertheless, clerical participation in nationalist movements in Britain did increase in the 1870s and 1880s for two reasons: first, because more Irish priests were filling posts within Irish parishes; secondly, because Home Rule became increasingly respectable.

Local branches were also subject to internecine wrangles and frequently drifted in and out of existence. The high mobility among migrants clearly did not help matters; nor did class-based divisions. This latter point was emphasised by the unwillingness of Butt, T. P. O'Connor and Captain Kirwan to embrace the self-improving aspects, such as sickness and burial funds, which helped to make Orangeism successful. The HRCGB was strongest in the big cities, where there was an identifiable middle class, and places such as Liverpool and Glasgow remained the focus for campaigns. The mid-1870s were marked by a continuing struggle to establish the HRCGB on a firm footing and by the ascension of Parnell, first to the executive (1876) and then to the presidency (1877). Parnell's elevation was a notable victory over Butt's conservative tutelage, though the movement in Britain continued to teeter on the brink of insolvency and apathy. When Parnell was inaugurated as president at the Liverpool convention of 1877, only 40 delegates were present.

The period of the Land War (1879–82) brought renewed optimism to the nationalist campaign. The widespread violence or upheaval which accompanied the bad harvest and hunger of 1879 injected a new mood of militancy into Irish politics, and eventually brought Fenian elements and constitutionalists together, under Parnell's control, initially through the Land League, which eventually replaced the HRCGB. During these crisis years, coercion remained a constant threat to Ireland, and Parnell was imprisoned in Kilmainham gaol for refusing to condemn rural violence. Moderates in particular were shaken in May 1882 by the murder in Phoenix Park of Lord Frederick Cavendish, the new Irish Secretary, and his under-secretary, T. H. Burke. The resumption of Fenian-style violence in Britain (organised through the American *Clan na Gael* movement), with attempts to blow up Liverpool Town Hall and three explosions in Glasgow in January 1883, also added greatly to the feverish atmosphere. The authorities, driven by anger and vengeance, arrested ten Irishmen for the Glasgow bombings, and their trials resulted in sentences ranging from seven years' imprisonment to penal servitude for life.[50] Against this background there were now branches of the Land League throughout the major Irish communities, especially in the north-west and Scotland.

In 1883 the Land League gave way to the Irish National League of Great Britain (INLGB), which was Parnell's way of reasserting his grip on Irish politics both inside Westminster and beyond. The Land League had been closely associated with Fenian operators, such as Davitt and Devoy, and the change of name symbolised a new constitutional turn and cooperation between Davitt and Parnell. Membership figures for the new organisation were impressive. In 1884 there were under 5000 INLGB members in Britain; within two years the figure was around 13 000; by 1889 this reached 34 000.[51] The success of the INLGB was as nothing compared with that of the Land League in America, where the movement seemed to represent a 'coming of age' in Irish American politics.

The Land League of America spread rapidly and by September 1881 it had more than 500 000 members organised into 1500 branches. This success was partly a measure of the effectiveness of middle-class leaders and the importance of modern communications. As well, the League was able to tap into the increasingly mature Irish political culture of many big American cities, uniting three strands of Irish politics: Devoy's revolutionary nationalism, Patrick Ford and Davitt's radical land reformism, and Parnell's constitutionalism. Yet it has been argued that the movement drew its strength more from Irish American experiences of hardship in the new country than solely from their exaggerated sense of Irishness. Brown argues that: 'The springs of Irish-American nationalism [in this period] are to be found in the realities of loneliness and alienation, and of poverty and prejudice'. Thus Irish American nationalism, the zealous adoption of the land question, represented a yearning for self-improvement, a desire to be respected in their new homes; but most of all, Brown claimed, 'the Irish wanted to be middle-class and respectable ... [and] in the Lace Curtain Irishman the rebel found fulfilment'.[52]

Critics have argued that Brown overlooked the activities of those Irish at the bottom of the pile and implicitly negated the diversity of class and ethnicity in 'Gilded Age America'. Others have emphasised the questions of class struggle which Brown's liberal self-improvement thesis ignores. For Foner, the successful mobilisation behind the Land League was the measure of another sort of coming of age: the welding together of Irish class and ethnic imperatives. For the first time, the Irish were being introduced to the American reform tradition, railing against one form of monopoly, the British government, in such a way that would prepare them for an important role in the fight against another form of monopoly, American capitalism. The League can thus be presented as an instrument in the American Irish community's 'assimilation ... with a strong emergent oppositional working class culture'.[53] While many Irish in Britain felt the same way, their organisation failed on both points: they could not break into the native political arena either by forming their own party or by dominating an existing party. The mature and conservative political culture of British life, and the absence of a large Irish middle class in most towns, save for Liverpool and Glasgow, made the political achievements of their American cousins an enviable dream, and something that would not be realised throughout industrial Britain until perhaps the 1920s, by which time Irishmen were playing a significant role in the then mainstream British Labour Party.

The 1880s in Britain were still marked by nationalist optimism. Up to the climactic election campaigns of 1885 and 1886, nationally renowned Irish figures such as T. P. O'Connor and Parnell himself visited far-flung Irish communities urging them to register as electors and to stand firm on the nationalist question. From 1886, the 'Plan of Campaign', a policy of tenant resistance in Ireland, including the infamous 'boycotting' system, gave renewed vigour and hope to expatriate supporters of the nationalist cause. The impact of Irish politics upon INLGB fortunes was perhaps greatest in Scotland, where Ulster migration and robust native Protestantism promoted both anti-Irish and intra-Irish sectarianism. Between 1883 and 1890 the number of Scottish branches rose from 52 to an impressive 630, while income grew from £400 to £4000 and membership from 4000 to 40 000. By 1890, Handley argues, the INLGB had 'canalised the Irish vote in the country not only in parliamentary but also in municipal elections'.[54] Gladstone's conversion to Home Rule in 1886 shifted the ground under the Irish National Party in Westminster and clearly impacted on the movement among the Irish in Britain. O'Day has argued that prior to the conversion, the HRCGB was a 'party of social integration' because it 'set the full bounds of the political culture of members'. By contrast, he argues, the commitment of Gladstone to Home Rule undermined the distinctiveness of Irish nationalist organisation and made the Parnellite party, and its supporters at home and in Britain, a prop for the Liberal Party. During the 1870s and 1880s the leadership failed to make the INLGB and its forebears a 'Tammany Hall-like machine' although it could reasonably be called 'the political voice of the Irish community'.[55]

The weaknesses of Irish nationalist organisation in Britain are shown up by reference to Liverpool's isolated success. Liverpool's Irish population was massive – totalling, at various times, about one-third of the city. The docks provided employment for vast armies of unskilled men; densely packed communities sprung up along the waterfront of Liverpool and the levels of overcrowding and residential clustering all added to the compact strength of the Irish community. Between the 1870s and the 1920s, the city was England's Irish nationalist capital. At various times there were as many as 10 000 members of the different Home Rule organisations. Irish nationalists in Liverpool won council seats regularly; like their Orange counterparts, they made a significant contribution to the political culture and social life of the city. Irish nationalists shared the government of the city for three years, and, as late as the early 1920s, were the official opposition, with 23 councillors. The real power of the Liverpool Irish nationalists was demonstrated by the return in the 1885 general election of T. P. O'Connor, 'spokesman of the Irish in Britain', in the city's Scotland parliamentary division. He held the seat until his death in 1929.[56]

If the 1870s and 1880s were marked by a failure to create a truly independent and powerful force in regional and national politics, the 1890s and early 1900s centred upon relations with Liberalism, Labour and Unionism. The Parnell divorce case of 1890 was a bitter blow to the aspirations of Irish nationalists. The *Glasgow Observer* captured the pessimistic mood when it lamented: 'What all the enemies of Ireland failed to do against Mr Parnell he has done to himself.'[57] The divorce, which scandalised conventional morality, ended Parnell's career, and some would say his life, for he died the following year after a series of bitter struggles to win a parliamentary seat. Handley argues that the shock of Parnell's fall from grace threw the INLGB into a state of 'temporary bewilderment'. This reaction should not detract from what Handley has seen as the striking capacity of the Irish in Scotland to work together. Handley ascribes this cooperation to the centripetal role of the Catholic parish, strong regional ties among migrants and the weakness of factors promoting integration or assimilation.[58] Despite the strength and identity of Irish groups in places like Glasgow and Lancashire, constitutional objectives precluded truly independent action. Having tried to return more MPs for mainland constituencies, Parnellite nationalists by the later 1880s accepted the central role which Liberalism must play if Ireland was to be independent. Fielding has argued that Gladstone's conversion made a nationalist–Liberal alliance inevitable, while the divorce scandal, and bitter divisions surrounding Parnell's demise, increased Gladstone's status and bridged gaps between Irish and Liberal reformers. Consequently, in Manchester Irishmen rose to prominence in ward and divisional Liberal parties. These included Dan Boyle and Dan McCabe, the latter of whom became Manchester's first Catholic Lord Mayor in 1913.[59]

In 1891 the INLGB became the United Irish League under the aegis of John Redmond, who became the most prominent figure in the split Irish party in Westminster. In Scotland this movement was especially prominent, with a spate of public campaigns after the failure of Gladstone's Home Rule Bill of 1893. During the late 1880s working-class leaders like Keir Hardie began to address nationalist gatherings in the hope of gaining support for the parliamentary candidates of the Independent Labour Party (ILP) and Labour Representation Committee. In 1906, for example, there was clearly strong Irish support for Labour candidates, such as George Barnes, who won Glasgow Hutchestown against Andrew Bonar Law, and Charlie Duncan, whose victory at Barrow-in-Furness saw the first Labour MP returned for any west coast constituency between Lancaster and Carlisle. Relations between the Irish and Labour were far from smooth, however, and despite the vigorous pro-Labour campaigns of the old Fenian and parliamentary nationalist Michael Davitt, the Irish still aligned themselves with the Liberals, a legacy of Gladstone's campaigns for Irish self-government. This link is certainly borne out by the affinities of the Irish in Keighley, the Yorkshire textile and engineering town, where members claimed in 1893 that the local INLGB contributed more to the Home Rule cause 'than either of the populous towns of Glasgow or Liverpool'. While the Keighley Irish were strongly attached to the Home Rule cause, it was the Liberal Party, not the Irish party or the ILP, which benefited. The ILP were irritated by the unswerving loyalty the local Irish showed to the Liberals; they were used, one ILP man claimed, by the Liberals 'as the hewers of wood and the drawers of water'.[60]

It would misleading to look only at the nationalist dimension of Irish politics in Britain, for the Unionists were not entirely without claims upon Irish votes. Little is known about the Protestant Irish in Britain and no evidence has surfaced to determine the national origins of grass-roots members of anti-Home Rule movements, such as the Orange Order. McFarland has shown that Orangeism in Scotland was almost universally a movement of Irish-born and their first-generation offspring, remaining this way till 1918.[61] Links between Orangeism and Conservatism seem to have been shakier than might be expected, though it is clear that through their networks of associations, job offers and general camaraderie, Tory dignitaries were able to draw a bloc of Irish voters away from the nascent labour movement which better-suited their class interests. The quest to secure votes for the Union required little exertion among a Protestant community with deep attachments to the homeland of Ulster whence a large majority of Protestant Irish came.

The position of the Orange Order in Lancashire is different from that in Scotland. First, fewer Orangemen there were Irish. Neal's work on Liverpool,[62] which was the main centre of English Orangeism, suggests that while Orangeism had been a movement of Irishmen in the first half of the century it quickly became a crucial part of the Liverpool Tory political machine, and thus exerted an influence on English and other working-class groups. By the 1870s, for example, Orangeism was a strong element in Liverpool's curious, American-style 'boss politics' culture; and it came to represent a very simple Englishness against the huge Irish nationalist population of the city. Violence was a part of Liverpool's political *modus operandi* as well as its leisure culture. While Liverpool returned Britain's only Irish nationalist MP in these years, the city was often dominated by militant Toryism. Liverpool had its own Protestant Party, which contested municipal elections, and Tories held on to most of its parliamentary seats, and the strength of the anti-nationalist, anti-Catholic culture remained so strong that the Labour Party did not win a seat in the city till after 1939.

Elsewhere in Lancashire, although Liberals were elected, the Orange influence was also considerable. In the Furness district of north Lancashire, as well as in west Cumberland, Orangemen kept their oar in local politics. The Orange vote in Whitehaven was strong enough to offset the influence of the large Catholic population. Labour members were not returned in the west Cumberland coal and iron belt until after World War I, and then Whitehaven was won by Charles Gavan Duffy, who had in the 1900s organised the local union in the Irish-dominated iron-ore mines. In Barrow-in-Furness, Orange and Green clashes abounded in the 1880s and 1890s. As the struggle against Parnell and Gladstone became increasingly fraught, Orange Unionist opposition to the national campaign was cloaked in terms of imperial conquest, and the need for Ulster to stand firm against Catholic nationalism was emphasised. The Irish question provided a unique opportunity for the Tory–Orange alliance to harness working-class support by playing upon fears of an eroding empire. In an echo of politics in Ireland, where Home Rule threw differing types of Irishness into sharp relief, local battle lines were also clearly drawn between Irish Protestants and Irish Catholics. Cumbrian Orangemen also drew on analogies between their mission and historic defence of Ireland in 1798 or earlier. 'To these ardent supporters of the constitution', argued one Orangeman in 1893, 'the safety of Ulster might be confidently entrusted'. Similar views doubtless were expressed in Preston, Oldham and in other towns and cities where the Irish cohort was large enough to play a part in local political affairs.[63]

Sinn Fein, World War I and the Formation of the Free State

The strength of Unionism, supported by the militant Orange Order in Ulster and Britain, undoubtedly played a part in the radicalisation of Irish politics which occurred after 1900. From then until World War I and the creation of the Irish Free State in 1922, Irish politics was marked by the initial success of constitutional methods and by the emergence of Sinn Fein. There were many other groups too which played for migrant sympathies, and the general tenor of Celtic revivalism, which gave rise to Race Conventions and other politico-cultural celebrations, drew in support from Irish communities across the world. The Gaelic Athletics Association, the Gaelic League and a variety of Irish friendly-type societies sought to link the day-to-day pursuits of Irish migrants with the imperatives of cultural and political nationalism, though they lacked the single-issue focus and large membership of earlier Home Rule groups. The United Irish League (which had its roots in the Land League) continued to be important, especially in Glasgow, with 2600 members in 1908, and in Leeds and London where there were 1800 and 1500, respectively. Many other towns and cities also had memberships that numbered well up in the hundreds. The 'raison d'être' of all Home Rule organisations in Britain was electoral',[64] though in this they remained unsuccessful. They spent money on numerous unsuccessful Irish candidatures in Britain. By the eve of World War I, the grass-roots constitutional reformers lacked previous examples of success, or any hope of success in the future. As Fitzpatrick has argued, 'Britain's immigrant population, apart from an aging core of enthusiasts still bedded in political culture, gave at best half-hearted support to the Nationalist cause'.[65]

It is against this background that, during the Edwardian era, the support of the Irish in Britain was also solicited by a number of cultural nationalists and hard-liners, like Patrick Pearse, Arthur Griffith and C. J. Dolan. Irish politics at this time became a battle between Sinn Fein republicanism and Redmondite constitutionalism. The *Glasgow Observer*, which continued to support Redmond, nevertheless reported the spread of Sinn Fein branches throughout central Scotland. At the same time, the moderate position in Glasgow was bolstered by Joe Devlin, the national president of the Ancient Order of Hibernians, who actively opposed Sinn Fein. In these years, the Irish vote in Glasgow was crucial to the fortunes of the Liberal Party and Scotland became an important battleground for political campaigners of various persuasions. Labour continued to campaign there, as did the extremes of Irish nationalism. At the same time, the demise of a truly independent Irish party, and the intimate connection with Liberalism, seems to have weakened the vigour with which national figures campaigned among the Irish in Britain. Sinn Fein naturally exploited this. In 1906 the *Glasgow Observer* spotted the problem: 'Till recent years the bigger centres [of Scotland] ... had visits from speakers of Cabinet rank, such as Redmond, Dillon, Blake and "T.P.". This year not one crosses the border.'[66] In 1908 Devlin was continuing his Scottish campaign for Home Rule by constitutional methods, but increasingly he and his kind were coming up against the Sinn Fein challenge.

The abolition of the House of Lords' veto on parliamentary legislation in 1911 encouraged the Redmondites. In that year, the Irish nationalist leader toured Scotland, following in the wake of Sir Edward Carson, the Ulster Unionist leader, answering the latter's speeches. Redmond was at the height of his powers and after one address he was escorted around Glasgow by 20 000–30 000 Irish nationalists and members of the Young Scots League. Yet the coming years would see the moderates outflanked. The outbreak of war was crucial for the radical programme of Sinn Fein. The Home Rule legislation which Parliament passed in 1914 was suspended until the war's end. In the meantime, Redmond supported the British war effort, and his position was endorsed in Scotland by a large public meeting. However, Redmond's decision not to join the coalition government was perhaps his greatest mistake. His main opponents, Carson, Bonar Law and Balfour, all accepted similar offers, and the presence of so many Unionists in the wartime Cabinet hardly furthered the prospects of a smooth transition to Home Rule once the war was over.

The Easter Rising of 1916 galvanised radical Irish nationalists in Britain. At the same time, even moderates were growing restless. As the war dragged on, questions were asked about the comfortable relationships enjoyed by salaried MPs in the wartime coalition. When Lloyd George's government tried to introduce conscription in Ireland, and had Sinn Fein leaders thrown into prison, Diamond (editor and proprietor) placed the *Glasgow Observer*'s not inconsiderable force behind the Sinn Feiners. Diamond's conversion to a more militant tradition typified the growing current of radicalism sweeping Irish politics along. In 1918, Diamond stood for the Labour Party in the 'Khaki elections'; in the following year he received a six months' prison sentence for an article in another of his newspapers which argued: 'There are Irishmen who consider that a state of war exists between themselves and their oppressors. They too kill. Is *their* killing murder? It depends.'[67] A deterioration of the imperial rule of law, not least the barely controlled violence of the 'Black and Tans', added further to the feelings of unrest and anger among the Irish in Britain.

In 1914 the Irish Catholics in Scotland had had their own companies of Irish Volunteers prepared to counteract Carson's Ulster Volunteers. Although the war had sent them underground, they continued to drill. Redmond managed to persuade some of these men to fight in France, but most stayed in the shadows, dedicated Sinn Feiners. Handley claims that such actions were indicative of broader Scots-Irish sympathies, for Sinn Fein's popularity was greater in Scotland than elsewhere in the Diaspora. By 1918 there was an extensive network for trafficking arms out of the Clyde and the Mersey to Ireland, and many more arms fell into Sinn Fein hands from Germany. In 1920, Glasgow alone had 4000 IRA volunteers, while police surveillance uncovered a network of arms gathering which took in most major towns of central Scotland. In the run-up to the establishment of the Free State, the Scots-Irish played an important and successful role – perhaps more successful than any other open or clandestine political organisation in Britain since the United Irishmen.

The radicalisation of the Scots-Irish at this time was not mirrored elsewhere. The exhortations of Sinn Fein largely passed by the Liverpool Irish, for whom moderate constitutionalism had become both accepted and successful. By the early 1900s Irish nationalism was part of Liverpool's official municipal political culture; winning council elections had become a habit, and a significant (if not majority) Irish working-class vote, brought together under a strong middle-class tutelage, perhaps made Liverpool different from any other British city. Irishmen controlled the major workplaces and influenced politics; their culture *was* Liverpool's culture, and both Liberals and Conservatives had to pay attention to Irish issues. At the same time, Liverpool was riven by sectarian conflict in a way that was unique in Britain. In this respect the city was more like Belfast than Manchester or Birmingham. As a consequence of the local power of Orangeism, Irish nationalism habitually melted into the wider imperatives of Catholicism and anti-Catholicism. The years 1912–14 saw huge pro-Carson demonstrations by Liverpool's Orangemen, and, though nationalism was radicalised during the war, Sinn Fein did not achieve more than a toehold in the city. The Sinn Fein victories in Ireland in the general election of 1918, their refusal to sit in Parliament, the death of Redmond and the retirement of John Dillon (the veteran nationalist campaigner, and son of the IUSA leader John Blake Dillon), had an enormous and bewildering effect upon constitutional nationalism in England. The movement collapsed, leaving Liverpool as the only properly functioning political centre.[68]

Many of the conundrums of Irish politics in Britain are distilled in the shape of the Irish Self-Determination League (ISDL), formed in 1919. The ISDL refrained from outright republicanism, and drew in many different groups, from old Home Rulers to priests. The ISDL limited its membership to those who were Irish, by birth or descent, and, in echoes of earlier Parnellite proscriptions, local branches were instructed to refrain from involvement in British politics. The ISDL utilised the well honed networks of parish Catholicism, selling newspapers after mass, and pushing local clergymen to become involved. In April 1922 the ISDL claimed to be the biggest Irish nationalist organisation of all time, with hundreds of branches, though, as Fitzpatrick has uncovered, 'In a more sober moment … the League's secretary complained that "the total membership of the League is at present only 26 000"'. There was no branch in Scotland and little activity in Liverpool. Without these major centres, the ISDL may have been well spread, but it remained largely marginal. The annual conference of April 1922 rejected outright republicanism and the ISDL dissipated quickly thereafter.[69]

Conclusions

According to Alan O'Day, the Irish failed 'to construct and maintain effective communal political institutions', which 'reflected indifference to their fate'.[70] Part of the problem was the fact that the various movements were divided: first, between Irish and English organis- ations, for example, repeal and Chartism, labour and nationalism; secondly, between clandestine and 'open' organisation, from the United Irishmen to Sinn Fein, from Catholic Emancipation to Home Rule. The contradictions between these styles of organisations and their modes of operation clearly impacted upon the political effective- ness of Irish migrant groups. Moreover, the participation of ordinary Irish settlers in these various political or labour movements is difficult to assess, for some of the most successful recruiters of Irish workers – such as the Ribbon Society or trade unions – are precisely those about which we know the least.

However, in the present discussion the traditional presentation of ethnicity as a primitive form of consciousness which Irish migrants needed to shake off before passing into the ranks of a class-conscious working class has been questioned. It has been demonstrated that, whatever the limitations of the sources, some ordinary Irish migrants at least were willing contributors to an array of class-based initiatives like trade unions, as well as many of their own 'national' or 'ethnic' movements, even though the latter sometimes sharpened differences between them and the wider community. Home Rule, for example, was clearly regarded as a bulwark against Irish support for the labour movement. Following the defeat of the ILP candidate, Robert Smillie, at the mid-Lanark by-election in 1894, Keir Hardie bitterly observed: 'In the readiness of the Irish to do the dirty scavenging work of the Liberal party lies the real danger to the home-rule cause'.[71] The real symbol of strength among Irish communities, however, was not political but religious. The Catholic Church was central in this respect. Political movements might have helped to maintain the migrants' ethnic consciousness, but, as O'Day has rightly argued, in all cases 'Faith proved much stronger than Fatherland'.[72]

6

A CULTURE OF ANTI-IRISHNESS

Introduction

Wherever in the world they settled, Irish migrants were often the victims of antipathy and violence. Big American cities, such as Philadelphia and New York, witnessed regular and often extreme outbursts of violence against such migrants, and the situation was little different in Liverpool and Glasgow, where sectarian riots remained a feature of communal life until World War II. Even smaller industrial towns in the Midwest of America or the north of England were prone to acute communal disorder, with savage fighting quite common and occasional fatalities. Even in the predominantly pastoral Canada, moreover, militant Orangeism was one of *the* defining features of national identity. While the social problems of industrialism partly help us to understand this culture of violence in Britain and the eastern United States, no amount of urban decay, workplace competition or poverty and hardship could explain the extraordinary passions that were inflamed by Irish migration. A more potent explanation is the fact that in both Britain and North America the dominant Protestant religion was vehemently anti-Catholic, and this acutely affected the reception that awaited the much-despised 'Paddy'. This Victorian image of 'Paddy' was of deeply historical formulation, attributable to what M. A. G. Ó Tuathaigh neatly describes as 'an odd compound of religious, social and political elements, of the rational and irrational'.[1] Whatever the admixture of factors, there can be little doubt that Irish migrants suffered considerable abuse at the hands of the native population.

Although anti-Irish behaviour was a part of British life from the Middle Ages, O'Day is perfectly correct to argue that the mid-Victorian years – between the Famine and the emergence of the Home Rule movement – witnessed by far the most intense examples.[2] Physical violence and psychological abuse were the result of living cheek by jowl in often poor neighbourhoods with fellow working-class toilers; but they were also a measure of native workers' inchoate and inarticulate enmity towards Ireland itself. Religion, perceived Irish criminality, workplace tension and organised sectarianism each contributed to the anti-Irish tenor of Victorian life, but so too did cultural and political differences between these nations. Discord imparted a sense of national identity. The fact that Irish migration reached previously unimaginable proportions in the turbulent period of industrialisation, and developments such as Catholic emancipation, Fenianism, Irish agrarian violence and the struggle for political independence each added colour to what was an already vivid palette of animosities. An attempt is made here to describe and explain some of the major factors promoting this uneasy situation.[3] An effort is made, moreover, to present a longer-run analysis than most other studies, by suggesting that anti-Irishness, while most notable in the generation after the Famine, actually lived on until the Edwardian period.

The 'Condition of England'

The timing of Irish migration offers a major explanation of the nature and extent of anti-Irishness in Victorian society. Without Irish settlers, the great conurbations of industrial Britain would still have been miserable and unhealthy places to live and work, as the novels of Dickens, Gaskell, Disraeli and others attest; however, with the Irish significantly represented, the same cities took on an even greater social relevance. The incoming group provided a ready-made scape-goat for the disease, overcrowding, immorality, drunkenness and crime of the urban world. For this reason, historians have tended to focus on the classic, stereotyped, texts of writers such as Carlyle or Engels, or on the often savage or lampooning caricatures that were the stock-in-trade of *Punch* and other such publications. Images of the Irish as drooling, half-crazed Fenian monkeys or wild Frankenstein's monsters dominate our perceptions of the way the Victorians perceived Ireland. Yet while famous figures such as J. A. Froude, the Anglo-Saxonist historian, could attack the Irish as being 'more like tribes of squalid apes than human beings',[4] there were in fact more mundane though equally pervasive influences at work. The harshest tones of anti-Irishness often sounded in local and provincial newspapers rather than in illustrated national journals, yet few historians have undertaken detailed study of the role of the provincial journalist in moulding the Irish stereotype. In all, few contemporary works, apart from Cornewall Lewis's magisterial essay of Irish life in the industrial north of Britain (1836), came close to an even-handed treatment of the Irish, though even here the appendices are loaded with the antipathies of a procession of petty provincial office-holders and employers whose outpourings Lewis tried vainly to temper.[5]

One of the starting points in the construction of the Irish migrant's negative identity is the work of the Manchester doctor and reformer J. P. Kay, who in a now infamous essay of 1833 denounced the Irish in his city as an insidious social problem. Kay believed the Irish were a threat to both the living standards and the morality of the native working class. In arguing that 'The Irish have taught the labouring classes of this country a pernicious lesson', Kay captured the essential features of what was becoming a pervasive contempt for the arrival of Irish workers:

Debased alike by ignorance and pauperism, they have discovered, with the savage, what is the minimum of the means of life, upon which existence may be prolonged. The paucity of the amount of means and comforts *necessary for the mere support of life*, is not known by a more civilised population, and this secret has been taught the labourers of this country by the Irish. As competition and the restrictions and burdens of trade diminished the profit of capital, and consequently reduced the price of labour, the contagious example of ignorance and a barbarous disregard of forethought and economy, exhibited by the Irish, spread. The colonisation of savage tribes has ever been attended with effect on civilization as fatal as those which have marked the progress of the sand flood over the fertile plains of Egypt.

The barbarity of this Irish horde was, for Kay, measured by many examples of their rude habits and unsavoury behaviour. Excess drinking was considered to be a particularly acute problem: 'What is superfluous to the mere exigencies of nature, is too often expended at the tavern', he remarked. In addition, one of the effects of Ireland having no Poor Law at this time was, he thought, the failure of the Irish to respect self-help or fear poverty. 'For the provision of old age and infirmity', Kay reckoned, the Irish 'too frequently trust either to charity, to the support of their children, or to the protection of the poor laws'.[6]

Such complaints grew in currency during the 1830s, but few were as supremacist as Thomas Carlyle's now infamous attack of 1839:

> The wild Milesian features, looking false ingenuity, restlessness, unreason, misery, and mockery, salute you on all highways and byways. The English coachman, as he whirls past, lashes the Milesian with his whip, curses him with his tongue; the Milesian is holding out his hat to beg. He is the sorest evil this country has to strive with. In his rags and laughing savagery, he is there to undertake all work that can be done by mere strength of hand and back – for wages that will purchase him potatoes. He needs only salt for his condiment, he lodges to his mind in any pig-hutch or dog-hutch, roosts in out-houses, and wears a suit of tatters, the getting on and off which is said to be a difficult operation, transacted only in festivals and the high tides of the calendar. The Saxon man, if he cannot work on these terms, finds no work. The uncivilised Irishman, not by his strength, but by the opposite of strength, drives the Saxon native out, takes possession in his room.[7]

Engels, who in 1845 was writing on the eve of the Famine, concurred with Carlyle's view, except for the latter's 'exaggerated and one-sided condemnation of the Irish national character'. Engels described in some detail the low habits of the Irish: their monotonous potato diet, their crude abodes, their drinking. He attacked their negative influence on indigenous labour, and their discovery, 'as Dr Kay says ... [of] the minimum of the necessities of life'.[8] Engels, like Kay, felt that the Irish worker's ability to live in such a basic way rubbed off on the English working class and reduced their physical and moral fibre.

Negative impressions such these were intensified by the mass influx of Famine victims, as is shown by the *Morning Chronicle* surveys of 1849, conducted by Henry Mayhew, A. B. Reach, Charles MacKay, Alexander MacKay and others. Reach, who was the Mayhew of the north, is particularly interesting in this regard. He surveyed the great industrial regions of Lancashire and Yorkshire, doing what Mayhew had achieved in rather more sensitive and skilful fashion in the capital.[9] Reach was obsessed with the Irish, choosing to comment on their inferior ways at almost every turn. Indeed, his impression of the 'Irish in Manchester' is one of the most vivid pieces of anti-Irish prose ever written:

> The last place we visited is, I am told, the 'worst cellar in all Manchester'. The outer room was like that of the others which I had seen, but, following a woman who held a light, we proceeded into the inner cellars. They were literally vaults, three of them opening from one to the other. The air was thick with damp and stench. The vaults were mere subterranean holes, utterly without light. The flicker of the candles showed their grimy walls, reeking with foetid damp, which trickled in greasy drops down to the floor. Beds were huddled in every corner; ... In one of these there was a man lying dressed, and beside him slept a well-grown calf. Sitting upon another bed was an old man, maudlin drunk, with the saliva running over his chin, making vain efforts to rid himself of his trowsers, and roaring for help. In the next cellar boys were snoring together in one bed, and beside them was a man sleeping in an old battered cap for a nightcap. 'Is he undressed?' I said. The police officer for an answer, twitched down the clothes, and revealed a stark man black with filth. The smell in this room was dreadful, and the air was at once hot and wet.[10]

For Reach, the English poor were different, maintaining a certain dignity in adversity. Such characteristics were, he felt, absent among the Irish: 'The contrast between this poor [English] family and their lazy Irish neighbours was very striking and very painful'.[11] In an effort to strengthen the case against the Irish, many of Reach's pen portraits were highly personalised. The following is one of the most loathsome of them all: 'A woman with skin so foul that she might have passed for a negress, was squatted on the ground; and a litter, I cannot call then a group, of children burrowed about her. The woman could barely talk English; yet she must have been more than a dozen years in the country'.[12] Views such as these were both influential and commonplace; they underpinned what self-confident Victorians already felt about the backward and boisterous sister isle, but also added to the anxieties which created the 'Condition of England' question. It is quite likely, too, that condemnation from such quarters added a perceived legitimacy to the antagonisms of the street or workplace.

The Question of Race

The savagery of these writers has led historians to wonder whether or not the Victorian view of the Irish was racist. Much debate has been generated in this area since the publication of L. P. Curtis's study of the Irish stereotype, with its central thesis that Victorian anti-Irishness was fundamentally racist.[13] Gilley, for example, questioned Curtis's arguments about racism on the basis that 'few ideas are more subtly influential than a nation's understanding of its "national character".' Gilley then argued that 'the English perception of the Irish was loaded with positive as well as negative assumptions', and that the 'English invoked the good points or the bad according to their temperament'.[14] He claimed that the Irish character, as perceived by both English and Irish, combined what the novelist Maria Edgeworth called 'that mixture of quickness, simplicity, cunning, carelessness, dissipation, disinterestedness, shrewdness and blunder'.[15] Gilley concludes that anti-Irishness in this period was more 'national' than 'racial'. Indeed, the Victorians caricatured what they perceived as the fundamental failings of Irish character – for example, drunkenness and violence – just as much as (if not more than) their alleged racial inferiority. At the same time, even when social reformers and cartoonists suggested genuine attempts to improve Ireland such as industrialisation and land reform, they could not help but refer to the old habits of this Celtic people. Although Gilley points out the ambiguities of Anglo-Saxonist perspectives on 'race' and 'national character', he does not doubt the supremacist overtones of many British writers.

Another contributor to this debate, M. A. G. Ó Tuathaigh, supported Curtis's thesis, arguing that Gilley underestimated the extent to which national differences were characterised in racial terms from the 1840s. (This was especially the case from the 1880s, when the language of Unionism levelled the charge against Home Rule campaigners that the Celtic race was incapable of self-determined government.) Ó Tuathaigh's claim is that, in the mid-Victorian period, 'the immigrant Irish benefited much less from the idealised and benign elements of the "Paddy" stereotype in cartoons and elsewhere than they suffered from its malign elements'. He further argues that irrespective of this balance between '"good" and "bad" images of the Irish' it remains the case that anti-Irish animosity grew enormously in the pre-Famine years, as industrial development and large-scale migration conflated with changes in the British labour market.[16]

The most recent words on the subject of racism and anti-Irishness has come from Roy Foster and Mary J. Hickman, the former aligning with Gilley, the latter with Curtis.[17] Foster, like Gilley, focuses on the ambiguity of anti-Irish stereotyping. He portrays this dimension of Anglo-Irish relations as loaded with contradictions over the Irish character (and, thus, stereotype), and points out that the caricatures in magazines like *Punch* – key evidence in Curtis's thesis – were just as likely to denigrate the English working class, while *Punch*'s Irish equivalents lampooned the English in similar fashion. Foster thus concludes that racial prejudice is too simple a generalisation to apply to the anti-Irish hostility of the British. He cites the fact that intermarriage between Irish and British partners was viewed as a process of conversion, rather than as miscegenation, to play down the allegedly racialist dimension. Indeed, Foster considers that 'class and religion were more central preoccupations in constructing an alien identity for the Irish than Curtis will admit', adding that the general feeling in Britain 'may relate more to resentment of the Irish attack on property [in Ireland] and the Union, and also resentment against Irish resentment of the Union. How *could* they know what was good for them? Certainly the attitude was colonial; the Irish were weaker brethren'.[18]

Hickman stress this final point, but takes the issue a step further, claiming that the Irish were the victims of what she calls 'colonial racism'. And indeed, anti-Irish attitudes undoubtedly were moulded by the long-lived colonial relationship between the two powers, one stronger and aggressive, the other weaker and resistant. This colonial relationship came to a head in the nineteenth century when challenges to the Act of Union (1801) separated Irish from Irish, Protestant from Catholic, English from Irish on the grounds of politics, religion, and, Hickman believes, 'race'. Hickman is particularly critical of Gilley's argument that, in the case of the Irish, there is no 'objective criterion of "race"': to suggest that racism can be expressed only towards a person or group with a different skin colour is, Hickman asserts, an 'unjustifiably narrow definition of racism'.[19]

There is perhaps no single 'right' or 'wrong' answer to this vexed question, though it is important to note that white-on-white attacks can be racist. At the same time, we need to acknowledge that Victorian definitions of racism were different from ours: they used the term 'race' much more casually, in a way which lacked the consistency and degree of determinism evinced by later exponents of race theory and eugenics. What we need to remember is that perceptions were an important part of the myth of Irish character and behaviour, and that the Victorians were quick to preference these perceptions over the reality of daily lives, in which the Irish were generally victims rather than perpetrators of crime and discord.

Crime and Violence

One of the key causes of middle-class antipathy was a widely held perception that the Irish were quick to violence. Irish society was recognised as being much more violent in the nineteenth century than the rest of the United Kingdom, even though Irish migrants tended not to bring the worst excesses of Irish rural life with them to Britain – in fact, Irish criminals in Britain tended to be petty larcenists and small-scale brawlers, though sometimes repeat offenders. However, the fact that they did not often commit murder, or the more serious types of physical assault, was not fully understood by the British public. Such reportage fuelled the anxieties of observers who were already fearful of the impact of urban growth. One consequence of this situation was that the Irish came to be viewed as part of a social residuum whose alien character and unruly disposition habitually exercised police officers and magistrates alike.

There are, however, grains of truth in most stereotypes and the Irish migrant's fondness for drink and quickness of temper were not wholly exaggerated. The figures in Table 6.1 illustrate the sometimes significant levels of Irish petty crime for a number of centres of settlement.

The Irish-born were persistently over-represented in magistrates' courts, being at least twice as likely to be brought before the bench, evidence suggests that their crimes were overwhelmingly haracter. McManus's research on Durham shows that charges

Table 6.1: Irish-born offenders summarily dealt with by magistrates, 1851–91

	1851		1861		1871		1881		1891	
	%	IO	%	IO	%	IO	%	IO	%	IO
Barrow	–	–	–	–	–	–	31	2.9	36	4.4
Bradford	–	–	19	3.3	24	4.2	15	3.5	–	–
Liverpool	–	–	37	2.0	34	2.2	24	1.9	16	2.1
Manchester	–	–	30	1.9	22	2.3	17	2.3	13	2.8
Preston	–	–	26	3.1	28	5.2	27	6.1	26	8.4
Wolverhampton	22	2.8	–	–	–	–	–	–	–	–
York	26	3.6	21	2.6	16	2.1	–	–	–	–

Source: R. Swift, 'Heroes or villains? The Irish, crime and disorder in Victorian Britain', *Albion*, 29 (1997), p. 401, n. 13; 'Chief constables' annual reports', *Borough of Barrow-in-Furness Treasurers' Accounts* (Barrow, 1881–1906). Irish-born as a percentage all offenders.

IO = index of over-representation, being the degree to which the percentage of Irish convictions was greater than their proportion of the population.

of drunkenness and of being drunk and disorderly accounted for 46 of a total of 96 'Irish' offences dealt with by the city's petty sessional court throughout 1861. A further 15 were various kinds of assaults (including three on police officers), while just 12 were brought up for larceny.[20] Although they were mainly petty offenders, however, the Irish were also 'five times as likely to go to prison as the English'.[21] In Scotland, Fitzpatrick has shown, the vista was similarly bleak, with around one-quarter of the inmates in Barlinnie gaol, Glasgow, being Irish-born.[22] Similarly, in Carlisle gaol in 1861, 23.4 per cent of males were Irish-born, and 12.6 per cent of women. Ten years later the figures were 18.9 and 16.6, respectively. As late as 1891, when the Irish-born population had fallen considerably from its mid-Victorian peak, Lancaster gaol still had a male population that was 23.1 per cent Irish-born, with 20.1 per cent for women. Throughout the second half of the nineteenth century the male Irish-born population of Preston gaol only once fell into single figures (9.2 per cent in 1870), while in the same years Durham gaol ranged between a high of 21.4 per cent and a low of 12.4.[23]

Such data perhaps indicate why, in Victorian minds, the Irish were closely associated with crime; providing an explanation of these levels is rather more difficult. For example, can such patterns be explained by reference to punitive and selective policing? Or is it partly accounted for by social geography, with the majority of Irish communities taking shape in the most policed parts of towns? At the same time, some have argued that Irish Catholics were the victims of oppressive policing because of the propensity of Irish Protestants to join the police.[24] While any of these might account for Irish crime rates, the attitudes of the Irish themselves must also be considered. Swift has shown, for example, that some of the more serious Irish-orientated 'street rows' that occurred in Wolverhampton 'fell into the category of anti-police disorders' because Irish pub culture was particularly contemptuous of the forces of law and order.[25] In the north Lancashire market town of Ulverston in September 1864, for example, John Grafton, an Irish labourer, was charged with assaulting two police constables, Stott and Marsden. The magistrates heard how the two officers had tried to prevent Grafton from fighting with a man named Hodgson, but because his response was so frenzied they had been compelled to bind his feet.[26]

The drink issue was also linked to a broader perception of the Irish migrant as a criminal nuisance. One of the most common causes of unease concerned relations between the police and the Irish. Drinking and violence were even noticed among small Irish populations, as Mulkern has shown of Coventry, where street disorder involving brutality was common.[27] While urban life in general was marked by high levels of drinking and drink-related crime, Irish (and indeed Gaelic) rural custom held alcohol in high cultural esteem, so that the rituals of drink were often much more than 'mindless' examples of 'escapist' overindulgence. In peasant Ireland, drink was a fundamental aspect of leisure culture, playing a central role in the main rituals of life: birth, marriage and death. The Gaelic name for whiskey, usquebaugh ('water of life') says much of its importance.[28]

Other aspects of Irish tradition also became enmeshed with the migrant drinking habits, with the result that outsiders often viewed the migrants as mere hedonists. This was certainly the case with the Irish 'wake', which was a particularly important cultural device, and a known setting for drink, music and song. On arrival in Britain or America, Irish migrants found that 'wakes' were frowned upon by the authorities and proscribed by the Church, and though this opposition did not stop workmates or families gathering to send off a friend in style, such ritualised expressions of collective mourning led to clashes with the authorities. Cumbrians, for example, viewed the 'Irish wake' with a mixture of disdain and humour, as was the case in February 1871 when a Cleator Moor landlord, Anthony Campbell, was fined 10*s* for allowing 16 men to drink in his public house at 6.30 one Sunday morning. The men were all miners gathered to mourn a colleague who had died in a pit accident. The men collected the body and gave the landlord '7*s* to be drunk, as it was a sort of "opening wake"'.[29] The near-universal occurrence of such incidents leads Gilley to assert that 'courtroom reports of Irish brawling ... more than any other single factor shaped the English idea of the Irishman in England'.[30]

Workplace Tensions

By the time of the Famine, many of the British working class would have agreed with Carlyle's assessment that the Irish labourer was a dangerous competitor because the poverty of life in Ireland imbued the migrant with lower expectations in terms of wages and conditions.[31] Engels agreed with Carlyle's view that Irish workers were a creeping and malign influence: 'Nothing else is therefore possible than that, as Carlyle says, the wages of the English working man should be forced down further and further in every branch in which the Irish compete with him'.[32] The fact that the majority of Irish migrants were economic opportunists, simply searching for better jobs than they had in Ireland, increased the prospects for workplace violence. The scale of that division was considerable. It picked up in times of hardship or dispute and became increasingly widespread as Irish settlers reached into major industrial areas. While historians have long acknowledged the importance of the workplace as a sphere for studying anti-Irish violence, there has been a tendency to accept the stereotypical view, held by contemporaries such as Carlyle and Engels, that the Irish *did* undercut the indigenous wage rate and *were* present as a reserve army of labour.

In fact, a clear understanding of this aspect of Irish settlement remains elusive, given the dearth of local studies on employment patterns among the Irish in Britain, and the absence of data on occupational breakdown in the pre-Famine period. Neal's work has highlighted tensions between Liverpool's ships' carpenters from about 1840, though this was the result of the declining fortunes of men whose livelihoods relied on wooden ships, rather than of Irish competition.[33] Fitzpatrick's suggestion that the Irish gravitated towards high-wage areas where labour was in short supply, rather than to places of stiff competition, provides a sure-footed approach to what is difficult historical terrain, and a significant advance on any blanket acceptance of the Irish as instruments of their employers or unwitting 'knobsticks'.[34] Those Irish who broke strikes were usually shipped in from Ireland for that purpose, and were not drawn from within the established community. This was certainly the case with Lord Londonderry's strike-breakers used during the miners' strike of 1842. What is more, the Irish in Britain (mainly Catholics in this example) generally sought out unskilled manual work, the sort of occupations for which peasant Ireland had prepared them, and had little success in, for example, mining and shipbuilding until much later in the century. They tended to come into contact with the more marginal sorts of workers in the new communities, for example black freemen in the United States, displaced Highlanders in Scotland and, more generally, those whose work the Irish might attempt with little training: labourers, navvies, agricultural workers and domestic textile workers.

It is clear that levels of violence against the Irish grew at a rate commensurate with the size of the migrant communities, because mass arrival coincided with the greatest upheavals in industrial and urban growth. Although there is evidence from the Middle Ages which suggests Irish paupers and clerks were unwanted burdens in the realm, it was not until the early eighteenth century that labour tensions became more intense and common. Violent reprisals were exacted in 1736, for example, against the Irish by English harvesters. In the same year English weavers rioted against Irish workers who allegedly undercut the going rate. In the aftermath of the Napoleonic Wars, middle-class ratepayers throughout the country began fretting about the burden of Irish paupers, while the native working class became increasingly restive over fears that Irish workers were beginning to colonise certain sectors of the economy, such as the construction industry. Complaints about Irish labour ranged from the peaceable protests of female market-gardeners in Richmond to the rather more robust protestations of northern miners or Scottish cottars.[35]

While Lancashire provides numerous examples of work-related anti-Irish violence, the problem was pervasive. The Irish in South Wales, for example, began in the 1820s to congregate in heavy manual labour, and, though not often in direct competition for skilled work, such as mining, they still met with an aggressive response. Violence erupted in 1826, for example, at the Bute ironworks in the Rhymney Valley with the news that cheap gangs of Irish labour were being employed to build new blast furnaces. Similarly in the early 1830s Irish workers were driven out of a Pontypool ironworks on the suspicion of working for lower wages, and such occurrences punctuated mid-nineteenth-century labour relations in Wales thereafter.[36] This idea that the Irish undercut wages was shared by ironworkers, dock labourers and navvies alike, as was the claim, made by striking textile workers in Preston in 1853, that the Irish were regularly used as strike-breakers.[37]

In few places was the Irish labourer as likely to be excoriated as in Scotland. Derived partly from historic divisions between Catholicism and Calvinism, the Scottish dimension provides us with some of the ugliest examples of anti-Irish violence. In the early part of the nineteenth century there were effectively two Scotlands: the Highland region and the industrialising central belt. Both were undergoing significant changes at the same time as Irish settlement was increasing, and in neither area were migrants welcomed as friendly fellow Celts. The Highland clearances of the early 1800s marked the final destruction of the clan system and with it went the livelihoods of thousands of peasant cottars and their black cattle, driven out by larger farm units and the ubiquitous sheep. New farming practices resulted in a great increase in demand for seasonal agricultural labourers, which further undermined the traditional peasant proprietor. Despite opportunities for migrants, either overseas or to the south in Glasgow and Edinburgh, many displaced Scottish cottars remained in the north, hoping to secure paid farming employment, and thus coming into contact and conflict with Irish harvesters. As Handley tells us, this new rural order in Scotland cast the Highlanders into exactly the same mould as the Irish spalpeen, wandering the country waiting for crops to ripen. The hardships of their lives, and the scanty resources they could accrue, were bound to nurture resentments. The same basic economic grievances, therefore, occupied Highlanders and the Irish as they worked or competed side by side. There were numerous ugly clashes between the two groups, not least in the early 1820s during the construction of the Caledonian and Union canals.[38] Indeed, some of the worst recorded incidents of serious fighting were among the railway builders of northern England and Scotland.

The era of 'railway mania' witnessed perhaps as many as a quarter of a million industrious and hard-living navvies toiling on the main north–south lines. Drinking, fighting and ribald leisure pursuits were key characteristics of these itinerant communities. Scots, Irish and English seemed unable or unwilling to work together and local farmers, townsfolk and the authorities loathed their presence. By mid-1845 the combined pressures of grim living conditions, hard work and national and regional tensions had these colonies in a highly agitated state. Yorkshiremen confronted Lancastrians; Scots fought the English; and all sections – Highlanders, lowlanders and northcountry men – attacked the Irish. Later, in 1845 the Lancaster, Carlisle and Edinburgh line became the site of rioting between separate encampments of Irish and English workers, one housed in Lockerbie, the other in Ecclefechan. Several days of rioting, drunkenness and beatings were halted only when a detachment of militia was brought in to support beleaguered constables. While employers generally tried to keep regional and national groups apart, one effect of the distance between them was to incubate rumours of imminent attacks and murderous plots. Although often non-existent, such threats usually resulted in violence on the navvies' monthly pay day, when drink was flowing and courage grew.

In early 1846 tensions erupted on the same line, with serious riots at Penrith, in Cumberland and at Gorebridge, near Edinburgh. There was also rioting between the Irish and English at Moffat and between the English and Scots at Dunblane. The Penrith incident, which allegedly broke out because an Irish navvy ignored his ganger's order to use a shovel and not his pick, resulted in 2000 rampaging Englishmen wildly attacking the Irish, who were fewer in number. The Irish eventually fled to Penrith, where they begged the magistrates for protection.

In general, the authorities were hard-pressed to maintain order at this time. Although such exchanges were much reduced by the 1850s, examples still occurred many years later. There was, for example, serious rioting during the construction of docks at Barrow-in-Furness in April 1864. Scottish and English navvies united and, 'with curses loud and deep', drove the 'Mickeys' from the town. A rumour had spread that the Irish were undercutting wages, but one witness blamed the proceedings on collective memories of the Penrith riots of two decades before when 'it appeared the Irishmen had the best of it'.[39]

These incidents add to our understanding of the social problems attendant upon rapid industrial and urban development, but they constitute only a partial picture. Economic issues apparently set off many battles between navvies. However, the reason why they occurred so often, and lasted so long, requires a discussion of aspects of culture and religion as well as work patterns.

Anti-Catholicism

It would be misleading to write of British anti-Catholicism as purely anti-Irish. Protestantism in England, Scotland and Wales, though adopting a variety of guises, was uniformly hostile to papal authority and the main tenets of the Catholic Church. The fact that Irish migrants were mainly Catholic, or were so viewed, increased many times native antipathy against the incomer. The process of Catholic revival deeply disturbed all those who believed Protestantism and the flight from Rome provided the cornerstones of the British constitution, and the keys which guaranteed the liberty and freedom and which set Britain apart from the enslaved masses of Catholic Europe. The Irish role in this renaissance could hardly go unnoticed.

The rabid anti-Catholicism of the eighteenth century, which had led to violent explosions such as the Gordon Riots (1780), never really died out after the French Revolution; indeed, events in the nineteenth century kept these feelings close to boiling point. The Act of Union, for example, threw up enormous problems for the Protestant Ascendancy: namely, how to deal with the Union of Protestant and Catholic cultures under the Anglican hegemony of the English state. Tory Ultras 'saw it as their highest duty to maintain the union of throne and altar',[40] thus thwarting Pitt's hope that greater Catholic freedoms would kill off the United Irish tradition and reinvigorate the Irish people.[41] O'Connell's Catholic emancipation movement – the first successful mass political mobilisation in United Kingdom politics – also strained relations between Protestants and Catholics, and his success in 1829 provided a spur for the Protestant evangelicalism that dominated religious debate in the period between emancipation and the Great Famine. The granting of Catholic freedoms, Colley has shown, stirred an astounding response. Countless local and regional meetings were held, alarm was registered and Parliament was presented with numerous petitions. Those from

Birmingham, Glasgow and Bristol carried 36 000, 24 000 and 38 000 signatures, respectively. Although Colley notes a previous softening of middle-class anti-Catholicism (something which Irish migration would reverse in the coming years), it is important to point out that the petitioners of Britain came not just from the big cities but also from small and isolated villages whose names the 'London and the big provincial newspapers hardly knew how to spell' and 'where a man from the next county, never mind an Irishman, would have been as rare as a dry summer'.[42]

The zeal of British Protestantism had serious implications for the Irish in Britain. While sporadic violence accompanied their support of O'Connell, or their resistance to proselytising advances from Protestants, anti-Catholicism at this time was building up a head of steam over the question of the Maynooth grant in 1845 (state funds for the priests' seminary in Ireland), the Famine influx soon afterwards and the 'Papal Aggression' of 1850. Such sentiments lingered on in the 1860s and 1870s, however, and were prevented from dying down by the controversy over the inspection of convents (which never happened) and the disestablishment and disendowment of the Church of Ireland (which did).

Anti-Catholic tendencies had been strengthened in the 1830s and 1840s by resistance to the Oxford, or Tractarian, Movement which sought to reassert the 'High Church' Catholic dimension of Anglicanism. Ritualism (the use of Catholic ceremonial procedures in the Anglican Church) was denounced by low churchmen and by Dissenters alike; most of all, though, it increased the wider anti-Catholic consciousness of British Protestants. The early to mid-Victorian period also witnessed a number of high-profile conversions to Catholicism, notably of Henry Newman, later to be a Catholic cardinal, and the famous architect A. W. N. Pugin, which encouraged the baser tendencies of popular Protestant opposition.

Anti-Catholicism was additionally promoted by a rich tradition of cheap literature. Some of the most famous publications included the classic reprint of Foxe's *Book of Martyrs* (1875) which, with its lurid images of Protestant sufferings, Norman remarked, was 'almost as familiar to the Victorians as the Bible itself'.[43] Organisations such as the Protestant Association and the Protestant Evangelical Mission and Electoral Union (PEMEU) produced copious pamphlets, books and posters denouncing Catholic priests, rule from Rome and the foundation of Catholic liturgy and practice. The PEMEU alone in

1869 claimed to have sold several million tracts. Nunneries and convents were common targets in this genre, denigrated as brothels and torture chambers in such gothic monstrosities as *The Awful Disclosures of Maria Monk*, allegedly the true story of a young nun who had escaped from a convent in Montreal, and Rebecca Reed's *Six Months' Residence in a Convent*, both fabricated texts which nevertheless enjoyed international sales.[44] Anti-Catholic writers claimed to expose the myths of celibacy and reveal in language overwrought but unspecific the unspeakable sexual vices of abbots and priests. The confessional, in particular, was lambasted as immoral and corrupting, and it was suggested that young women were defenceless quarry for licentious priests who used the intimacy of the confessional to press for sexual favours. More generally, Protestants shuddered at the thought of women divulging the details of their sex lives for the pleasure of lecherous priests. Consequently, *The Confessional Unmasked* became one of the most widely read of the PEMEU's catalogue of pamphlets; it crystallised Protestant fears about Catholicism by describing the confessional as 'a FOUL BLASPHEMY and worthy to be execrated of mankind'.

By the 1850s, for a variety of religious, cultural and economic reasons, violent reprisals against the Irish in Britain had become widespread. One reason was the failure of Chartism, which has been regarded by some Labour historians as the final breaking point of a radical–Irish alliance. As well, the wider social and economic pressures of the Famine undoubtedly exacerbated tensions. Most specific, however, was the politico-religious tension of the 'Papal Aggression' of 1850 (see Chapter 3). This action prompted a remarkably intense reaction, providing clear evidence of the average Briton's love of Protestantism and hatred of Catholicism. Meetings, often ecumenical, were held in most towns and cities of England and Wales to protest at this perceived incursion by an alien power. *The Times* dubbed the term 'Papal Aggression', which entered the imagination of the British people, while thousands of petitions flooded Westminster to demand that the government of Lord John Russell take firm action. In a letter to the Bishop of Durham, which was subsequently published in *The Times*, Russell expressed regret at the Pope's action: 'My Dear Lord, I agree with you in considering the "late aggression on our Protestantism" as "insolent and insidious", and I therefore feel as indignant as you do upon the subject'.[45] Up and down the country, journalists took a lead from their Prime Minster and the country's foremost daily newspaper, joining in the denunciation. The *Liverpool Standard*, 29 October 1850, considered that the restoration showed how 'Rome scoffs at the authority of the Protestant Sovereign of the British Empire, and resolved to treat her dominions as if they were a fief under its absolute control'; and on the same day the *Cumberland Paquet* explained how every newspaper in the land was filled with details of the 'insidious Popish manoeuvre'. Ordinary Protestants were stirred up by this issue, and tempers were hardly doused when the new Archbishop of Westminster, Cardinal Wiseman, issued a pastoral address which boasted of 'Catholic England ... restored to its orbit in the ecclesiastical firmament from which its light had long vanished'. Bishop Ullathorne of Birmingham attempted to calm the situation, but Wiseman's talk of 'governing' the counties of his diocese was impolitic to say the least, for it 'reactivated traditional English fears of Romish plots, doubtful Catholic loyalties and foreign influences'.[46] If these anxieties were not in themselves enough, the continuing inflow of Famine Irish sharpened fears. The reaction was not, however, simply inspired by the large numbers of Irish, though their presence increased the prospect of violent reaction from agitators. The hysterical reactions of Victorian Protestants allied vague notions of national identity with more focused political realities. Since the 1830s, the Tory press had been a constant critic of the O'Connellite connections of the Whigs, with *The Times* and the *Quarterly Review* leading the way in reasserting the age-old view that Catholicism was backward, disloyal, superstitious, sacerdotal and thoroughly out of character with rational, liberal British institutions. The migrants simply provided physical targets for existing prejudices.[47]

The issue of the Papal Aggression brought the impartiality of the state into question, a development which became most apparent on 27 November 1850, when there was serious trouble in Birkenhead after local magistrates called a meeting at the town hall to discuss the Papal Aggression. Irish Catholics were incensed, and their priest, Father Browne, said he would attend, while appealing for his co-religionists to stay calm. However, allegations of insensitive and inadequate policing led to a great disturbance. The town hall was stoned by angry Irish Catholics and the Riot Act was read. When Father Browne appeared at a broken window, and raised his arm, the effect was reportedly magical, with calm suddenly falling over the crowd. This example of the priest's power captures the gulf separating the two sides on the issue of papal authority. The following summer was also tense, and the Orange Order's marching season in Liverpool in July was marred by the wielding of weapons and the firing of shots, as well as the usual drunken punch-ups. Quite a stir was caused by the death of two men, one of whom was Irish, and the dismissal from the force of PC Green because he was an Orange lodge member. Such intelligence simply confirmed Catholic suspicions – suspicions that were hardly allayed during the turbulent 'no-popery' atmosphere of the election year of 1852, when, amidst the general turmoil, a pregnant woman died after being kicked in the stomach by a policeman. The Orange demonstrations that followed closely after this incident caused unusual exasperation, and the Lord Chief Justice banned all such processions within the city's boundaries.[48]

One of the most infamous incidents of post-1850 violence occurred when the Cheshire town of Stockport was hit on several occasions in June 1852 by violence associated with the Papal Aggression. The immediate catalyst was the Tory government's issue of a ban on Catholic processions just three weeks before the general election. The move was intended to prevent trouble, although Liberals dismissed it as electioneering and pandering to sectarian passions. In Stockport, where Catholics had held an annual parade for nearly two decades, Lord Derby's instruction was met with polarised opinions. While Catholics were angered, Orangemen used the ban to publicise their own political views and air their anti-Catholic rhetoric. Despite Orange protestations, the procession went ahead without incident. The next day, however, saw effigies of Catholic clergy being burned by the local Protestant Association. Thereafter, the situation began to deteriorate, with fighting breaking out around the town. The residents of an Irish enclave called Rock Row were dragged out and beaten, and their homes were ransacked. Although a detachment of troops was mustered and the Riot Act read, the inflamed mob still managed to ransack Stockport's two Catholic chapels as well as a priest's house and nearby vestries. Several days later, 24 Irish families were without homes and one of their countrymen was dead. Although the Irish were clearly the aggrieved party, only two of the 113 arrested were English. This intense outburst of riotous behaviour was clearly promoted by the general no-popery atmosphere pervading the early 1850s, but Millward demonstrates that the activities of a group of local Tory politicians and clerics, who encouraged sectarian animosities for party political ends, were clearly to blame for the scale of the Stockport example. The waning fortunes of the local Tories between 1847 and 1852 had increased their sense of desperation and thus it was that the Orange card was deployed with such wanton disregard for the town's communal stability.[49]

Popular Protestantism and Orangeism

Some of the earliest and most sustained bouts of anti-Irish and intra-Irish violence were whipped up by the advent of the Orange parading tradition. As early as 1807, there was a large and bloody riot associated with the Manchester celebrations of the 'Glorious Twelfth', though Liverpool did not experience similar occurrences until 1819 and 1820. Although the authorities often banned these marches, violence continued to light up the 'Glorious Twelfth' throughout the 1820s and 1830s.[50] By the time of the Famine and the 'Papal Aggression', the Orange presence was widespread and pervasive, ready and able to take advantage of the animosities which these events were bringing to the surface.

The anti-Catholic momentum of this period was strongly en-couraged by 'no-popery' lecture campaigns throughout the industrial regions. Popular Protestantism was kept alive and in some cases reinvented by the incendiary and swaggering style of demagogues such as Father Gavazzi, the Baron de Camin, Henry Mead and William Murphy, who made dangerous livings in the 1850s and 1860s by denouncing popery in towns and villages with often large and turbulent Irish Catholic communities. In addition, each locality threw up its own examples, such as 'Ranter Dick', who led a sustained assault on the 'Papal Aggression', and John Sayers Orr, the self-styled 'Archangel Gabriel', whom Handley has described as 'an illiterate half-wit'. Orr had a fancy for dressing up in the style of 'pious woodcuts, letting his hair sweep down over his shoulders and summoning his audiences with blasts of his trumpet'. In the afterglow of the Restoration of the Hierarchy (a similar edict did not affect Scotland till the 1870s), Orr whipped up a section of working-class Scots into a frenzy. On 12 July 1851, for instance, Greenock's Catholic chapel and the priest's house were attacked by a mob. On the following day the homes of Irish workers in nearby Gourock were ransacked and, though innocent, many of the Irish were dismissed by nervous employers to reduce tensions. Meanwhile, the 'Archangel Gabriel' ascended from the trouble and flew from the town.[51]

Similarly serious disturbances of this kind occurred in Oldham in 1861 and were blamed, in contemporary accounts, on the numerical increase of the Irish population. However, Foster argues that anti-Irishness was a measure of the false consciousness of English workers, mediated by the revivification of anti-Catholic organisations like the Orange Order, the Protestant Association and the Pastoral Aid Society. A sign of both native aggression and the Irish response, Foster asserts, was that small, socio-geographical, ethnic enclaves emerged as 'the Irish communities solidified and turned in on themselves'. The same historian also notes that whereas in the 1840s some Irishmen had defied the priesthood in their support for Chartism, the next decade bore witness to a reaffirmation of clerical control.[52]

Divisions between native workers and Irish migrants are sometimes explained in terms of the competition between class and ethnic affiliations. The so-called Garibaldi Riots of 1862 provide good examples of this. When Garibaldi and his Red Shirts began their march on Rome, there was a great wave of support from non-Catholic members of the working class for Garibaldi's brand of secular nationalism, though, by contrast, Irish Catholics offered a strident defence of the Pope. This pro-Catholic behaviour was denounced by the likes of Gavazzi and the 'Baron de Camin', who were quick to turn Garibaldi's march on Rome into a crusade against the papacy.[53] With their prompting, the Garibaldi issue quickly became anti-Catholic, and riots occurred in Wakefield, Bradford, Leeds and Tralee in Ireland.[54] The worst outbursts, however, and those most directly linked to the Garibaldi issue, broke out in London and Birkenhead. When Garibaldian sympathisers, like Charles Bradlaugh, gathered in Hyde Park, their meeting was broken up by Irish Catholics; while in Birkenhead, where rioting was more intense, soldiers as well as policemen were required before order could be restored. In the aftermath of the latter episode, severe sentences were passed, including transportation, which angered Catholics up and down the country.[55]

Any remaining pro-Irish sympathies were, however, all but destroyed by the Fenian episodes of the later 1860s, which had made worse the internecine enmities splitting the working class since the 'Papal Aggression'. When the Fenians launched their bombing campaigns in 1867 and 1868, as well as various raids on gaols and arsenals, the middle class bewailed the ingratitude of the Irish, while members of the working class responded with their fists. Many members of the Irish community were clearly dismayed by the Fenian activities. However, the execution of the 'Manchester Martyrs' (as Larkin, Allen and O'Brien became known), as well news of the victimisation of Irish workers, and a mixture of angst and a siege mentality, caused some to adopt at least passive forms of support for Fenianism. Throughout 1867 and 1868 the newspapers were full of rumours that the Fenians were about to attack some barracks, gasworks or else a national treasure, like St Paul's Cathedral. Local journalists were swept along with the tide, so that even ordinary Irish drunks or brawlers suddenly became malevolent troops on their way to join the Fenian campaign which culminated in an abortive rising in Dublin in 1867. There were many reasons for public opinion turning against the Irish, but most of them were more apparent than real. Against this background of fear and reprisal, William Murphy, the most famous of all the Protestant demagogues, turned a brief flickering of national celebrity into sustained infamy.

Murphy's no-popery career provides a useful case study in anti-Catholic and anti-Irish turbulence. He was well known in mid-Victorian England. His tours were documented in both the newspapers, not least in *The Times*, and in the steady flow of correspondence between local magistrates, police chiefs and the Home Office. Murphy came from a family of no-popery lecturers, claiming his father, Michael, had been killed by a Catholic mob. He began his English career under the aegis of the PEMEU, which sponsored his lectures, and he also enjoyed the support of maverick MPs, such as the anti-Catholic stalwart George Whalley, who made sure Murphy's grievances against turbulent Irish Catholics sometimes made the pages of *Hansard*.[56] Murphy spent most of the mid-1860s working in and around Birmingham and the Midlands. He was first brought to the attention of the Home Office when one of his meetings in Wolverhampton led to serious rioting.

A meeting in Birmingham in June 1867 catapulted Murphy to national celebrity, and his name became 'a household word as the "lecturer against Romanism"'. This gathering of 3000 people was short lived, for, when he described the Pope as a 'rag and bone picker', a throng of Irish labourers fell on the meeting and serious rioting commenced. The unrest went on for several days, with mobs of his supporters descending on Birmingham's Irish district, ransacking a number of houses. Similar events occurred throughout the winter of 1867 as Murphy travelled around the Midlands, speaking in Stafford, Walsall and other smaller places.

Similar events unfolded in the following year when, encouraged by the backlash against Fenianism, Murphy made Lancashire the target of his crusade. In the face of violent threats, Murphy demanded Home Office protection and the right to freedom of speech, though the Home Secretary, Gathorne Hardy, left matters to the local authorities. Consequently, there was a mêlée in Rochdale which resulted in a policeman being shot by Murphy's assistant, George Mackay, who was then arrested. Early in April 1868, a public debate between Murphy and a man named Edward Mooney on the priesthood and confessional passed without violence, but the same could not be said of his appearances in Stalybridge, Blackburn, Bacup and Ashton-under-Lyne, which led to serious street disorders, during which property was stoned, weapons wielded and a number of people received serious beatings. In the following month, May, Oldham was also gripped by the violence and upheaval that followed Murphy's entourage. The general election of 1868 offered the itinerant lecturer further opportunities to increase his infamy, and he even threatened to stand as a candidate for the city. Although he never did, his tours of south Lancashire undoubtedly helped to gel working-class anti-Catholicism and anti-Irishness with opposition to the Liberalism of their mill-owning employers, and this in turn resulted in Lancashire turning decisively Tory in 1868 and emphatically so in 1874.

The news of Murphy's lectures was usually met with mixed responses. While Manchester authorities chose to arrest him, their counterparts in Liverpool refused to let Murphy set foot in their powder-keg of a city. In Tynemouth in 1869 he was met by an army of 250 Irishmen who threatened to kill him in the Oddfellows Hall, while numerous other Northumberland towns barred his entry. The Mayor of Birmingham acted similarly in June 1869, prompting outrage among his parliamentary sponsors, Whalley and Charles Newdegate, who declared that Murphy's exclusion had particularly serious implications for freedom of speech in a liberal country. Despite this rash of bans, Murphy was allowed to air his intemperate views in enough places to become a national celebrity; indeed, he may well have regretted the libertarian sentiments of the Whitehaven magistrates who in April 1871 decided to allow him to speak in their town. Rather like in the Tynemouth episode, Murphy was attacked in Oddfellow's Hall – but this time by 300 well drilled iron-ore miners, from the nearby pit village of Cleator Moor. The police, caught unawares and hopelessly outnumbered, could do little for him, and, before a rescue could be effected, Murphy was horribly beaten. It took some weeks before he recovered sufficiently to face his attackers in court. In the meantime Whitehaven throbbed with the anticipation of more violence. In the end, five men were given 12 months with hard labour and two got three months. Murphy came back to the town in December, despite the entreaties of the local magistrates, but events passed off relatively smoothly. In March 1872, the town was again rocked by the news that Murphy had relapsed after his beating. He died, Birmingham surgeons claimed, because of the lingering effects of the savage assault dished out by those Cleator Moor miners.[57] The press was horrified that a man could die for his views, however intemperate they might be; Irish Catholics rejoiced at the passing of this enemy of their faith; but in west Cumberland the 'Martyr Murphy' became the focus for a staggering Orange re-generation. From a small and inconsequential cluster of like-minded shopkeepers and artisans, Orangeism in the region became a genuinely popular force, parading, patrolling and strutting defiantly in the face of hissing Catholic crowds. Murphy may have been dead, but his legacy remained.

Later Victorian Violence

Historians tend to view the short Fenian and Murphyite period (1866–71) as the final burst of sustained anti-Irish violence in Victorian Britain, with recent writings pointing out the apparent speed with which mid-Victorian street violence came to a halt.[58] However, this perspective is informed as much by a lack of research into the later period as by any evidence in its favour. It is true that many of the worst and most intense episodes of violence occurred between the Famine and the early 1870s, but many types of aggression continued to occur until the Edwardian period. Indeed, Murphy actually died at the beginning, rather than at the end, of a period of Orange regeneration that was responsible for significant examples of anti-Irish and intra-Irish friction. In the north-west of England the 1870s and 1880s were routinely marked with outbreaks of street disorder, especially on the 'Glorious Twelfth' of July. By the mid-1870s, most notable towns in Scotland, Lancashire and Yorkshire were staging impressive displays of Orange solidarity, and it took very little provocation for lines of jeering Catholics to send down a shower of stones and for a riot to ensue. The sound of the bands playing 'Croppies Lie Down', 'To Hell with the Pope' or 'Boyne Water' was itself enough to prompt violent retribution.

Brought about by Irish Protestant immigrants and strengthened by the resolve of native Protestant workers, Orangeism was perhaps the most potent symbol of divisions among the Irish in both old and new communities. With the emergence and spread of the constitutional Home Rule campaign, the meaning of Orangeism became more overtly political and thus more inflammatory. At the same time, the Orangemen's domination of the public stage was for the first time challenged by the other side. In Glasgow and Liverpool, Irish nationalist leaders could often count on crowds of 10 000 to attend their Home Rule meetings, while smaller, but not insignificant numbers were mustered by, for example, the pro-Irish meetings of the Newcastle Radical MP Joseph Cowen.

Orangeism represented a significant coming together of anti-Home Rulers, pro-empire Unionists, MPs and ordinary working people – even though those who played the Orange card in Liverpool or central Scotland always ran the risk of violence. In 1886, for example, with the first Home Rule Bill providing an important topical issue, Liverpool's Orangemen were active on the street long before the election. There were many different engagements between Orangemen and Catholics, from small scuffles outsides pubs to much larger mêlées during which slates were ripped from roofs and used as missiles. Local observers reckoned that in the 1880s Liverpool was more divided than it had been 40 years earlier, when the Famine and the Protestant agitator Hugh McNeile, and various Protestant societies, had shaped the cultural terrain. The police were powerless to prevent often very serious outbreaks of rioting; and even priests could not always be relied upon to 'countermand the influences of hot summer days, boredom and drink'.[59]

It is perhaps surprising, given these continuities in Liverpool's Irish history, that the worst incident of Orange Day violence in 1880s England should occur in the small iron-mining colony of Cleator Moor. The Cleator Irish had been responsible for the beating of William Murphy and local Orangemen had never forgotten or forgiven the fact. Therefore, the provincial lodge's decision to hold the 1884 celebrations of the 'Glorious Twelfth' was both aggressive and unwise. The authorities and the Liberal press were alarmed, though local lodgemen glibly complained that it was an insult to think they needed extra police vigilance. The event went off quite calmly at first, with thousands of Orangemen descending on the small town by train. They marched through the streets to their meeting place, but, on returning to the station, a large Catholic crowd, certainly numbering thousands, began stoning the processors. Gun shots were heard, the police were attacked, and, though most Orangemen escaped without injury, both sides sustained casualties that included severe wounds caused by swords and pistol shots. One youth, a 17-year-old postal worker and Irish National League member named Henry Tumelty, was shot in the head and died. The locality was awash with speculation about lax and pro-Orange policing. Local priests exculpated the Irish by attacking the swaggering brutality of the Orangemen and their insulting music. The iron-ore mining belt around Whitehaven and Cleator remained in a disturbed state for months, especially when no one was convicted of Tumelty's murder.[60]

By the 1890s, the Home Rule issue had given the Orange Order a position of near respectability on the Unionist wing of British politics. Having carved out a niche as a staunch opponent of Home Rule, the movement gave expression to inarticulate working-class visions on such subjects as independence for Ireland. Orangeism was also at the forefront of the renewed campaign against ritualism which came to the surface in the 1890s. The Orangemen's concern with the state of the Church of England served as a spur to evangelical outfits such as John Kensit's Protestant Truth Society (1899), which was a major player in the last campaign against 'Romanisation' in the Anglican Church. In the north of England, the promotion of Low Church worship, through the denunciation of Catholicism, was sure to bring out turbulent Irish opponents. So great was the tide of reaction against ritualism that, in the early 1900s, a parliamentary commission was established to report into its alleged effects on the established Church. Kensit's Protestant Truth Society recruited preachers to be the apostles of his particular gospel, and there were a number of offshoot groups. One of the most notable of these was the Wickliffe Preachers (1902), who spread the Kensitite message throughout Britain and Ireland, meeting varying degrees of opposition wherever they went. By 1903 there were 30 of these preachers, and in that year alone they held 2561 meetings in 441 places, distributing 200 000 pamphlets as they went. Machin calls them 'young militants', though they were less rabble-rousing than William Murphy or than one of their contemporaries, Pastor George Wise, the Liverpool-based demagogue whose rhetoric was noted for its trails of violence and uproar. In the early 1900s circumstances catapulted Kensit and Wise into each other's orbit. Both were Londoners (Wise born in 1855 and Kensit in 1853) and trained in the capital's thriving evangelical Protestant tradition. In 1888 Wise moved to Liverpool, where his anti-Catholicism fitted neatly into Britain's sectarian capital. In 1902, at the height of the ritualism debate, Kensit and his father had launched a nationwide tour which eventually led the younger man to Wise's Liverpool, where the atmosphere was predictably electric. Kensit Junior had an immediate effect, clashing regularly with local Irish Catholics, just as Wise had been doing for over a decade, and something of a power struggle emerged between the two vain exponents of a fading art. When Kensit Junior was imprisoned after one particular outburst, Wise attempted to reimpose his power base, though Kensit Senior arrived in town to further his son's efforts. However, this notion was snuffed out in dramatic fashion during a turbulent meeting in Birkenhead, during which Kensit Senior was pole-axed by a blow to the head from a two-pound iron file. He died in hospital on 8 October 1902. Competition between Wise and Kensit Junior continued into 1903 as the latter continued his quest by establishing a Wickliffe mission in Liverpool. Wise was arrested a number of times in the 1900s and played a major part in the establishment of Liverpool's independent Protestant Party, which was still winning council seats after World War II. Although Wise died in 1917, Kensit continued 'to champion ultra-Protestantism until the 1940s'.[61] While Wise and Kensit represented tensions within popular Protestantism, in truth they shared much common ground.

The links between Kensit and Wise, as well as their differences, were highlighted in one particularly turbulent trip to Barrow-in-Furness on 31 July and 1 August 1903, when local Catholic temperatures were raised by two visits: first, by Wise, who inflamed local Catholics before quickly departing; and, secondly, by the Wickliffe Preachers, who reaped Wise's whirlwind. Before the latter were able to utter one word at a specially planned meeting before a crowd of over 1000, they were 'subjected to the most strenuous opposition'. Despite the claims of one of their number that the Wickliffe Preachers 'were not in any way fighting directly against the Roman Catholic church', and an emphatic denial that they were associated with Wise, the proceedings degenerated into a series of localised arguments before 'a rush was made for the Preachers', and 'blows and kicks were freely given and taken, and sticks were used on the heads and shoulders of any who chanced in the way'. The next day, Sunday 2 August, gave rise to further unrest. The Kensitites tried to lecture again, but before they could speak their banner, which bore 'a large picture ... representing two martyrs burning at the stake', was seized, torn down and trodden upon with 'excited cries of exaltation'. The crowd apparently yelled 'We killed Kensit and will kill you', and the police protected the preachers from the jostling mob before arresting them all for causing a breach of the peace. They were brought before magistrates, along with three Irish Catholics who were charged with public order offences. The three men were bound over for six months but the Wickliffe lecturers refused to be similarly restricted because it would have prevented them from conducting further meetings. Instead, they were imprisoned for one month. This sentence led to uproar in the Protestant community; even George Wise came to their defence (albeit in an open letter to the press), and John Kensit and other preachers came to the town to complain about their colleagues' perceived ill-treatment. So great was the public outcry that the magistrates back-peddled some days later and freed the men. Although Sir Charles Cayzer, the town's Conservative MP, threw his weight behind the preachers' campaign, it was a petition of over 30 000 names and a series of large demonstrations in the town that won the day. Stanley Parker, the Methodist organiser of the Barrow campaign, captured this point well: 'The people are omnipotent, if they only knew it. The people can do anything they please.'[62]

In Liverpool, where the extreme Protestant tradition was most turbulent, one of the most explosive series of events occurred under the aegis of George Wise. Events were sparked by the Catholic Eucharistic Congress of 1908, what Bohstedt describes as 'a sort of religious world fair',[63] a celebration of faith which resulted in a huge surge of anti-Catholic feeling. The climax of the Congress was to see the host, the consecrated wafer (which according to the doctrine of transubstantiation represented the body of Christ, and an emblem which reviled ultra-Protestants), being paraded through the streets of London. The Archbishop of London claimed this act would test whether or not the Catholic Emancipation Act (which prohibited Catholic clergymen from conducting services or wearing their holy vestments outside their churches) was still in force. There was a huge outcry, with Wise and his followers in Liverpool at the vanguard. Such was the reaction that the Prime Minister intervened and the procession of the host was dropped. This decision had significant implications for Britain's rather battered doctrine of liberty, and so Catholics in several towns and cities, including Manchester, decided to go ahead with their parades in the spring of 1909. It was against these acts of Catholic assertiveness or defiance that Wise reacted.

In May 1909 Liverpool witnessed a huge Catholic march, with an altar being erected in the streets, without the authorities' consent, and an Orange demonstration was organised to match it. The Catholic Holy Cross parade (so called to celebrate 60 years of the 'Famine church') attracted between 4000 and 5000 marchers with impromptu altars and shrines erected *en route*. The police were out in force, as were the crowds, keeping a watchful or curious eye on what Catholic propagandists were calling the finest display of Catholicity in Liverpool's history. This was just the kind of language which incensed Wise and his supporters. At this stage, there was much political to-ing and fro-ing over the legality of the event, but little violence. Events continued in June, however, with Orange demonstrations and street fights between the rival communities. Another Catholic procession was planned for 20 June and with it a predictable Orange counter-demonstration. This time, the police requested that the marchers carry no images (viewed as profane by ultra-Protestants like Wise), but it was too late to achieve this end and a huge riot occurred. The police were attacked, Catholic houses destroyed and fierce hand-to-hand fighting took place. During the summer Wise fanned the flames with a series of speeches at his favourite venue, St Domingo Pit. 'For four months, Pastor Wise and other speakers assailed Catholic treachery and police favouritism, posing as martyrs for law and freedom in the face of police tyranny.' There was trouble after many of these meetings, and when Wise planned a parade of his own for 27 June, and refused to obey police instructions to cancel it, he was arrested. Wise spent only a few days in gaol, and he, like the Wickliffe Preachers before him, refused to be bound over. The summer was thus marked by an endless series of disturbances and legalistic discussions about Wise's case. Wise's hearing was postponed several times and when he was finally imprisoned, he was escorted by 100 000 sympathisers, what Bohstedt called 'a great procession of state'.[64]

Conclusions

A balance must be struck in any account of anti-Irish violence, between the various mix of reasons for the aggression. Perhaps too few accounts take cognisance of the wider political scene: the Irish question exercised Parliament to an inordinate degree in the second half of the nineteenth century, and, allied to Irish agrarian unrest, numerous risings and rebellions, the Fenian campaigns and the formation of an effective transatlantic Home Rule movement, clearly impacted upon the way Irish issues were perceived, and, consequently, how the Irish in Britain were treated. There were of course organisations which made headway by promoting the image of a backward and divided Ireland. The Orange Order, for example, presented its members as defenders of the more mature, loyal, and even superior, of the 'Two Irelands', thus driving a wedge between the Protestant and Catholic Irish abroad. But this situation alone cannot explain the degree of violence which accompanied Orange Day parades in Scotland, Lancashire or Cumberland. Religion undoubtedly was the key: but it took more than the 'show trumpery' of Orangeism to bring it to the fore. If anti-Catholicism simply had been the product of intra-Irish squabbling, then Victorians would have said little about it. The reaction to Catholic Emancipation (1829), the 'Papal Aggression' (1850), as well as other alleged concessions to 'popery' illustrates with stark clarity the deep-seated loathing that linked proletarian Ulster-born Orangemen with the very heart of the British state – those who saw the unity of church and state as sacrosanct and who defended it unfailing throughout our period. Therefore, whether measured in terms of historical animosity or contemporary cultural difference, Catholicism was absolutely central to the Victorian idea of Englishness, Scottishness or Britishness, as it was to the type of reception that awaited the arrival of Irish settlers.

CONCLUSION

The Irish were by far the most important migrant group in Britain during the nineteenth century. They appeared in all of the growing urban centres of the Midlands, the north of England and the central lowlands of western Scotland, performing a vital economic role wherever they settled. Although most of the men found work as general labourers, skilled tradesmen were not entirely absent from their ranks. Contemporaries noted how much Irish work was dirty, hard and unappealing; yet more desirable outlets such as customs houses, shipping agencies and hotels also provided work for a significant body of white-collar migrants, more so as the century wore on. While it is true that the Irish arrived in greatest numbers in the 1830s and 1840s, when the problems of industrialism were most acute, we must also remember that they had been disembarking in significant numbers at ports such as Whitehaven since the seventeenth century and continued to do so long after the early Victorian zenith. This logic of Irish migration was not simply to provide labour power for the Industrial Revolution, important though this is. The Irish in Britain also exerted a considerable cultural influence, whether by boosting the fortunes of the Catholic Church in Britain or by introducing Orange lodges. Some migrants also became involved with the radical and working-class political movements of the period, as well as promoting their own nationalist causes – which they did despite sometimes fierce opposition. Yet none of these factors can explain the deep-seated animosity which so regularly faced the Irish in Britain. To understand this dimension of the Irish experience, we have also had to probe some of the historic and cultural divisions that separated the sender and receiver countries.

Two of the most compelling reasons for anti-Irish reaction were the size of the Irish communities and the timing of their establishment. One-third of *all* Irish-born settlers in the years 1841 to 1871 were located in the major settlements of London, Liverpool, Manchester

185

and Glasgow. In the great northern cities, the Irish-born approached one-fifth of the population, as they did in several Scottish towns, such as Dundee, and in small iron-ore colonies, such as Cleator Moor in Cumberland. In certain towns, therefore, the male labour force could be considerably more than one-third Irish-born. This question of concentration clearly affected the reception that awaited them. Tensions were also aroused by the Irish tendency to cluster in key occupational groups, notably the building trades, often to the exclusion of others. While social historians today are rightly moving away from the idea of the ghetto Irish (though not necessarily denying the reality and importance of residential concentrations), the fact remains that the Irish were noted for spatial as well as occupational clustering. But factors such as communal and workplace cohesion are not unique to Irish migrants, and might easily be observed among other incoming groups. Where the Irish *were* unique was in the absolute size of these major settlements: in 1891, for example, the Irish-born population of Liverpool (at more than 66 000) was over 30 per cent larger than the entire German-born population of Britain (50 000). If the size of the Irish communities impacted on the native community, then the timing of their construction is a related factor when explaining levels of anti-Irishness.

Large Irish communities were a relatively new phenomenon in the nineteenth century. Although migration from Ireland to Britain was centuries old, and despite the existence of Irish enclaves in London since the sixteenth century, nothing that went before could have prepared Britons for the influx witnessed in the century after 1760. Irish migrants, such as paupers and tinkers, may have been viewed as an undesirable element since the Middle Ages, but developments after 1800 solidified previously vague notions of the Irish as a burden on British society. Moreover, migration worsened British attitudes towards Ireland and Irish society in a more diffuse sense. Migration was created by a complex weave of 'push' and 'pull' factors; the greater these became, the more migration flowed; and the more it flowed, the more the 'push' elements of poverty and landownership forced themselves on the attentions of Britons. Ireland's own problems may have been enough to push many thousands of migrants from 'the old country', but the effect of these preconditions was greatly exacerbated by one of the greatest economic leaps in human history – the British 'Industrial Revolution'. The fact that this British experience was followed by an even more impressive series of developments in the United States gave the Irish an almost irresistible incentive to leave. Migration quickened after 1815, expanding almost annually until the Great Famine, at which point the torrent of leavers dwarfed all previous departures. The migrants to Britain in this period found themselves entering the sorts of dystopian urban centres that were so vividly captured in the novels and social commentaries of the day, and this immediately and inexorably increased reactions against them. Victorian cities were dark and brooding places, whose populations were disproportionately young, and where even non-Irish residents were often incomers from different worlds. Such urban centres grew at a pace beyond previous experience, making demands on the fledgling infrastructure which, down to the 1840s and beyond, simply could not be met. And when the Victorians looked for a scapegoat, they saw an Irish migrant.

Although these matters of timing and concentration are vital, and gave added impetus to many forms of class-orientated conflict between British and Irish workers, the amalgamating ingredient for most acts of violence was religion. Irish Catholics in Britain were guaranteed a rocky reception because the native population viewed anti-Catholicism as a mainstay of their Protestant identity. Negative attitudes were endemic, dangerous and malevolent features of British cultural life, and were worsened by the vanguard role which Irish Protestant migrants played in promoting the Protestant ideal, principally through the Orange Order. The reasons for religious discord, and its place in migrants' lives, as well as the shapes it assumed, have been major themes of the preceding discussion.

The Victorian urban world was a turbulent arena for human interactions, often reflecting or distilling age-old misunderstandings and prejudices, but it is also important to remember that our consideration of what might be termed the darker side of culture was counterpointed with reference to the more positive aspects of migrant life (Chapters 3–5). One of the most remarkable features of the new communities was a resourcefulness in forming social, political and cultural attachments. The Catholic religion may have been a reason for division, but it was also one of the main symbols of migrant identity; and through it Irish arrivals from a disparate array of regional backgrounds came together as 'Irish' and as 'Catholic'. A deep social and spiritual attachment to Catholicism, and the way that was shaped and adapted, and how it in practice functioned, was a key aspect of our investigations in Chapter 3. For the first time in a study such as this, moreover, we were able to consider (in Chapter 4) the Protestant dimension, looking not just at patterns of Protestant settlement, but also at the types of social and cultural bodies that Protestants, like their Catholic counterparts, created.

The lives of the Irish in Britain were varied and rich, even though a stark contrast between achievement and animosity so often marked out their lives. This book has attempted to uncover positive aspects of Irish communal life to place alongside the better-known stories of aggression, violence and contempt. Most Irish lives were ordinary lives; and yet they often stood out for the reasons discussed here. Migration to Britain was but part of a wider set of cultural, political and economic interactions between Britain and Ireland; thus anti-Irish hostility in, for example, Liverpool was, in many respects, the 'Irish problem' writ small. Expressions of hatred and incidents of violence reflected deeper feelings which so many Britons harboured towards Ireland and the Irish in general. This migration reminds us of the problems of integration which all migrant groups can face; but it also tells us something yet more important about the particularly strained historical relationship between the various countries of the Atlantic archipelago.

NOTES

Introduction

1. Editors' introduction, R. Swift and S. Gilley (eds), *Irish in the Victorian City* (London, 1985), p. 9.
2. The continued importance of the Irish in the post-Famine period is clearly announced in two fine essays by David Fitzpatrick: '"A peculiar tramping people": the Irish in Britain, 1801–70', and 'The Irish in Britain, 1871–1921', in W. E. Vaughan (ed.), *A New History of Ireland*, vol. V, *Ireland Under the Union, I: 1801–1870* (Oxford, 1986) and vol. VI, *Ireland Under the Union, II: 1870–1921* (Oxford, 1996).
3. Fitzpatrick, 'Irish in Britain', correctly stresses the continuing 'apartness' of Irish settlers.
4. O. Handlin, *Boston's Immigrants* (London, 1941) and *The Uprooted: The Epic Study of the Great Migrants that Made the American People* (Boston, 1951). The quotation is from the first page of the latter.
5. See W. F. Adams, *Ireland and Irish Emigration to the New World from 1815 to the Famine* (New Haven, 1932); T. F. Blegen, *Norwegian Migration to America, 1820–1860* (Northfield, Carolina, 1931); M. L. Hansen, *The Atlantic Migration, 1607–1860: A History of the Continuing Settlement of the United States* (Cambridge, 1940).
6. As C. Holmes, *John Bull's Island: Immigration and British Society, 1871–1971* (Basingstoke, 1987), amply attests.
7. C. Ó Gráda, 'A note on nineteenth century Irish emigration statistics', *Population Studies*, 29 (1975).
8. E. Delaney, *Demography, State and Society: Irish Migration to Britain, 1921–1971* (Liverpool, forthcoming).
9. This is, though, the argument of Ruth-Ann Harris, *The Nearest Place that Wasn't Ireland: Early Nineteenth-Century Labor Migration* (Ames, Iowa, 1994).
10. D. Fitzpatrick, *Oceans of Consolation: Personal Accounts of Irish Migration to Australia* (Cork, 1994), pp. 334–58.
11. Frank Neal, 'The famine Irish in England and Wales', in Patrick O'Sullivan (ed.), *The Irish World-Wide*, vol. VI, *The Meaning of the Famine* (Leicester, 1997), pp. 63–4. The Sullivans' harrowing story is recounted more fully in *idem, Black '47: Britain and the Famine Irish* (Basingstoke, 1997), pp. 51, 177–9.
12. These two phrases are employed by David Fitzpatrick to illustrate the cohesiveness as well as the variety of Irish lives in Britain: 'A curious

middle place: the Irish in Britain, 1871-1921', in R. Swift and S. Gilley (eds), *The Irish in Britain, 1815-1939* (London, 1989), and '"A peculiar tramping people"'.

13. Alan Mayne, *The Imagined Slum: Newspaper Representations in Three Cities, 1870–1914* (Leicester, 1993), p. 1.
14. *Ibid.*, pp. 9–10.
15. This point is compellingly argued by Lynn Hollen Lees, *Exiles of Erin: Irish Migrants in Victorian London* (New York and Manchester, 1979).
16. As well as being a brilliant reconstruction of imperial expansion and a shrewd examination of the world view of Irish colonisers, D. H. Akenson's *If the Irish Ruled the World: Monserrat, 1630–1730* (Liverpool, 1997), also provides clear guidance on the range of identities which existed within Ireland and how these fared in the New World under Irish and other leadership.

1 ECONOMY, POVERTY AND EMIGRATION

1. Problems abound with emigration data. See C. Ó Gráda, 'A note on nineteenth-century Irish emigration statistics', *Population Studies*, 29 (1975).
2. See D. Fitzpatrick, *Irish Emigration, 1801–1921* (Dublin, 1984); *idem*, 'Emigration, 1801–1870', in W. E. Vaughan (ed.), *A New History of Ireland*, vol. V, *Ireland Under the Union, I: 1801–1870* (Oxford, 1986), pp. 562–622; D. H. Akenson, *Small Differences: Irish Catholics and Irish Protestants, 1815–1922* (Dublin, 1988), Appendix H, p. 182.
3. E. J. Hobsbawm, *The Age of Capital, 1848–1875* (London, 1962), p. 196.
4. Marcus Lee Hansen, *The Immigrant in American History* (Cambridge, Massachusetts, 1942), pp. 158–9.
5. See, for example, T. G. Fraser, 'Ireland and India', in K. Jeffrey (ed.), *'An Irish Empire'? Aspects of Ireland and the British Empire* (Manchester, 1996).
6. Fitzpatrick, *Irish Emigration*, p. 7.
7. David Fitzpatrick, 'Emigration, 1870–1921', in W. E. Vaughan (ed.), *A New History of Ireland*, vol. VI, *Ireland Under the Union, II: 1870–1921* (Oxford, 1996), pp. 612–13; C. Ó Gráda, *Ireland: A New Economic History, 1780–1939* (Oxford, 1994), pp. 225–8. For female migration, also see two essays by David Fitzpatrick: '"A share of the honeycomb": education, emigration and Irishwomen', *Continuity and Change*, 1 (1986), and 'The modernisation of the Irish female', in P. O'Flanagan, P. Ferguson and K. Whelan (eds), *Rural Ireland, 1600–1900: Modernisation and Change* (Cork, 1986).
8. While it would be wrong to compare historians today with the nationalists of yesterday, the language of 'exile' runs through much recent writing. See, for example, Kerby A. Miller, *Emigrants and Exiles: Ireland and the Irish Exodus to North America* (New York and Oxford, 1985), and L. H. Lees, *Exiles of Erin: Irish Migrants in Victorian London* (New York and Manchester, 1979).
9. Quoted in T. W. Freeman, *Pre-Famine Ireland: a Study in Human Geography* (Manchester, 1956), p. 38.

10. Differing views are found in J. Mokyr and C. Ó Gráda, 'Emigration and poverty in pre-famine Ireland', *Explorations in Economic History*, 19 (1982), and S. Nicholas and P. R. Shergold, 'Human capital and the pre-famine Irish emigration to England', *Explorations in Economic History*, 24 (1987).

11. The best short introduction to this area is L. Kennedy and L. A. Clarkson, 'Birth, death and exile: Irish population history, 1700–1921', in B. J. Graham and L. J. Proudfoot (eds), *An Historical Geography of Ireland* (London, 1993).

12. K. T. Hoppen, *Ireland Since 1800: Conflict and Conformity* (London, 1989), pp. 35.

13. *Ibid.*, p. 36.

14. W. F. Adams, *Ireland and Irish Emigration to the New World from 1815 to the Famine* (New Haven, 1932), ch. 1; R. Crotty, *Irish Agricultural Production: Its Volume and Structure* (Cork, 1966), ch. 2; J. Mokyr, *Why Ireland Starved: A Quantitative and Analytical History of the Irish Economy, 1800–1850* (London, 1983). An excellent overview of the debate is Ó Gráda, *Ireland*, especially chs 4–7.

15. L. M. Cullen, *An Economic History of Ireland Since 1660* (London, 1993), ch. 5 (first published 1972), provides a trenchant account of this period of crisis.

16. S. H. Cousens, 'The regional variation in emigration from Ireland between 1821 and 1841', *Transactions of the Institute of British Geographers*, 37 (1965).

17. D. Fitzpatrick, *Oceans of Consolation: Personal Accounts of Irish Migration to Australia* (Cork, 1994), pp. 14–15; Cousens, 'Emigration from Ireland', pp. 18–19.

18. Fitzpatrick, *Irish Emigration*, p. 11.

19. North American data in this paragraph are derived from two sources which are as reliable as can be obtained: Adams, *Ireland and Irish Emigration*, pp. 413–14; and W. E. Vaughan and A. J. Fitzpatrick, *Irish Historical Statistics: Population 1821–1971* (Dublin, 1978), p. 259.

20. Arthur Young, *A Tour in Ireland. With General Observations on the Present State of that Kingdom Made in the Years 1776, 1777 and 1778* (Cambridge, 1925), pp. 198–9.

21. Mokyr, *Why Ireland Starved*, ch. 2.

22. Ó Gráda, *Ireland*, pp. 69–71.

23. T. R. Malthus, *An Essay on the Principle of Population* (Cambridge, 1992), p. 15 (first published 1798).

24. See L. A. Clarkson and M. Crawford, 'Dietary directions: a topographical survey of Irish diet, 1836', in R. Mitchison and P. Roebuck (eds), *Economy and Society in Ireland, 1500–1939* (Edinburgh, 1989).

25. B. M. Walsh, 'A perspective on Irish population patterns', *Eire–Ireland*, 4 (1969), p. 5.

26. Young, *Tour in Ireland*, p. 185.

27. The major work on the potato is P. M. A. Bourke, '*The Visitation of God': the Potato and the Great Irish Famine* (Dublin, 1993).

28. Malthus, *Essay on the Principle of Population*, p. 127.

29. Bourke, *Visitation of God*, pp. 36–7.

30. J. R. Donnelly, 'Excess mortality and emigration', in W. E. Vaughan (ed.), *A New History of Ireland*, vol. V, p. 352.

31. See B. M. Kerr, 'Irish seasonal migration to Great Britain, 1800–38', *Irish Historical Studies*, 3 (1942–3); J. H. Johnson, 'Harvest migration from nineteenth-century Ireland', *Transactions of the Institute of British Geographers*, 41 (1967); C. Ó Gráda, 'Seasonal migration and post-Famine adjustment in the west of Ireland', *Studia Hibernica*, 13 (1973); A. O'Dowd, *Spalpeens and Tatie Hokers: History and Folklore of the Irish Migratory Agricultural Worker in Ireland and Britain* (Dublin, 1991); S. Barber, 'Irish migrant agricultural labourers in nineteenth century Lincolnshire', *Saothar*, 8 (1982).

32. Kerr, 'Irish seasonal migration', pp. 365–6.

33. *Ibid.*, pp. 371, 377.

34. Ó Gráda, 'Seasonal migration', pp. 50, 55–66.

35. Mokyr, *Why Ireland Starved*, p. 278.

36. L. A. Clarkson, 'Population change and urbanisation, 1821–1911', in L. Kennedy and P. Ollerenshaw (eds), *An Economic History of Ulster, 1820–1940* (Manchester, 1985).

37. Young, *Tour in Ireland*, p. 183.

38. Wakefield, quoted in C. Ó Gráda, *Ireland Before the Famine and After* (Manchester, 1988), p. 14; H. D. Inglis, *Ireland in 1834* (London, 1835), vol. I, pp. 11, 13.

39. J. G. Kohl, *Ireland* (London, 1844), p. 7.

40. D. Clark, *The Irish in Philadelphia: Ten Generations of Urban Experience* (Philadelphia, 1973), p. 25.

41. For Mill's Irish commentaries, see E. D. Steele, 'J. S. Mill and the Irish question: the principles of political economy, 1848–1865', *Historical Journal*, 13 (1970). For this, and the wider context of his attitude towards land, see D. E. Martin, *John Stuart Mill and the Land Question* (Hull, 1981).

42. *Morning Chronicle*, 7 October 1846.

43. Crotty, *Irish Agricultural Production*, ch. 2.

44. Young, *Tour in Ireland*, pp. 183–4.

45. *Ibid.*, p. 187.

46. Kohl, *Ireland*, p. 23.

47. See Eoin O'Malley, 'The decline of Irish industry in the nineteenth century', *Economic and Social Review*, 13 (1981), pp. 21–42; Brenda Collins, 'Proto-industrialisation and pre-famine emigration', *Social History*, 7 (1982), pp. 127–46.

48. Jan de Vries, *European Urbanisation, 1500–1800* (London, 1984), table 3.8, pp. 45–8.

49. S. H. Cousens, 'Regional patterns of emigration the Great Irish Famine from 1846 to 1851', *Transactions of the Institute of British Geographers*, 28 (1960), p. 125.

50. D. Fitzpatrick, *Irish Emigration, 1801–1921* (Dundalk, 1984), p. 32.

51. An excellent discussion of the effects of the Famine on national memory is given by J. S. Donnelly, 'The construction of the memory of the Famine in Ireland and the Irish Diaspora, 1850–1900', *Eire–Ireland*, 31 (1996).

52. Cousens, 'Regional patterns', pp. 55–74; Mokyr, *Why Ireland Starved*, p. 267; Donnelly, 'Excess mortality', pp. 350–3 .

53. Cullen, *Economic History of Ireland*, p. 132. Donnelly, 'Excess mortality', provides a trenchant and most convincing exposition on the Famine as a national disaster.
54. Donnelly, 'Excess mortality', p. 350.
55. O. MacDonagh, 'Irish emigration to the United States and the British colonies during the Famine', in O. Dudley Edwards and T. D. Williams (eds), *The Great Famine: Studies in Irish History, 1845–52* (Dublin, 1994), p. 319 (first published 1956).
56. Fitzpatrick, 'Emigration, 1801–70', p. 582.
57. Miller, *Emigrants and Exiles*, p. 291.
58. C. Kinealy, *This Great Calamity: The Irish Famine, 1845–52* (Dublin, 1994), tables 25, 26, pp. 304, 310.
59. Cousens, 'Regional patterns', pp. 15–30; Donnelly, 'Excess mortality', pp. 354–6.
60. T. M. Devine, *The Great Highland Famine: Hunger, Emigration and the Scottish Highlands in the Nineteenth Century* (Edinburgh, 1988), pp. 86–7.
61. Cousens, 'Regional patterns', p. 126.
62. Devine, *Highland Famine*, p. 81.
63. Cousens, 'Regional patterns', pp. 127–8, 129–33.
64. C. Ó Gráda, 'Seasonal migration and post-Famine adjustment', p. 48.
65. *Ibid.*, pp. 48–9.
66. Fitzpatrick, 'Emigration, 1870–1921', p. 606.
67. *Ibid.*, p. 607.
68. T. W. Guinnane, *The Vanishing Irish: Households, Migration and the Rural Economy in Ireland* (Princeton, 1996). For Connell's work on marriage, and so on, see 'Peasant marriage in Ireland: its structure and development since the famine', *Economic History Review*, 14 (1962); 'Peasant marriage in Ireland after the great famine', *Past and Present*, 12 (1957); 'Marriage in Ireland after the famine: the diffusion of the match', *Journal of the Statistical and Social Inquiry Society of Ireland*, 19 (1955–6).
69. Ó Gráda, 'Seasonal migration', p. 63.
70. This has been discussed by D. Fitzpatrick, 'The disappearance of the Irish agricultural labourer, 1841–1912', *Irish Economic and Social History*, 7 (1980).
71. Royal Commission on the Condition of the Poorer Classes in Ireland, Appendix G, *Report into the State of the Irish Poor in Great Britain*, Parliamentary Papers (1836), p. 136.

2 Concentration and Dispersal: Irish Labour Migration to Britain

1. R. F. Foster, *Modern Ireland, 1600–1972* (London, 1988), p. 345.
2. Royal Commission on the Condition of the Poorer Classes in Ireland, Appendix G, *Report into the State of the Irish Poor in Great Britain*, Parliamentary Papers (1836), p. 141.
3. I Hen. V, c. 8: A. Redford, *Labour Migration in England, 1800–1850* (Manchester, 1926), p. 114; Patrick Fitzgerald, '"Like crickets to the crevice of a brew-house": poor Irish migrants in England, 1560–1640', in

P. O'Sullivan (ed.), *The Irish World Wide: History, Heritage, Identity*, vol. I, *Patterns of Migration* (Leceister, 1992), p. 13.

4. Redford, *Labour Migration*, p. 114.

5. Fitzgerald, 'Poor Irish migrants', p. 19; John McGurk, 'The Irish in European armies (sixteenth to eighteenth centuries)', in P. O'Sullivan (ed.), *The Irish World Wide: History, Heritage, Identity*, vol. I, *Patterns of Migration* (Leceister, 1992), pp. 36–62.

6. B. M. Kerr, 'Irish seasonal migration to Great Britain, 1800–38', *Irish Historical Studies*, 3 (1942–3), pp. 370–4.

7. W. Cobbett, *Manchester Lecturer* (London, 1832), p. 163.

8. Kerr, 'Irish seasonal migration', p. 377.

9. See Ann O'Dowd, *Spalpeens and Tatie Hokers: History and Folklore of the Irish Migratory Agricultural Workers in Ireland and Britain* (Dublin, 1991), *passim*.

10. T. Coleman, *The Railway Navvies* (London, 1968 edn), p. 103.

11. J. A. Patmore, 'A navvy gang of 1851', *Journal of Transport History*, 5 (1962); D. Brooke, 'Railway navvies on the Pennines 1841–71', *Journal of Transport History*, 3 (1975–6); J. E. Handley, *The Navvy in Scotland* (Cork, 1970).

12. *Report on the Poor Law* (1817), vi, p. 85. See D. M. MacRaild, *Culture, Conflict and Migration: The Irish in Victorian Cumbria* (Liverpool, 1998), pp. 30–2.

13. L. H. Lees, *Exiles of Erin: Irish Migrants in Victorian London* (New York and Manchester, 1979), p. 45.

14. Dorothy George, 'The London coal-heavers: attempts to regulate water-side labour in the eighteenth and nineteenth centuries', *Economic History Supplement to the Economic Journal* (May 1927).

15. P. J. Waller, *Democracy and Sectarianism: a Political and Social History of Liverpool, 1868–1939* (Liverpool, 1981), p. 7.

16. *State of the Irish Poor*, pp. 146, 151–2. See also J. E. Handley, *The Irish in Scotland, 1798–1845* (Cork, 1943), ch. 4, especially pp. 75–85; and N. Murray, *The Scottish Handloom Weavers, 1790–1850: a Social History* (Edinburgh, 1979), *passim*.

17. *State of the Irish Poor*, pp. 156–7.

18. A. Fell, *The Early Iron Industry of Furness and District* (London, 1968), pp. 363–7 (first published 1908); J. D. Marshall, *Furness and the Industrial Revolution* (Beckermet, 1981), pp. 104–9 (first published 1958).

19. *State of the Irish Poor*, pp. 149–55.

20. *State of the Irish Poor*, pp. 132, 133–4. For discussions of Paisley, see B. Collins, 'Irish emigration to Dundee and Paisley during the first half of the nineteenth century', in J. M. Goldstrom and L. A. Clarkson (eds), *Irish Population, Economy and Society* (Oxford, 1981).

21. Frank Neal, *Sectarian Violence: the Liverpool Experience, 1819–1914* (Manchester, 1988), p. 4.

22. For a discussion of this, see I. C. Taylor, 'The court and cellar dwelling: the eighteenth-century origins of the Liverpool slum', *Transactions of the Historic Society of Lancashire and Cheshire*, 62 (1970).

23. E. A. Parkes and J. S. Burdon-Sanderson, *Report on the Sanitary Condition of Liverpool* (London, 1871), p. 50, quoted in *ibid.*, p. 67.

24. Handley, *Irish in Scotland*, p. 85.
25. *State of the Irish Poor*, evidence of Reverend James Crook, p. 61, and Peter Ewart, p. 64.
26. *Ibid.*, evidence of Samuel Holme, p. 29.
27. *Ibid.*, pp. 61, 63, 64, 65.
28. *Ibid.*, p. 66.
29. *Ibid.*, pp. 67, 68.
30. *Ibid.*, p. 44.
31. *Ibid.*, p. 48.
32. *Ibid.*, pp. 1–2.
33. *Ibid.*, pp. 1–2, and the evidence of James Holmes, p. 3.
34. *Ibid.*, p. xiii.
35. *Ibid.*, evidence of the Reverend Gover, Liverpool St Peter's parish, p. 22.
36. See Frank Neal, *Black '47: Britain and the Famine Irish* (Basingstoke, 1997) for a moving and richly detailed analysis of the migration of this period.
37. See A. P. Coney, 'Mid-nineteenth-century Ormskirk: disease, over-crowding and the Irish in a Lancashire market town', *Transactions of the Historic Society of Lancashire and Cheshire*, 84 (1989).
38. R. J. Scally, *The End of Hidden Ireland: Rebellion, Famine and Emigration* (Oxford, 1995), ch. 9. For Liverpool's role in the emigration trade, also see Neal, *Sectarian Violence*, chs 1–3, and *idem*, 'Liverpool and the Irish steamship companies and the Famine Irish', *Immigrants and Minorities*, 5 (1986).
39. *Ibid.*, p. 33.
40. Neal, *Sectarian Violence*, p. 80.
41. *Ibid.*, p. 82.
42. *Ibid.*, p. 82.
43. E. M. Crawford, 'Migrant maladies: unseen lethal baggage', in *idem* (ed.), *The Hungry Stream: Essays on Emigration and Famine* (Belfast, 1997), pp. 137–50.
44. F. Neal, 'Lancashire, the famine and the poor laws', *Irish Social and Economic History*, 22 (1995), p. 33.
45. *Ibid.*, p. 92.
46. *Ibid.*, p. 33.
47. *Ibid.*, table 4, p. 38.
48. C. Kinealy, *This Great Calamity: the Irish Famine, 1848–52* (Dublin, 1994), p. 336.
49. *Ibid.*, pp. 33–5.
50. Frank Neal, 'The famine Irish in England and Wales', in P. O'Sullivan (ed.), *The Irish World Wide*, vol. VI, *The Meaning of the Famine* (Leicester, 1997), pp. 61–2, quoting the *Bristol Gazette*, 25 February 1847, and the *Newcastle Journal*, 27 March 1847.
51. Neal, *Black '47*, ch. 6; quotations from J. E. Handley, *The Irish in Modern Scotland* (Cork, 1947), pp. 25–30.
52. Frances Finnegan, *Poverty and Prejudice: a Study of Irish Immigrants in York, 1840–1875* (Cork, 1982), pp. 22–3.
53. Neal, 'Famine Irish in England and Wales', table 3.7, p. 71.
54. *Ibid.*, p. 155.

55. D. Fitzpatrick, 'The Irish in Britain, 1871–1921', in W. E. Vaughan (ed.), *A New History of Ireland*, vol. V, *Ireland under the Union, II: 1870–1921* (Oxford, 1986).

56. *Ibid.*, p. 656.

57. *Ibid.*, p. 663.

58. T. Dillon, 'The Irish in Leeds, 1851–1861', *Thoresby Society*, miscellany, 16 (1973), table 4, pp. 6–7; C. Richardson, 'Irish settlement in mid-nineteenth-century Bradford', *Yorkshire Bulletin of Economic and Social Research*, 20 (1968), table 4, p. 42; F. Finnegan, *Poverty and Prejudice: a Study of Irish Immigrants in York 1840–1875* (Cork, 1982), pp. 4, 20–1, 69, 70, 94–5; John Herson, 'Irish migration and settlement in Victorian England: a small-town perspective', in R. Swift and S. Gilley (eds), *The Irish in Britain, 1815–1939* (London, 1989), p. 89.

59. MacRaild, *Culture, Conflict and Migration*, table 2.5, pp. 42–3, 47.

60. P. Norris, 'The Irish in Tow Law, Co Durham, 1851 and 1871', *Durham Local History Society Bulletin*, 33 (1984), p. 42.

61. MacRaild, *Culture, Conflict and Migration*, ch. 3; Alan B. Campbell, *The Lanarkshire Miners: A Social History of their Trade Unions, 1775–1874* (Edinburgh, 1979), pp. 178–81.

62. MacRaild, *Culture, Conflict and Migration*, p. 12; Norris, 'Tow Law', p. 44.

63. An excellent overview of the spread of later Irish migration to Britain is C. G. Pooley, 'Segregation or integration? The residential experience of the Irish in mid-Victorian Britain', in R. Swift and S. Gilley (eds), *The Irish in Britain, 1815–1939* (London, 1989), pp. 60–83.

64. Finnegan, *Poverty and Prejudice*, tables 28 and 29, pp. 108–9. The question of skill is discussed by Pooley, 'Segregation or integration?', pp. 70–1.

65. MacRaild, *Culture, Conflict and Migration*, pp. 71, 79.

66. R. D. Lobban, 'The Irish community in Greenock in the nineteenth century', *Irish Geography*, 6 (1971).

67. R. A. Burchell, *The San Francisco Irish, 1848–1880* (Manchester, 1979), tables 6–7, pp. 56–7.

68. W. J. Lowe, *The Irish in Mid-Victorian Lancashire: the Shaping of a Working Class Community* (New York, 1990), table 11, p. 81.

69. Material on Cumbria and the north-east is contained in the penultimate, 'Letter XV'. See H. Heinrick, *A Survey of the Irish in England (1872)*. First published in the *Nation*. Edited with an introduction by A. O'Day (London, 1990), pp. 115–22. It is rarely clear whether Heinrick's 'Irish' means 'Irish-born' or a wider sense of an Irish community.

70. J. Denvir, *The Irish in Britain from the Earliest Times to the Fall and Death of Parnell* (London, 1892), p. 444.

71. *Ibid.*, pp. 442–4.

72. Pooley, 'Segregation or integration?', pp. 80–1.

3 SPIRITUAL AND SOCIAL BONDS: THE CULTURE OF IRISH CATHOLICISM

1. Evidence to Cornewall Lewis, Royal Commission on the Condition of the Poorer Classes in Ireland, Appendix G, *Report into the State of the Irish Poor in Great Britain*, Parliamentary Papers (1836), p. 2.

2. There is some debate over the figures. The English context of Catholicism is analysed brilliantly in John Bossy, *The English Catholic Community, 1750–1850* (London, 1975). For excellent introductions to the subject, see G. Parsons, 'Victorian Roman Catholicism: emancipation, expansion and achievement', in *idem, Religion in Victorian Britain* (Manchester, 1988). The best, brief overview of the development of English Catholicism is S. Gilley, 'Roman Catholic Church in England, 1780–1940', in S. Gilley and W. J. Sheils (eds), *A History of Religion in Britain: Practice and Belief from Pre-Roman Times to the Present* (Oxford, 1994).

3. For more on this, see G. F. A. Best, 'The Protestant constitution and its supporters, 1800–1829', *Transactions of the Royal Historical Society*, 5th series, 8 (1958).

4. See T. F. Moriarty, 'The Irish American response to Catholic emancipation', *Catholic Historical Review*, 66 (1980); J. H. Treble, 'The Irish agitation', in J. T. Ward (ed.), *Popular Movements, c.1830–50* (London, 1970).

5. See Emmet Larkin, 'The devotional revolution in Ireland 1850–75', *American Historical Review*, 77 (1972); D. W. Miller, 'Irish Catholicism and the Great Famine', *Journal of Social History*, 9 (1975).

6. Larkin, 'Devotional revolution', pp. 626–7; Miller, 'Irish Catholicism', p. 83.

7. S. Gilley, 'The Roman Catholic Church and the nineteenth-century Irish Diaspora', *Journal of Ecclesiastical History*, 35 (1984), pp. 206–7. This is an enormously important comparative statement, rich in ideas and examples.

8. P. O'Farrell, *Ireland's English Question: Anglo-Irish Relations, 1534–1970* (London, 1971); Gilley, 'Irish Diaspora', p. 195.

9. R. Samuel, 'An Irish religion', in *idem* (ed.), *Patriotism: the Making and Unmaking of British National Identity*, vol. II, *Minorities and Outsiders* (London, 1989), p. 94.

10. L. H. Lees, *Exiles of Erin: Irish Migrants in Victorian London* (New York and Manchester, 1979), pp. 164–212; Lowe, *Irish in Lancashire*, pp. 109–43.

11. G. P. Connolly, '"Little brother be at peace": the priest as holy man in the nineteenth-century ghetto', in W. J. Sheils (ed.), *Studies in Church History*, vol. XIX, *The Church and Healing* (Oxford, 1982), p. 191. See also his 'The transubstantiation of myth: towards a new popular history of nineteenth-century Catholicism in England', *Journal of Ecclesiastical History*, 35 (1984).

12. Gilley, 'Irish Diaspora', p. 206.

13. J. F. Champ, 'The demographic impact of Irish immigration on Birmingham Catholicism, 1800–1850', in W. J. Shiels and D. Wood (eds), *Studies in Church History*, vol. XXV, *The Church, Ireland and the Irish* (Oxford, 1989), pp. 233–7.

14. Charles Booth, quoted in Hugh McLeod, *Class and Religion in the Victorian City* (London, 1974), p. 34.

15. B. Aspinwall, 'The formation of the Catholic community in the west of Scotland: some preliminary outlines', *Innes Review*, 33 (1982); Lowe, *Irish in Lancashire*, pp. 112–13.

16. W. J. Lowe, *The Irish in Mid-Victorian Lancashire: the Shaping of a Working-Class Community* (New York, 1990), p. 109; McLeod, *Class and Religion*, p. 34, quoting a *Daily News* census; Booth claimed around one-third.

17. Frank Neal, *Sectarian Violence: the Liverpool Experience, 1819–1914* (Manchester, 1988), especially pp. 125–8. For London, see McLeod, *Class and Religion*, pp. 35, 40.

18. See Champ, 'Demographic impact of Irish immigration', pp. 239–41.

19. S. E. Baker, 'Orange and Green: Belfast, 1832–1912', in H. J. Dyos and M. Wolffe (eds), *The Victorian City: Image and Reality* (London, 1973); A. C. Hepburn, 'Irish Catholic in Belfast and Glasgow: connections and comparisons', in S. J. Connolly, R. A. Houston and R. J. Morris (eds), *Conflict. Identity and Economic Development: Ireland and Scotland, 1600–1939* (Preston, 1995), pp. 212, 214, 215; J. E. Handley, *The Irish in Modern Scotland* (Cork, 1947), p. 283.

20. M. C. Bishop, 'The social methods of Roman Catholicism in England', *Contemporary Review*, 39 (1877), p. 612.

21. See D. M. MacRaild, *Culture, Conflict and Migration: the Irish in Victorian Cumbria* (Liverpool, 1998), ch. 4.

22. James Hennesey, *American Catholics: a History of the Roman Catholic Community in the United States* (New York and Oxford, 1981), p. 75.

23. Henry Mayhew, quoted by R. Samuel, 'The Roman Catholic Church and the Irish poor', in R. Swift and S. Gilley, *The Irish in the Victorian City* (London, 1985), pp. 275–6.

24. *Ibid.*, p. 275.

25. *York Gazette*, 2 and 9 October 1847, quoted in F. Finnegan, *Poverty and Prejudice: a Study of Irish Immigrants in York, 1840–1875* (Cork, 1982), p. 16.

26. W. G. Todd, 'The Irish in England', *Dublin Review*, 41 (1856).

27. J. P. Dolan, *The Immigrant Church: New York's Irish and German Catholics, 1815–65* (London, 1983), p. 63.

28. *Ibid.* For details of the Catholic calendar, see M. Heinmann, *Victorian Catholic Devotion* (Oxford, 1985), *passim.*

29. Bishop, 'Social methods of Roman Catholicism', p. 607.

30. Booth's survey quoted in Samuel, 'Roman Catholic Church', p. 278.

31. Owen Dudley Edwards, 'The Irish priests in North America', in W. J. Sheils and D. Wood (eds), *Studies in Church History*, vol. XXV, *The Church, Ireland and the Irish* (Oxford, 1989), pp. 346, 351.

32. See J. M. Feheney, 'Delinquency among Irish Catholic children in Victorian London', *Irish Historical Studies*, 23 (1983).

33. Dolan, *Immigrant Church*, pp. 121–7.

34. S. Gilley, 'Heretic London, holy poverty and the Irish poor, 1830–1870', *Downside Review*, 89 (1971), p. 65.

35. *The Table*, 3 July 1847, quote in *ibid.*

36. Dolan, *Immigrant Church*, p. 127; B. Aspinwall, 'The Welfare State within the state: the Saint Vincent de Paul Society in Glasgow, 1848–1920', in W. J. Sheils and D. Wood (eds), *Voluntary Religion* (Oxford, 1986), pp. 445–59.

37. Lowe, *Irish in Lancashire*, pp. 123–5; Aspinwall, 'Catholic community', pp. 49–50.

38. M. J. Hickman, *Religion, Class and Identity* (Aldershot, 1995), p. 166, which is useful, more generally, on the Catholic education issue.

39. MacRaild, *Culture, Conflict and Migration*, pp. 101–3.

40. See J. R. Barrett, 'Why Paddy drank: the social importance of whiskey in pre-Famine Ireland', *Journal of Popular Culture*, 11 (1977).

41. See E. Malcolm, *'Ireland Sober, Ireland Free': Drink and Temperance in Nineteenth-Century Ireland* (New York and Dublin, 1986), ch. 3; also, H. F. Kearney, 'Fr Mathew: apostle of modernisation', in Art Cosgrove and D. McCartney (eds), *Studies in Irish History* (Dublin, 1979).

42. Lees, *Exiles of Erin*, pp. 209–12; Lowe, *Irish in Lancashire*, pp. 130–1; Aspinwall, 'Catholic community', p. 45.

43. Lowe, *Irish in Lancashire*, p. 130; Aspinwall, 'Catholic community', p. 52.

44. S. Fielding, *Class and Ethnicity: Irish Catholics in England, 1880–1939* (Buckingham, 1993), pp. 73–7; also see *idem*, 'The Catholic Whit Walk in Manchester and Salford, 1890–1939', *Manchester Region History Review*, 1 (1987).

45. MacRaild, *Culture, Conflict and Migration*, pp. 122–8.

46. For New York, see Hennesey, *American Catholics*, especially pp. 120, 163, 179–82. The best source for the north-west of England is Lowe, *Irish in Lancashire*, p. 133. See also Owen Dudley Edwards and P. J. Storey, 'The Irish press in Victorian Britain', in R. Swift and S. Gilley (eds), *The Irish in the Victorian City* (London, 1985).

47. T. Gallagher, *Glasgow, the Uneasy Peace: Religious Tension in Modern Scotland* (Manchester, 1987), p. 54.

48. Gilley, 'Irish Diaspora', pp. 206–7.

4 THE PROTESTANT IRISH

1. D. H. Akenson, *Small Differences: Irish Catholics and Irish Protestants, 1815–1922* (Dublin, 1988), p. 3.

2. It is impossible to indicate the full range of writings on Irish Protestants in North America. The earliest academic study on the American dimension is H. J. Ford, *The Scotch-Irish in America* (London, 1915), which is now rather dated. Other good studies are J. G. Leyburn, *The Scotch-Irish: A Social History* (Chapel Hill, 1962); E. E. R. Green, *Essay in Scotch-Irish History* (London, 1969), pp. 46–68; K. A. Miller, *Emigrants and Exiles: Ireland and the Irish Exodus to North America* (New York and Oxford, 1985), especially chs 4–6. For the Canadian dimension, see C. J. Houston and W. J. Smyth, *Irish Emigration and Canadian Settlement: Patterns, Links and Letters* (Toronto and Belfast, 1990) and *idem*, *The Sash Canada Wore: a Historical Geography of the Orange Order in Canada* (Toronto, 1980).

3. T. W. Moody, 'The Ulster Scots in colonial and revolutionary America', *Studies*, 34 (1945), pp. 211–21.

4. Although see D. H. Akenson, 'The historiography of Irish in the United States', in P. O'Sullivan (ed.), *The Irish World Wide*, vol. II, *Irish in the New Communities* (Leicester, 1992).

5. Leyburn, *Scotch-Irish*, p. 272.

6. W. J. Lowe, *The Irish in Mid-Victorian Lancashire: the Shaping of a Working-Class Community* (New York, 1990), pp. 2–3.

7. Houston and Smyth, *Canadian Settlement*, pp. 8, 188–9.

8. Trevor Parkhill, 'Convicts, orphans, settlers: patterns of emigration from Ulster to Australia, 1790–1860', in John O'Brien and Pauric Travers (eds), *The Irish Emigrant Experience in Australia* (Dublin, 1991), pp. 12–13.

9. D. Fitzpatrick, *Oceans of Consolation: Personal Accounts of Irish Migration to Australia* (Dublin, 1994), p. 14. The controversy over measuring Catholic and Protestant populations is examined in Akenson, *Small Differences*, pp. 62–3, in which is criticised the method of O. MacDonagh, 'The Irish in Victoria, 1851–91', in T. D. Williams (ed.), *Historical Studies* (Dublin, 1971).

10. See Ian S. Wood (ed.), *Scotland and Ulster* (Edinburgh, 1994), and E. W. McFarland, *Ireland and Scotland in the Age of Revolution: Planting the Green Bough* (Edinburgh, 1994), for this connection.

11. See McFarland, *Ireland and Scotland*, ch. 2.

12. C. Ó Gráda, *Ireland: a New Economic History, 1780–1939* (Oxford, 1994), p. 283.

13. G. Walker, 'The Protestant Irish in Scotland', in T. M. Devine (ed.), *Irish Immigrants and Scottish Society in the Nineteenth and Twentieth Centuries* (Edinburgh, 1994), pp. 45–6.

14. E. P. Thompson, *The Making of the English Working Class* (London, 1986), pp. 468–71 (first published 1963).

15. Royal Commission on the Condition of the Poorer Classes in Ireland, Appendix G, *Report into the State of the Irish Poor in Great Britain*, Parliamentary Papers (1836), p. v.

16. D. F. Macdonald, *Scotland's Shifting Population, 1770–1850* (Glasgow, 1937), p. 78; Walker, 'Protestant Irish in Scotland', p. 48.

17. N. Murray, *The Scottish Handloom Weavers, 1790–1850* (Edinburgh, 1979), pp. 31–2.

18. *State of the Irish Poor*, pp. 151–2.

19. E. McFarland, *Protestants First: Orangeism in Nineteenth Century Scotland* (Edinburgh, 1990), p. 104.

20. T. Gallagher, *Glasgow, the Uneasy Peace: Religious Tension in Modern Scotland* (Manchester, 1987), p. 27; Walker, 'Protestant Irish in Scotland', p. 49.

21. J. F. C. Barnes, 'The trade unions and radical activities of the Carlisle handloom weavers', *Transactions of the Cumberland and Westmorland Antiquarian and Archaeological Society*, 78 (1978), p. 150.

22. J. D. Marshall and J. K. Walton, *The Lake Counties from 1830 to the Mid-Twentieth Century* (Manchester, 1981), pp. 9–11, 22–4, 244.

23. A. Redford, *Labour Migration in England, 1800–1850* (Manchester, 1926), pp. 32–4.

24. See A. C. Hepburn, *A Past Apart: Studies in the History of Catholic Belfast, 1850–1950* (Belfast, 1996), especially chs 4–7.

25. Lynda Letford and Colin Pooley, 'Geographies of migration: Irish women in mid-nineteenth-century Ireland', in P. O'Sullivan (ed.), *The Irish World Wide: History, Heritage, Identity*, vol. IV, *Irish Women and Irish Migration* (Leicester, 1995), pp. 103–4.

26. Tom Gallagher, '"A tale of two cities": communal strife in Glasgow and Liverpool before 1914', in R. Swift and S. Gilley (eds), *The Irish in the Victorian City* (London, 1985), p. 110.

27. Walker, 'Protestant Irish in Scotland', p. 57.

28. A. B. Campbell, *The Lanarkshire Miners: a Social History of their Trade Unions, 1775–1874* (Edinburgh, 1979), pp. 178–81.

29. D. M. MacRaild, *Culture, Conflict and Migration: the Irish in Victorian Cumbria* (Liverpool, 1998), ch. 3.

30. S. Pollard and P. Robertson, *The British Shipbuilding Industry, 1870–1914* (Cambridge, Mass. and London, 1979), p. 163; McFarland, *Protestants First*, pp. 85–8.

31. These figures correspond with the estimates of C. G. Pooley, 'Segregation or integration? The residential experience of the Irish in mid-Victorian Britain', in R. Swift and S. Gilley (eds), *The Irish in Britain, 1815–1939* (London, 1989), pp. 60–83.

32. The point is made about the Ribbon tradition in Liverpool, but also applies to Orangeism. See John Belchem, '"Freedom and friendship to Ireland": Ribbonism in early nineteenth-century Liverpool', *International Review of Social History*, 39 (1994).

33. McFarland, *Protestants First*, p. 31.

34. D. W. Miller, 'The Armagh Troubles, 1784–95', in S. Clark and J. S. Donnelly (eds), *Irish Peasants: Violence and Political Unrest 1780–1914* (Manchester, 1983), pp. 162–3; Peter Gibbon, *The Origins of Ulster Unionism: the Formation of a Popular Protestant Politics and Ideology in Nineteenth-Century Ireland* (Manchester, 1975).

35. See Miller, 'Armagh Troubles', pp. 155–91; F. Neal, *Sectarian Violence: the Liverpool Experience, 1819–1914* (Manchester, 1988), pp. 19–36; *idem*, 'The Manchester origins of the English Orange Order', *Manchester Region History Review*, 4 (1990–1), table 2, p. 19; McFarland, *Protestants First*, ch. 3; Gallagher, *Glasgow*, ch. 2.

36. Neal, 'Manchester origins', p. 20; Lowe, *Irish in Mid-Victorian Lancashire*, p. 153.

37. Neal, *Sectarian Violence*, pp. 68–70, and *idem*, 'Manchester origins', pp. 20–1; McFarland, *Protestants First*, pp. 55–61.

38. Neal, *Sectarian Violence*, pp. 70–1, 171.

39. *Ibid.*, p. 184.

40. *Glasgow Herald*, 16 July 1873, suggested 40 000 to 50 000. Quoted in McFarland, *Protestants First*, p. 71.

41. *Ibid.*, p. 70–2.

42. Walker, 'Protestant Irish in Scotland', pp. 51–5; McFarland, *Protestants First*, pp. 47–94.

43. See Graham Walker, 'The Orange Order in Scotland between the wars', *International Review of Social History*, 37 (1992); Gallagher, '"A tale of two cities", pp. 107–29; *idem*, *Glasgow*, especially chs 1–3; see also Joan Smith, 'Class, skill and sectarianism in Glasgow and Liverpool, 1880–1914', in R. J. Morris (ed.), *Class, Power and Social Structure in British Nineteenth-Century Towns* (Leicester, 1986).

44. *Whitehaven Herald*, 13 July 1872.

45. MacRaild, *Culture, Conflict and Migration*, table 5.1, pp. 145–6.
46. *Whitehaven News*, 18 July 1875; *Whitehaven Herald*, 18 July 1874.
47. *Whitehaven News*, 16 July 1874.
48. Houston and Smyth, *Sash Canada Wore*, pp. 85–6.
49. *Barrow Herald*, 15 July 1882.
50. *Ibid.*, 14 July 1877.
51. D. M. MacRaild, '"Principle, party and protest": the language of Victorian Orangeism in the north of England', in S. West (ed.), *The Victorians and Race* (Leicester, 1996), pp. 136–9.
52. Neal, *Sectarian Violence*, pp. 224–49; John Bohsedt, 'More than one working class: Protestant–Catholic riots in Edwardian Liverpool', in J. Belchem (ed.), *Popular Politics, Riot and Labour: Essays in Liverpool History, 1790–1940* (Liverpool, 1992), pp. 173–216; Walker, 'Orange Order in Scotland between the wars', p. 182; T. Gallagher, *Edinburgh Divided* (Edinburgh, 1988); C. Holmes, 'Alexander Ratcliffe: militant Protestant and anti-semite', in T. Kusher and K. Lunn (eds), *Traditions of Intolerance: Historical Perspectives on Fascism and Race Discourse in Britain* (Manchester, 1989), pp. 196–217.
53. McFarland, *Protestants First*, ch. 2, is the best attempt to theorise on the Order.
54. *Ibid.*, pp. 88–90.
55. See the numerous examples in T. G. Fraser (ed.), *'We'll Follow the Drum': the Parading Tradition in Ireland* (Basingstoke, forthcoming).
56. D. Hempton, *Religious and Political Culture in Britain and Ireland* (Cambridge, 1996), p. 106.
57. R. Colls, 'Englishness and political culture', in *idem* and P. Dodds (eds), *Englishness: Politics and Culture, 1880–1920* (London, 1986), p. 40.
58. *Ibid.*, 15 March 1875.
59. Neal, *Sectarian Violence*, p. 52; Bohsedt, 'Protestant–Catholic riots', p. 207.
60. McFarland, *Protestants First*, p. 104.
61. Walker, 'Orange Order in Scotland', p. 178.
62. McFarland, *Protestants First*, p. 104.
63. Walker, 'Orange Order in Scotland', pp. 184–5.
64. *Carlisle Express*, 26 July 1884.

5 POLITICS, LABOUR AND PARTICIPATION

1. For a trenchant overview see John Belchem, *Popular Radicalism in Nineteenth-Century Britain* (Basingstoke, 1996).
2. For a critique, see Steve Fielding, *Class and Ethnicity: Irish Catholics in England, 1880–1939* (Buckingham, 1993), pp. 1–18 (quotation, p. 18).
3. Dorothy George, 'The London coal-heavers: attempts to regulate waterside labour in the eighteenth and nineteenth centuries', *Economic History Supplement to the Economic Journal* (1927), p. 236.
4. N. Murray, *The Scottish Handloom Weavers, 1790–1850* (Edinburgh, 1979), p. 208; M. J. Bric, 'The Irish and the evolution of "New Politics" in America', in P. J. Drudy (ed.), *The Irish in America: Emigration, Assimilation and Impact* (Cambridge, 1985), pp. 143–67.

5. G. Walker, 'The Protestant Irish in Scotland', in T. M. Devine (ed.), *Irish Immigrants and Scottish Society in the Nineteenth and Twentieth Centuries* (Edinburgh, 1994), p. 46; M. Elliot, *Partners in Revolution: The United Irishmen in France* (London, 1982), pp. 144–50.

6. These characters and their milieu are brilliantly illuminated by I. McCalman, *The Radical Underworld: Prophets, Revolutionaries and Pornographers in London, 1795–1840* (Cambridge, 1988). Elliot, *Partners in Revolution*, p. 144.

7. See B. Dobrée and G. E. Mainwaring, *The Floating Republic* (London, 1937, 3rd edn); Elliot, *Partners in Revolution*, pp. 136–43.

8. E. P. Thompson, *The Making of the English Working Class* (London, 1986), p. 187 (first published 1963); Elliot, *Partners in Revolution*, pp. 183–5.

9. T. Pakenham, *The Year of Liberty: the History of the Great Irish Rebellion of 1798* (London, 1969); Elliot, *Partners in Revolution*, pp. 163–240.

10. Elliot, *Partners in Revolution*, p. 307.

11. The only comprehensive treatment of Ribbonism is John Belchem, '"Freedom and friendship to Ireland": Ribbonism in early nineteenth-century Liverpool', *International Review of Social History*, 39 (1994).

12. *Ibid.*, pp. 34–50.

13. Thompson, *English Working Class*, p. 471. More generally, see R. G. Kirby and A. E. Musson, *The Voice of the People: John Doherty, 1798–1854: Trade Unionist, Radical and Factory Reformer* (Manchester, 1975).

14. J. H. Treble, 'The attitude of the Roman Catholic Church towards trade unionism in the north of England', *Northern History*, 5 (1970), pp. 96–9.

15. Royal Commission on the Condition of the Poorer Classes in Ireland, Appendix G, *Report into the State of the Irish Poor in Great Britain*, Parliamentary Papers (1836), p. xxiii.

16. Treble, 'Attitude of the Roman Catholic Church', pp. 100–1.

17. *Ibid.*, p. 102.

18. G. P. Connolly, 'The Catholic church and the first Manchester and Salford trade unions in the age of the Industrial Revolution', *Transactions of the Lancashire and Cheshire Antiquarian Society*, 135 (1985); *idem*, '"Little brother be at peace": the priest as holy man in the nineteenth century ghetto', in W. J. Sheils (ed.), *Studies in Church History*, vol. XIX, *The Churches and Healing* (Oxford, 1982), p. 204.

19. I. Prothero, *Artisans and Politics in Early Nineteenth-Century London* (Folkestone, 1979), pp. 114–16, 129.

20. T. F. Moriarty, 'The Irish American response to Catholic emancipation', *Catholic Historical Review*, 66 (1980).

21. Dorothy Thompson, 'Ireland and the Irish in English radicalism before 1850', in J. Epstein and D. Thompson (eds), *The Chartist Experience: Studies in Working-Class Radicalism and Culture, 1830–1860* (London, 1982); M. Hovell, *The Chartist Movement* (Manchester, 1918), pp. 92–7, contains an unflattering and one-sided assessment of O'Connor.

22. Thompson, 'Irish in English radicalism', p. 129.

23. See J. H. Treble, 'O'Connor, O'Connell and the attitude of Irish immigrants towards Chartism in the north of England, 1838–48', in J. Butt and I. F. Clarke (eds), *The Victorians and Social Protest: a Symposium*

(Newton Abbot, 1973); R. O'Higgins, 'The Irish influence in the Chartist movement', *Past and Present*, 20 (1961). Thompson, 'Irish in English radicalism', *passim*

24. Thompson, 'Irish in English radicalism', p. 123.
25. J. Saville and J. Bellamy (eds), *Dictionary of Labour Biography*, vol. VI (London, 1982), pp. 59–63; *Biographical Dictionary of Modern British Radicals*, vol. II (London, 1984), pp. 138–41.
26. Thompson, 'Irish in English radicalism', *passim*.
27. Thompson, *English Working Class*, p. 483; Thompson, 'Irish in English radicalism', pp. 120–4; G. Davis, *The Irish in Britain, 1815–1914* (Dublin, 1991), pp. 170–1.
28. Two excellent works are J. Saville, *1848: the British State and the Chartist Movement* (Cambridge, 1987), and J. Belchem, 'Nationalism, republicanism and exile: Irish emigrants and the revolution of 1848', *Past and Present*, 146 (1995).
29. Belchem, *ibid.*, p. 124.
30. *Ibid*, pp. 123–8; John Belchem, 'Liverpool in the year of revolution: the political and associational culture of the Irish immigrant community in 1848', in *idem* (ed.), *Popular Politics, Riot and Labour: Essays in Liverpool History, 1790–1940* (Liverpool, 1992), table 4.1, p. 96.
31. Belchem, 'Nationalism, republicanism and exile', pp. 127–8.
32. See, for example, N. Kirk, *The Growth of Working-Class Radicalism in Mid-Victorian England* (Urbana and Chicago, 1985), ch. 7; Belchem, '1848: Feargus O'Connor and the collapse of the mass platform', in J. Epstein and D. Thompson (eds), *The Chartist Experience: Studies in Working-Class Radicalism and Culture* (London, 1982); W. J. Lowe, *The Irish in Mid-Victorian Lancashire: the Shaping of a Working-Class Community* (New York, 1990), pp. 185ff.
33. *The Times*, 10 April 1848, quoted in John Belchem, 'English working-class radicals and the Irish, 1815–1850', in R. Swift and S. Gilley (eds), *Irish in the Victorian City* (London, 1985), p. 93.
34. Lowe, *Irish in Lancashire*, p. 186.
35. *Punch*, 15 (1848), pp. 154–5.
36. R. F. Foster, *Modern Ireland, 1600–1972* (London, 1988), p. 316.
37. R. V. Comerford, *The Fenians in Context: Irish Politics and Society 1848–1882* (Dublin, 1985).
38. For transatlantic connections, see W. D'Arcy, *The Fenian Movement in the United States, 1856–1886* (New York, 1971); V. A. Walsh, 'Irish nationalism and land reform: the role of the Irish in America', in P. J. Drudy (ed.), *The Irish in America: Emigration, Assimilation and Impact* (Cambridge, 1985), pp. 253–69.
39. J. Denvir, *The Irish in Britain from the Earliest Times to the Fall and Death of Parnell* (London, 1892), p. 182.
40. *Glasgow Herald*, 17 October 1867.
41. J. Denvir, *Life Story of an Old Rebel* (Dublin, 1910), pp. 81–5; P. Quinlivan and P. Rose, *The Fenians in England, 1865–1872: a Sense of Insecurity* (London, 1982), pp. 16–32.
42. Quinlivan and Rose, *Fenians in England*, especially pp. 50–3.

43. J. E. Handley, *The Irish in Modern Scotland* (Cork, 1947), p. 268.

44. *Barrow Herald*, 14 December 1866.

45. *The Times*, 12 February 1868, quoted in Alan O'Day, 'The political organisation of the Irish in Britain, 1867–90', in R. Swift and S. Gilley (eds), *The Irish in Britain, 1815–1939* (London, 1989), p. 188.

46. Handley, *Irish in Modern Scotland*, pp. 261–8, 274.

47. Owen Dudley Edwards and P. J. Storey, 'The Irish press in Victorian Britain', in R. Swift and S. Gilley (eds), *The Irish in Victorian Britain* (London, 1985), pp. 158–78.

48. O'Day, 'Political organisation', p. 190.

49. W. Walker, 'Irish immigrants in Scotland: their priests, politics and parochial life', *Historical Journal*, 15 (1972).

50. K. R. M. Short, *The Dynamite Wars: Irish-American Bombers in Victorian Britain* (London, 1979); Handley, *Irish in Modern Scotland*, p. 274.

51. O'Day, 'Political organisation', p. 204.

52. T. N. Brown, *Irish-American Nationalism, 1870–1890* (Westport, Connecticut, 1996), pp. 23, 41, 46. See also Walsh, 'Irish nationalism and land reform'.

53. E. Foner, 'Class, ethnicity and radicalism in the Gilded Age: the Land League and Irish America', *Marxist Perspectives*, 1 (1978), pp. 6, 43.

54. Handley, *Irish in Modern Scotland*, pp. 279–80.

55. O' Day, 'Political organisation', pp. 204–7.

56. For O'Connor's Liverpool connections, see L. W. Brady, *T. P. O'Connor and the Liverpool Irish* (London, 1983); also B. O'Connell, 'Irish nationalism in Liverpool, 1873–1923', *Eire–Ireland*, 10 (1975), pp. 24–37.

57. *Glasgow Observer*, 18 July 1891.

58. Handley, *Irish in Modern Scotland*, pp. 280–3.

59. Fielding, *Class and Ethnicity*, pp. 88–91.

60. *Keighley News*, 22 September 1893, and *Keighley Labour Journal*, 24 October 1896, cited in D. James, *Class and Politics in a Northern Industrial Town: Keighley 1880–1914* (Keele, 1995), p. 69.

61. E. McFarland, *Protestants First: Orangeism in Nineteenth Century Scotland* (Edinburgh, 1990), ch. 5.

62. F. Neal, *Sectarian Violence: the Liverpool Experience, 1819–1914* (Manchester, 1988), *passim*.

63. D. M. MacRaild, '"Principle, party and protest": the language of Victorian Orangeism in the north of England', in S. West (ed.), *The Victorians and Race* (Leicester, 1996).

64. D. Fitzpatrick, '"A curious middle place": the Irish in Britain, 1871–1921', in R. Swift and S. Gilley (eds), *The Irish in Britain, 1815–1939* (London, 1989), pp. 35–46.

65. *Ibid.*, p. 38.

66. Handley, *Irish in Modern Scotland*, pp. 291–4; A. C. Hepburn, 'Irish Catholics in Belfast and Glasgow in the early twentieth century: connections and comparisons', in S. J. Connolly, R. A. Houston and R. J. Morris (eds), *Conflict, Identity and Economic Development: Ireland and Scotland, 1600–1939* (Preston, 1995), p. 212.

67. *Catholic Herald*, 27 December 1919.

68. O'Connell, 'Irish nationalism in Liverpool', pp. 32–7.
69. The details in this paragraph are derived from Fitzpatrick, '"A curious middle place"', pp. 43–4.
70. Alan O'Day, 'The political representation of the Irish in Britain, 1850–1940', in G. Alderman, J. Leslie and K. E. Pollmann (eds), *Comparative Studies on Governments and Non-Dominant Ethnic Groups*, vol. IV, *Governments, Ethnic Groups and Political Representation* (New York and Aldershot, 1993), p. 79.
71. Labour Leader, 7 April 1894, quoted in T. W. Moody, 'Michael Davitt and the British labour movement, 1882–1906', *Transactions of the Royal Historical Society*, 5th series, 4 (1953), p. 72.
72. O'Day, 'Representation of the Irish', p. 79.

6 A CULTURE OF ANTI-IRISHNESS

1. M. A. G. Ó Tuathaigh, 'The Irish in nineteenth-century Britain: problems of integration', in R. Swift and S. Gilley (eds), *The Irish in the Victorian City* (London, 1985), p. 20.
2. A. O'Day, 'Varieties of anti-Irish behaviour, 1846–1922', in P. Panayi (ed.), *Racial Violence in Britain in the Nineteenth and Twentieth Centuries* (Leicester, 1996).
3. See R Swift, 'Heroes or villains: the Irish, crime and disorder in Victorian Britain', *Albion*, 29 (1997), for an excellent overview of the mid-Victorian period till the early 1870s.
4. Quoted in C. Kinealy, *This Great Calamity: the Irish Famine, 1845–52* (Dublin, 1994), p. 331.
5. Royal Commission on the Condition of the Poorer Classes in Ireland, Appendix G, *Report into the State of the Irish Poor in Great Britain*, Parliamentary Papers (1836).
6. *The Moral and Physical Condition of the Working Class* (Manchester, 1833), pp. 21–2.
7. T. Carlyle, *Chartism* (London, 1888 edn), p. 18.
8. F. Engels, *The Condition of the Working Class in England* (London, 1987), p. 124 (first published 1845).
9. Mayhew's *Morning Chronicle* journalism grew into a much larger project and was eventually published as *London Labour and the London Poor* (1851–62).
10. Reprinted in J. Ginswick (ed.), *Labour and the Poor in England and Wales, 1849–1851*, vol. I (London, 1983), p. 78.
11. *Ibid.*, p. 160.
12. *Ibid.*, p. 176.
13. L. P. Curtis, *Apes and Angels: the Irishman in Victorian Caricature* (London, 1971).
14. S. Gilley, 'English attitudes to the Irish in England, 1780–1900', in C. Holmes (ed.), *Immigrants and Minorities in British Society* (London, 1978), pp. 81, 85.
15. *Ibid.*, p. 89; M. Edgeworth, *Castle Rackrent* (London, 1801), pp. 181–2.
16. Ó Tuathaigh, 'Problems of integration', pp. 20–1.

17. R. F. Foster, 'Paddy and Mr Punch', in *idem*, *Paddy and Mr Punch: Connections in Anglo-Irish History* (London, 1993), pp. 171–94.

18. *Ibid.*, p. 193.

19. M. J. Hickman, *Religion, Class and Identity* (Aldershot, 1995), pp. 52–3.

20. M. McManus, 'Folk devils and moral panics? Irish stereotyping in mid-Victorian Durham', *Bulletin of the Durham County Local History Society*, 53 (1994), table 4, p. 35.

21. From R. Swift, 'Crime and the Irish in nineteenth-century Britain', in R. Swift and S. Gilley (eds), *The Irish in Britain, 1815–1939* (London, 1989), p. 165.

22. D. Fitzpatrick, '"A curious middle place": the Irish in Britain, 1871–1921', in R. Swift and S. Gilley (eds), *The Irish in Britain, 1815–1939* (London, 1989), table 1.6, p. 28.

23. *Judicial Statistics for England and Wales: Police and Criminal Proceedings – Prisons*, Parliamentary Papers (1860–91).

24. See Swift, 'Crime and the Irish'; S. J. Davies, 'Class and police in Manchester, 1829–80', in A. J. Kidd and K. W. Roberts (eds), *Class, City and Culture: Studies of the Social Policy and Cultural Production in Victorian Manchester* (Manchester, 1985); F. Neal, 'A criminal profile of the Liverpool Irish', *Transactions of the Historic Society of Lancashire and Cheshire*, 140 (1991). For an earlier period, P. Linebaugh, *The London Hanged* (London, 1991).

25. See R. Swift, '"Another Stafford Street row": law, order and the Irish presence in mid-Victorian Wolverhampton', *Immigrants and Minorities*, 3 (1984), p. 10; see also W. J. Lowe, 'The Lancashire constabulary, 1845–70: the social function of a Victorian police force', *Criminal History*, 4 (1983), p. 45.

26. *Barrow Herald*, 10 September 1864.

27. P. Mulkern, 'Irish immigrants and public disorder in Coventry, 1845–1975', *Midland History*, 21 (1996).

28. J. R. Barrett, 'Why Paddy drank: the social importance of whiskey in pre-Famine Ireland', *Journal of Popular Culture*, 11 (1977), p. 156.

29. *Whitehaven Herald*, 2 February 1871.

30. Gilley, 'English attitudes to the Irish', p. 85.

31. Carlyle, *Chartism*, p. 18.

32. Engels, *Condition*, p. 125.

33. F. Neal, 'Patriots or bigots? The political allegiances of the Liverpool ships' carpenters, 1815–51', in L. Fischer (ed.), *From Wheelhouse to Counting House: Essays in Maritime Business History*, International Maritime Economic History Association, *Research in Maritime History*, 2 (1992), pp. 27–8.

34. D. Fitzpatrick, '"A peculiar tramping people": the Irish in Britain, 1801–70', in W. E. Vaughan (ed.), *A New History of Ireland*, vol. V, *Ireland Under the Union, I: 1801–70* (Oxford, 1989), p. 643.

35. A. Redford, *Labour Migration in England, 1800–1850* (Manchester, 1926), pp. 115, 136, 138; Ian Gilmour, *Riots, Risings and Revolutions: Governance and Violence in Eighteenth-Century England* (London, 1993), p. 253 (first published 1992); A. Campbell, *The Lanarkshire Miners: a Social History of their Trade Unions, 1775–1974* (Edinburgh, 1979), pp. 178–201.

36. P. O'Leary, 'Anti-Irish riots in Wales, 1826–1882', *Llafur*, 5 (1991), pp. 28–30; Fitzpatrick, '"A peculiar tramping people"', p. 643; J. Hickey, *Urban Catholics* (London, 1967), pp. 53–4.

37. F. Neal, 'English–Irish conflict in the north west of England: economics, racism, anti-Catholicism or simple xenophobia?', *North West Labour History*, 16 (1991–2), p. 24.

38. J. E. Handley, *The Navvy in Scotland* (Cork, 1970), pp. 267–320.

39. Terry Coleman, *The Railway Navvies: a History of the Men Who Made the Railways* (London, 1965). For the Barrow incident, see D. M. MacRaild, *Culture, Conflict and Migration: the Irish in Victorian Cumbria* (Liverpool, 1998), pp. 172–7.

40. E. R. Norman, 'Church and state since 1800', in S. Gilley and W. J. Sheils (eds), *A History of Religion in Britain: Practice and Belief from Pre-Roman Times to the Present* (Oxford, 1994), p. 277.

41. J. H. Treble, 'The Irish agitation', in J. T. Ward (ed.), *Popular Movements, c. 1830–50* (London, 1970), especially pp. 152–3. Also see G. F. A. Best, 'The Protestant constitution and its supporters, 1800–1829', *Transactions of the Royal Historical Society*, 8 (1958), pp. 105–27; G. I. T. Machin, *The Catholic Question in English Politics, 1820–1830* (Oxford, 1964).

42. L. Colley, *Britons: Forging the Nation, 1707–1837* (New Haven and London, 1992), pp. 330–4.

43. E. R. Norman, *Anti-Catholicism in Victorian England* (London, 1968), p. 13.

44. For the Canadian dimension see J. R. Miller, 'Anti-Catholic thought in Victorian Canada', *Canadian Historical Review*, 66 (1985).

45. W. R. Ralls, 'The Papal Aggression of 1850: a study of Victorian anti-Catholicism', in G. Parsons (ed.), *Religion in Victorian Britain*, vol. IV, *Interpretations* (Manchester, 1988).

46. G. Parsons, 'Victorian Roman Catholicism: emancipation, expansion and achievement', in *idem* (ed.), *Religion in Victorian Britain*, vol. I, *Traditions* (Manchester, 1988), p. 148; Ralls, 'Papal Aggression', p. 116.

47. Ralls, 'Papal Aggression', pp. 118–19.

48. *Ibid.*, pp. 131–42, 156–7.

49. P. Millward, 'The Stockport riots of 1852: a study of anti-Catholic and anti-Irish sentiment', in R. Swift and S. Gilley (eds), *The Irish in the Victorian City* (London, 1985).

50. F. Neal, *Sectarian Violence: the Liverpool Experience, 1819–1914* (Manchester, 1988), pp. 17, 21, 30–1.

51. J. E. Handley, *The Navvy in Scotland* (Cork, 1970), pp. 269–70.

52. John Foster, *Class Struggle and the Industrial Revolution* (London, 1974), pp. 243–6.

53. S. Gilley 'The Garibaldi Riots of 1862', *Historical Journal*, 16 (1973); F. Neal, 'The Birkenhead Garibaldi Riots of 1862', *Transactions of the Historic Society of Lancashire and Cheshire*, 131 (1982).

54. Gilley, 'Garibaldi Riots', p. 703.

55. Neal, *Sectarian Violence*, pp. 176–83.

56. For Murphy, see W. L. Arnstein, 'The Murphy Riots: a Victorian dilemma', *Victorian Studies*, 19 (1975); W. J. Lowe, *The Irish in Mid-Victorian Lancashire: the Shaping of a Working-Class Community* (New York,

1990), pp. 151–73; R. Swift, '"Another Stafford Street row"', pp. 94–104; MacRaild, *Culture, Conflict and Migration*, pp. 177–83; P. Joyce, *Work, Society and Politics* (Brighton, 1980), pp. 255–61.

57. MacRaild, *Culture, Conflict and Migration*, p. 180–1.
58. A. O'Day, 'Anti-Irish behaviour'.
59. Neal, *Sectarian Violence*, pp. 186–7.
60. MacRaild, *Culture, Conflict and Migration*, pp. 183–9.
61. The details in this paragraph derive from G. I. T. Machin, 'The last Victorian anti-ritualism campaign, 1895–1906', *Victorian Studies*, 25 (1982); Neal, *Sectarian Violence*, pp. 200, 207–13; P. J. Waller, *Democracy and Sectarianism: a Political and Social History of Liverpool, 1868–1939* (Liverpool, 1981), p. 191.
62. MacRaild, *Culture, Conflict and Migration*, p. 195.
63. John Bohsedt, 'More than one working class: Protestant–Catholic riots in Edwardian Liverpool', in J. Belchem (ed.), *Popular Politics, Riot and Labour: Essays in Liverpool History, 1790–1940* (Liverpool, 1992), p. 178.
64. *Ibid.*, pp. 185–7.

BIBLIOGRAPHICAL ESSAY

The following list is indicative rather than exhaustive. Many other studies are cited in the text. Note that London is the place of publication, unless otherwise stated.

Important theoretical contexts are discussed in two fine works which, despite their titles, have important implications for the study of Irish and other emigrant flows to Britain and the United States: Binley Thomas, *Migration and Economic Growth: a Study of Great Britain and the Atlantic Economy* (Cambridge, 1954) and D. E. Baines, *Migration in a Mature Economy: Emigration and Internal Migration in England and Wales, 1861–1900* (Cambridge, 1985). The best short analyses of the Irish in Britain are two by David Fitzpatrick, '"A peculiar tramping people": the Irish in Britain, 1801–70' and his 'The Irish in Britain, 1871–1921', both of which appear in W. E. Vaughan (ed.), *A New History of Ireland*, vol. V, *Ireland Under the Union, I: 1801–1870* (Oxford, 1986) and vol. VI, *Ireland Under the Union, II: 1870–1921* (Oxford, 1996); and Roger Swift's *The Irish in Britain, 1815–1914: Perspectives and Sources* (1991). For more detailed treatments, see J. A. Jackson's *The Irish in Britain* (1963); Graham Davis, *The Irish in Britain, 1815–1914* (Dublin, 1991), which is particularly strong on historiography; and three volumes edited by R. Swift and S. Gilley: *The Irish in Britain, 1815–1939* (1989), *The Irish in the Victorian City* (1985) and *The Irish in Victorian Britain: the Local Dimension* (Dublin, forthcoming). Ruth-Ann Harris, *The Nearest Place that Wasn't Ireland: Early Nineteenth-Century Labor Migration* (Ames, Iowa, 1994) is controversial for taking Engels at face value and for arguing that the majority of the Irish in Britain were temporary sojourners. Patrick O'Sullivan's monumental series on the Irish Diaspora contains many good essays on the British dimension: *The Irish World Wide: History, Heritage, Identity*, six vols (Leicester, 1992–7), I, *Patterns of Migration*; II, *Irish in the New Communities*; III, *The Creative Migrant*; IV, *Irish Women and Irish Migration*; V, *Religion and Identity*; VI, *The Meaning of the Famine* (see particularly Swift's essay in vol. II). Two contemporary accounts, H. Heinrick, *A Survey of the Irish in England, 1872* (1990; edited with an introduction by A. O'Day) and J.

Denvir, *The Irish in Britain from the Earliest Times to the Fall and Death of Parnell* (1892), provide fascinating insights into the Irish in Britain. The best books on the Scottish dimension are still J. E. Handley, *The Irish in Scotland, 1789–1845* (Cork, 1943) and his *The Irish in Modern Scotland* (Cork, 1947), although T. M. Devine (ed.), *Irish Immigrants and Scottish Society in the Nineteenth and Twentieth Centuries* (Edinburgh, 1991) contains a number of good essays.

The best short introductions to emigration from Ireland are two essays by David Fitzpatrick: 'Emigration, 1801–70' and 'Emigration, 1871–1921', which both appear in Vaughan (ed.), *A New History of Ireland*, vols V and VI. A superlative introduction to the wider population issue is L. Kennedy and L. A. Clarkson, 'Birth, death and exile: Irish population history, 1700–1921', in B. J. Graham and L. J. Proudfoot (eds), *An Historical Geography of Ireland* (1993). The standard book-length treatment of pre-famine population is K. H. Connell, *The Population History of Ireland, 1750–1845* (Oxford, 1950), and on the later period it is T. W. Guinnane, *The Vanishing Irish: Households, Migration and the Rural Economy in Ireland* (Princeton, 1996). Detailed treatment of the economic background can be found in J. Mokyr, *Why Ireland Starved: a Quantitative and Analytical History of the Irish Economy, 1800–1850* (1983) and in two volumes by C. Ó Gráda, *Ireland Before and After the Famine: Explorations in Economic History, 1800–1925* (Manchester, 1988) and *Ireland: a New Economic History, 1780–1939* (Oxford, 1994). The famine is now well covered in a single-authored volume, C. Kinealy, *This Great Calamity: the Irish Famine, 1845–52* (Dublin, 1994), although E. Margaret Crawford (ed.), *The Hungry Stream: Essays on Emigration and Famine* (Belfast, 1997) includes much excellent up-to-date research. For the Famine's affect on Britain, see Frank Neal, *Black '47: Britain and the Famine Irish* (Basingstoke, 1997), which expertly marshals masses of statistical data.

Several book-length studies provide an introduction to the regional dimension of Irish settlement: F. Finnegan, *Poverty and Prejudice: a Study of Irish Immigrants in York, 1840–1875* (Cork, 1982); L. H. Lees, *Exiles of Erin: Irish Migrants in Victorian London* (New York and Manchester, 1979); W. J. Lowe, *The Irish in Mid-Victorian Lancashire: the Shaping of a Working-Class Community* (New York, 1990); and D. M. MacRaild, *Culture, Conflict and Migration: the Irish in Victorian Cumbria* (Liverpool, 1998).

The social geography of Irish communities in Britain has been the subject of some debate. Contributors include: E. P. Thompson, *The Making of the English Working Class* (1963); J. M. Werly, 'The Irish in Manchester, 1832–49', *Irish Historical Studies*, 18 (1972–3); Graham Davis, *Irish in Britain* and his 'Little Irelands', in Swift and Gilley (eds), *Irish in Britain, 1815–1939*; M. A. Busteed, R. I. Hodgson and T. F. Kennedy,

'The myth and reality of Irish migrants in mid-Victorian Manchester: a preliminary study', in O'Sullivan (ed.) *The Irish World Wide*, vol. II, *Irish in the New Communities*; M. A. Busteed, 'The Irish in nineteenth-century Manchester', *Irish Studies Review*, 18 (1997); Colin G. Pooley, 'The residential segregation of migrant communities in mid-Victorian Liverpool', *Transactions of the Institute of British Geographers*, 2 (1977) and his 'Segregation or integration? The residential experience of the Irish in mid-Victorian Britain', in Swift and Gilley (eds), *Irish in Britain, 1815–1939*. Studies of Irish lives and living conditions include: J. Haslett and W. J. Lowe, 'Household structure and overcrowding among the Lancashire Irish, 1851–1871', *Histoire Sociale*, 10 (1977); and L. H. Lees, 'Patterns of lower-class life: Irish slum communities in nineteenth-century London', in S. Therstrom and R. Sennett (eds), *Nineteenth Century Cities* (New Haven, 1969) and his 'Mid-Victorian migration and the Irish family economy', *Victorian Studies*, 20 (1976).

The debate over Irish labour is encapsulated by E. H. Hunt, *Regional Wage Variations in Britain, 1850–1973* (Oxford, 1973), who argues that the Irish *did* affect wages levels in Britain, and by J. G. Williamson, 'The impact of the Irish on British labor markets during the Industrial Revolution', *Journal of Economic History*, 46 (1986), who comes from an econometric perspective to argue that they *did not*.

The clearest introduction to the subject of Catholicism in England is S. Gilley, 'Roman Catholic Church in England, 1780–1940', in S. Gilley and W. J. Sheils (eds), *A History of Religion in Britain: Practice and Belief from Pre-Roman Times to the Present* (Oxford, 1994). The religious transformation of post-Famine Ireland is debated by Emmet Larkin, 'The devotional revolution in Ireland 1850–75', *American Historical Review*, 77 (1972); and D. W. Miller, 'Irish Catholicism and the Great Famine', *Journal of Social History*, 9 (1975). Major studies of Irish Catholics in Britain are Steve Fielding, *Class and Ethnicity: Irish Catholics in England, 1880–1939* (Buckingham, 1993); and M. J. Hickman, *Religion, Class and Identity* (Aldershot, 1995). G. P. Connolly has written a clutch of important essays on Irish migrants and the Victorian Catholic Church, including 'The transubstantiation of myth: towards a new popular history of nineteenth-century Catholicism in England', *Journal of Ecclesiastical History*, 35 (1984), and 'Irish and Catholic: myth or reality? Another sort of Irish and the renewal of the clerical profession among Catholics in England, 1791–1918', in Swift and Gilley (eds), *Irish in the Victorian City*. Gilley's contribution is enormous – in addition to essays in his own volumes (edited with Swift), see 'The Roman Catholic Church and the nineteenth-century Irish Diaspora', *Journal of Ecclesiastical History*, 35 (1984) and 'Catholic faith of the Irish slums: London, 1840–70', in H. J. Dyos and

M. Wolff (eds), *The Victorian City: Image and Reality*, vol. II (1973). Other important works include those of Raphael Samuel, in particular 'Comers and goers', in Dyos and Woolf (eds), *The Victorian City*, 'The Roman Catholic Church and the Irish poor', in Swift and Gilley (eds), *Irish in the Victorian City*, and 'An Irish religion', in R. Samuel (ed.), *Patriotism: the Making and Unmaking of British National Identity*, vol. II, *Minorities and Outsiders* (1989). For some American comparisons, see J. P. Dolan, *The Immigrant Church: New York's Irish and German Catholics, 1815–65* (1983); and H. McLeod, 'Popular Catholicism in New York', in W. J. Shiels and D. Wood (eds), *Studies in Church History*, vol. XXV, *The Church, Ireland and the Irish* (Oxford, 1989). The role of the priest is vital. For his training, see P. Doyle, 'The education and training of Roman Catholic priests in the nineteenth century', *Journal of Ecclesiastical History*, 35 (1984); for his power among the Irish, see G. P. Connolly, '"Little brother be at peace": the priest as holy man in the nineteenth century ghetto', in W. J. Shiels (ed.), *Studies in Church History*, vol. XIX, *The Churches and Healing* (Oxford, 1982); for his involvement in politics, see W. A. Walker, 'Irish immigrants in Scotland: their priests, politics and parochial life', *Historical Journal*, 15 (1972); and for an excellent investigation of the American dimension, see Owen Dudley Edwards, 'The Irish priests in North America', in Sheils and Wood (eds), *Studies in Church History*, vol. XXV.

The important area of popular Protestantism and anti-Catholicism yields much on the Irish. The best introductions are E. R. Norman, *Anti-Catholicism in Victorian England* (1968), which contains many useful documents, and D. G. Paz, *Popular Anti-Catholicism in Mid-Victorian England* (Stanford, California, 1992). Periodical literature, a vital conduit for anti-Catholic ideas, is considered in D. G. Paz, 'Anti-Catholicism, anti-Irish stereotyping and anti-Celtic racism in mid-Victorian working-class periodicals', in *Albion*, winter (1986). The 'popular' dimension of anti-Catholicism and anti-Irish violence has yielded many fascinating books and essays, including Tom Gallagher, *Glasgow, the Uneasy Peace: Religious Tension in Modern Scotland* (Manchester, 1987); and Frank Neal, *Sectarian Violence: the Liverpool Experience, 1819–1914* (Manchester, 1988). For Scotland, also see Steve Bruce, *No Pope of Rome: Militant Protestantism in Modern Scotland* (Edinburgh, 1985). The tensions between class and ethnicity have been demonstrated in two fine essays by Joan Smith: 'Labour tradition in Glasgow and Liverpool', *History Workshop*, 17 (1984); and 'Class, skill and sectarianism in Glasgow and Liverpool, 1890–1914', in R. J. Morris (ed.), *Class, Power and Social Structure in British Nineteenth-Century Towns* (Leicester, 1986). The best contextual study of the mid-Victorian years is Alan O'Day, 'Varieties of anti-Irish behaviour, 1846–1922', in P. Panayi (ed.), *Racial Violence in Britain in the Nineteenth and*

Twentieth Centuries (Leicester, 1996). For the so-called 'Papal Aggression', see W. L. Ralls, 'The Papal Aggression of 1850: a study of Victorian anti-Catholicism', in G. Parsons (ed.), *Religion in Victorian Britain*, vol. IV, *Interpretations*; and P. Millward, 'The Stockport riots of 1852: a study of anti-Catholic and anti-Irish sentiment', in Swift and Gilley (eds), *Irish in the Victorian City*. For the 'no-popery' lecturing career of William Murphy, see: W. L. Arnstein, 'The Murphy Riots: a Victorian dilemma', *Victorian Studies*, 19 (1975), D. M. MacRaild, 'William Murphy, the Orange Order and communal violence: the Irish in west Cumberland, 1971–84', in P. Panayi (ed.), *Racial Violence in Britain 1840–1950* (Leicester, 1993). The Murphy Riots, Irish crime and violence more generally are the subject of Roger Swift's important essay '"Another Stafford Street row": law, order and the Irish presence in mid-Victorian Wolverhampton', *Immigrants and Minorities*, 3 (1984). See also S. Gilley, 'The Garibaldi Riots of 1862', *Historical Journal*, 16 (1973); and Frank Neal, 'The Birkenhead Garibaldi Riots of 1862', *Transactions of the Historic Society of Lancashire and Cheshire*, 131 (1982). Essays emphasising Liverpool's pre-eminent position in this respect include: Tom Gallagher, '"A tale of two cities": communal strife in Glasgow and Liverpool before 1914', in Swift and Gilley (eds), *Irish in the Victorian City*; Anne Bryson, 'Riotous Liverpool, 1815–60', and John Bohstedt, 'More than one working class: Protestant and Catholic riots in Edwardian Liverpool', both of which appear in J. Belchem (ed.), *Popular Politics, Riot and Labour: Essays in Liverpool History, 1790–1940* (Liverpool, 1992). The continuing English obsession with Romanisation (which had an Irish dimension) is examined by G. I. T. Machin, 'The last Victorian anti-ritualism campaign, 1895–1906', *Victorian Studies*, 25 (1982).

A number of books and articles deal with the Orange Order, including: F. Neal, 'Manchester origins of the English Orange Order', *Manchester Region History Review*, 4 (1990–1); E. McFarland, *Protestants First: Orangeism in Nineteenth Century Scotland* (Edinburgh, 1990); G. Walker, 'The Orange Order in Scotland between the wars', *International Review of Social History*, 37 (1992); and D. M. MacRaild, '"Principle, party and protest": the language of Victorian Orangeism in the north of England', in Shearer West (ed.), *The Victorians and Race* (Leicester, 1996). Excellent material on the North American dimension is located in: C. D. Gimpsey, 'Internal ethnic friction: Orange and Green in nineteenth-century New York, 1868–1872', in *Immigrants and Minorities*, 1 (1982); M. A. Gordon, *The Orange Riots: Irish Political Violence in New York City, 1870 and 1871* (Ithaca and London, 1993); C. J. Houston and W. J. Smyth, *The Sash Canada Wore: a Historical Geography of the Orange Order in Canada* (Toronto, 1980) and their 'Transferred loyalties: Orangeism in the United States and Ontario', *American Review of Canadian Studies*, 14 (1984).

The debate about anti-Irish 'racism' was begun by L. P. Curtis in his two books *Anglo-Saxons and Celts: a Study of Anti-Irish Prejudice in Victorian England* (New York, 1968) and *Apes and Angels: the Irishman in Victorian Caricature* (1971). He was subsequently challenged by S. Gilley in an essay, 'English attitudes to the Irish in England, 1780–1900', in C. Holmes (ed.), *Immigrants and Minorities in British Society* (London, 1978). Since then, several others have weighed with their views, including: M. A. G. Ó Tuathaigh, 'The Irish in nineteenth-century Britain: problems of integration', in R. Swift and S. Gilley (eds), *The Irish in the Victorian City* (London, 1985) (first published in *Transactions of the Royal Historical Society*, 5th series, 31 (1981)); R. F. Foster, 'Paddy and Mr Punch', in his *Paddy and Mr Punch: Connections in Anglo-Irish History* (1993); and M. J. Hickman, *Religion, Class and Identity* (Aldershot, 1995). See also F. Neal, 'English–Irish conflict in the north west of England: economics, racism, anti-Catholicism or simple xenophobia?', *North West Labour History*, 16 (1991–2). The idea of Ireland and the Irish as 'outsiders' under the Act of Union is discussed in a perceptive essay by D. G. Boyce, '"Marginal Britons": the Irish', in R. Colls and P. Dodds (eds), *Englishness: Politics and Culture* (London, 1986), which is a good starting point. Proof that English lampooning of the Irish is an age-old phenomenon is illustrated by John Gillingham in his essay 'The origins of English imperialism', *History Today*, 37 (1987). P. O'Farrell, *Ireland's English Question: Anglo-Irish Relations, 1534–1970* (1971) provides much useful context.

The best starting points on Irish criminality are two essays by Roger Swift: 'Crime and the Irish in nineteenth-century Britain', in Swift and Gilley (eds), *Irish in Britain*, and 'Heroes or villains? The Irish, crime and disorder in Victorian Britain', *Albion*, 29 (1997). Excellent local case studies include P. Mulkern, 'Irish immigrants and public disorder in Coventry, 1845–1975', *Midland History*, 21 (1996); and M. McManus, 'Folk devils and moral panics? Irish stereotyping in mid-Victorian Durham', *Bulletin of the Durham County Local History Society*, 53 (1994). S. J. Davies, 'Class and police in Manchester, 1829–80', in A. J. Kidd and K. W. Roberts (eds), *City, Class and Culture: Studies of the Social Policy and Cultural Production in Victorian Manchester* (Manchester, 1985) suggests that Irish crime rates might have been explained by the number of Protestant Irish who joined the police, while Frank Neal, 'A criminal profile of the Liverpool Irish', *Transactions of the Historic Society of Lancashire and Cheshire*, 140 (1991), cites religious hostility.

The politics of the Irish community was wide and varied. Little has been written on the French Revolutionary phase, although the Irish in Britain appear regularly in Marianne Elliot's brilliant study *Partners in Revolution: the United Irishmen in France* (1982), while Maurice J. Bric, 'The

Irish and the evolution of "New Politics" in America', in P. J. Drudy (ed.), *The Irish in America: Emigration, Assimilation and Impact* (Cambridge, 1985) explains the Irish role in American radicalism. The links between Irish and British radicalism and the effect of Irish issues on British politics in the pre-1850 period are discussed by J. H. Treble, 'The Irish agitation', in J. T. Ward (ed.), *Popular Movements, c. 1830–50* (1970); and John Belchem, 'English working-class radicalism and the Irish, 1815–1850', in Swift and Gilley (eds), *Irish in the Victorian City*. For trade union politics, the Irish and their church, see G. P. Connolly, 'The Catholic Church and the first Manchester and Salford trade unions in the age of the Industrial Revolution', *Transactions of the Lancashire and Cheshire Antiquarian Society*, 135 (1985); and J. H. Treble, 'The attitude of the Roman Catholic Church towards trade unionism in the north of England, 1833–42', *Northern History*, 5 (1970). The organic associationalism of Irish community life has been the subject of incisive essays by John Belchem: '"Freedom and friendship to Ireland": Ribbonism in early nineteenth-century Liverpool', *International Review of Social History*, 39 (1994), and 'The immigrant alternative: ethnic and sectarian mutuality among the Liverpool Irish during the nineteenth century', in O. Ashton, R. Fyson and S. Roberts (eds), *The Duty of Discontent: Essays for Dorothy Thompson* (1995). The Irish involvement in Chartism is discussed in several important works, including R. O'Higgins, 'Irish trade unions and politics, 1830–50', *Historical Journal*, 4 (1961) and her 'The Irish influence in the Chartist movement', *Past and Present*, 20 (1961); and in J. H. Treble, 'O'Connor, O'Connell and the attitudes of Irish immigrants towards Chartism in the north of England, 1838–48', in J. Butt and I. F. Clarke (eds), *The Victorians and Social Protest: a Symposium* (Newton Abbot, 1973); and D. Thompson, 'Ireland and the Irish in English radicalism before 1850', in J. Epstein and D. Thompson (eds), *The Chartist Experience: Studies in Working-Class Radicalism and Culture, 1830–1860* (1982). Feargus O'Connor is examined by John Belchem, '1848: Feargus O'Connor and the collapse of the mass platform', in Epstein and Thompson (eds), *The Chartist Experience*. The momentous year of 1848 is also covered in a number of important works: John Saville's excellent *1848: the British State and the Chartist Movement* (Cambridge, 1987), and three shorter pieces by John Belchem: 'The Year of Revolutions: the political and associational culture of the Irish immigrant community in 1848', in Belchem (ed.), *Popular Politics, Riot and Labour*, 'Republican spirit and military science: the "Irish brigade" and Irish-American nationalism in 1848', *Irish Historical Studies*, 24 (1994), and 'Nationalism, republicanism and exile: Irish emigrants and the revolutions of 1848', *Past and Present*, 146 (1995). The descent into sectarian politics in Lancashire is dissected by Neville

Kirk, 'Ethnicity, class and popular Toryism, 1850–1870', in K. Lunn (ed.), *Hosts, Immigrants and Minorities: Historical Responses to Newcomers in British Society, 1870–1914* (Folkestone, 1980). The next important phase is the 'Fenian scare' of the 1860s, which has been well documented by T. W. Moody, *Davitt and the Irish Revolution 1846–82* (Oxford, 1981), which focuses on a key leader; R. V. Comerford, *The Fenians in Context: Irish Politics and Society 1848–1882* (Dublin, 1985), which is the best general study; and P. Quinlivan and P. Rose, *The Fenians in England, 1865–1872: a Sense of Insecurity* (1982), which provides a detailed narrative of the British aspects. K. R. M. Short, *The Dynamite Wars: Irish-American Bombers in Victorian Britain* (1979) examines the resurgence of the 1880s. Alan O'Day is the main historian of the Home Rule phase, and his works include: *The English Face of Irish Nationalism* (London, 1977), 'Irish influence on parliamentary elections in London, 1885–1914: a simple test', in Swift and Gilley (eds), *Irish in the Victorian City*, 'The political organisation of the Irish in Britain, 1867–90', in Swift and Gilley (eds), *Irish in Britain, 1815–1939*, and 'The political representation of the Irish in Great Britain, 1850–1940', in G. Alderman, J. Leslie and K. E. Pollmann (eds), *Comparative Studies on Governments and Non-dominant Ethnic Groups in Europe*, vol. IV, *Governments, Ethnic Groups and Political Representation* (New York and Aldershot, 1993). L. W. Brady, *T. P. O'Connor and the Liverpool Irish* (1983) and B. O'Connell, 'Irish nationalism in Liverpool, 1873–1923', *Eire–Ireland*, 10 (1975), discuss the important Liverpool aspect. On the Scottish dimension, see Ian S. Wood, 'Irish nationalism and radical politics in Scotland, 1880–1906', *Bulletin of the Scottish Labour History Society*, 9 (1975), and 'Irish immigrants and Scottish radicalism, 1880–1906', in I. MacDougall (ed.), *Essays in Scottish Labour History* (Edinburgh, 1978). Discussions of the American scene at this time are found in Thomas N. Brown, *Irish-American Nationalism, 1870–1890* (Westport, Connecticut, 1966); Eric Foner, 'Class, ethnicity and radicalism in the Gilded Age: the Land League and Irish America', *Marxist Perspectives*, 1 (1978); David N. Doyle, 'Unestablished Irishmen: new immigrants and industrial America, 1870–1910', in Dirk Hoeder (ed.), *American Labor and Immigration History, 1877–1920s: Recent Research* (Urbana and London, 1983); and Victor A. Walsh, 'Irish nationalism and land reform: the role of the Irish in America', in Drudy (ed.), *The Irish in America*, which should be read in tandem.

Relatively little has been written about the Irish in the British labour movement. Ian S. Wood considers the Scottish scene through the activities of one important figure in 'John Wheatley, the Irish and the labour movement in Scotland', *Innes Review*, 31 (1980). For the English aspect, see Steve Fielding, 'Irish politics in Manchester and Salford,

1890–1939', *International Review of Social History*, 33 (1988), and the later chapters of his *Class and Ethnicity: Irish Catholics in England*. T. W. Moody, 'Michael Davitt and the British labour movement, 1882–1906', *Transactions of the Royal Historical Society*, 5th series, 4 (1953) examines the limitations of Irish–British cooperation in the political sphere.

The importance of temporary sojourners and itinerant labourers has been the focus of several important studies, including: J. H. Johnson, 'Harvest migration from nineteenth-century Ireland', *Transactions of the Institute of British Geographers*, 41 (1967); B. M. Kerr, 'Irish seasonal migration to Great Britain, 1800–38', *Irish Historical Studies*, 3 (1942–3); C. Ó Gráda, 'Seasonal migration and post-Famine adjustment in the west of Ireland', *Studia Hibernica*, 13 (1973); G. Moran, '"A passage to Britain": seasonal migration and social change in the west of Scotland, 1870–1890', *Saothar*, 13 (1988); Sarah Barber, 'Irish migrant agricultural labourers in nineteenth century Lincolnshire', *Saothar*, 8 (1982); and Ann O'Dowd, *Spalpeens and Tattie Hokers: History and Folklore of Irish Migratory Agricultural Workers in Ireland and Britain* (Dublin, 1991). The navvies have been uncovered in a number of works, including Terry Coleman, *The Railway Navvies: a History of the Men Who Made the Railways* (1965), and J. E. Handley, *The Navvy in Scotland* (Cork, 1970), which are the best.

Little has yet been written about either Irish women, the middle class or Protestants. Lees, 'Patterns of lower-class life', 'Mid-Victorian migration and the Irish family economy' and *Exiles of Erin*, and an essay by Lynda Letford and Colin Pooley, 'Geographies of migration: Irish women in mid-nineteenth-century Ireland', in O'Sullivan (ed.), *The Irish World Wide*, vol. III, are among the very few exceptions. And only G. Walker, 'The Protestant Irish in Scotland', in Devine (ed.), *Irish Immigration and Scottish Society in the Nineteenth and Twentieth Centuries*, has written solely about Irish Protestants.

Finally, much is to be gained by comparing the Irish in Britain with those in others countries. Four excellent essays in Vaughan (ed.), *A New History of Ireland*, are the best to start with. These are (in vol. V): P. O'Farrell, 'The Irish in Australia and New Zealand', and David N. Doyle, 'The Irish in North America, 1776–1845'; and (in vol. VI): P. O'Farrell, 'The Irish in Australia and New Zealand, 1870–1990', and D. N. Doyle, 'The re-making of Irish America, 1845–80'. The best comparative work is D. H. Akenson's *Small Differences: Irish Catholics and Irish Protestants, 1815–1922* (Dublin, 1988). For a study which explains the rural traditions of some Irish in North America, see D. H. Akenson, *The Irish in Ontario: a Study in Rural History* (Montreal, 1984). Kerby A. Miller, *Emigrants and Exiles: Ireland and the Irish Exodus to North America* (New York and Oxford, 1985) is a sweeping and much-criticised study of the stresses and strains of migrant life. Perhaps the best single location studies are R. A. Burchell, *The San Francisco Irish, 1848–1880* (Manchester, 1979); R. H. Bayor and T. J. Meagher (eds), *The New York Irish* (New York and London, 1996); and T. H. O'Connor, *The Boston Irish: a Political History* (Boston and London, 1995). An excellent study of small-town America is D. M. Emmons, *The Butte Irish: Class and Ethnicity in an American Mining Town, 1875–1925* (Urbana and Chicago, 1989). For Canada, see C. J. Houston and W. J. Smyth, *Irish Emigration and Canadian Settlement: Patterns, Links and Letters* (Toronto and Belfast, 1990). For Australia, see P. O'Farrell, *The Irish in Australia* (Kensington, New South Wales, 1987); and J. O'Brien and P. Travers (eds), *The Irish Emigrant Experience in Australia* (Dublin, 1991). David Fitzpatrick's magisterial study, *Oceans of Consolation: Personal Accounts of Irish Migration to Australia* (Dublin, 1994), is an important methodological breakthrough in the use of emigrants' letters.

INDEX